Wireless#
Certification Official Study Guide
(EXAM PW0-050)

Tom Carpenter

McGraw-Hill

New York Chicago San Francisco Lisbon London Madrid
Mexico City Milan New Delhi San Juan Seoul Singapore Sydney Toronto

The McGraw·Hill Companies

McGraw-Hill books are available at special quantity discounts to use as premiums and sales promotions, or for use in corporate training programs. For more information, please write to the Director of Special Sales, Professional Publishing, McGraw-Hill, Two Penn Plaza, New York, NY 10121-2298. Or contact your local bookstore.

Wireless# Certification Official Study Guide (Exam PW0-050)

1234567890 CUS CUS 019876

ISBN 0-07-226342-3

Sponsoring Editor Timothy Green	**Copy Editor** LeeAnn Pickrell	**Composition** International Typesetting and Composition
Editorial Supervisor Janet Walden	**Proofreader** Susie Elkind	**Illustration** International Typesetting and Composition
Project Manager Samik Roy Chowdhury (Sam)	**Indexer** WordCo Indexing Services, Inc.	**Series Design** Scott Turner
Acquisitions Coordinator Jennifer Housh	**Production Supervisor** James Kussow	**Cover Designer** Jeff Weeks
Technical Editor James Michael Stewart		

The CWNP® Program

The CWNP Program is the industry standard for wireless LAN training and certification, and is intended for individuals who administer, install, design, troubleshoot, and support IEEE 802.11 compliant wireless networks. Achieving CWNP certification will help you to design, install, and maintain wireless LANs that are more secure, cost-effective, and reliable.

The CWNP Program certifications cover all aspects of wireless LANs.

Wireless# is the entry-level wireless certification for the IT industry. Your Wireless# certification will help get you started in your IT career by ensuring you have a solid base of applicable knowledge of the latest cutting edge technologies, including Wi-Fi, WiMAX, RFID, Bluetooth, ZigBee, Infrared, and VoWLAN.

CWNA certification will get you started in your enterprise wireless career by ensuring you have the skills to successfully administer a wireless LAN. CWNA is a career differentiator that shows you are a technical leader with the ability to successfully implement wireless solutions for your organization or client.

CWSP advances your career by ensuring you have the skills to successfully secure wireless networks from hackers. CWSP offers the most thorough information available on how attacks occur and how to secure your wireless network from them.

CWAP ensures you have the skills to maximize the performance of a wireless network and reduce the time spent troubleshooting problems. You will be able to confidently analyze and troubleshoot any wireless LAN system using any of the market leading software and hardware analysis tools.

CWNE credential is the final step in the CWNP Program. By earning the CWNE certification, network engineers and administrators will have demonstrated that they have the most advanced skills available in today's wireless LAN market.

Acknowledgments

I would like to acknowledge the helpful staff at McGraw-Hill Professional for their guidance throughout this project. Tim Green and Jenni Housh were tremendously helpful and understanding along the way. I would also like to thank Devin Akin and Kevin Sandlin at CWNP, for their insights and assistance along the way. Devin, your late nights really paid off when I needed a response to my emails after one o'clock in the morning—thanks.

I would also like to acknowledge all the people who have made me who I am today. You are too many to list individually and too important not to be mentioned. You know if you know me and, if you do, you have helped me through what you do when you are you.

About the Author

Tom Carpenter is a technical experts' expert. He teaches in-depth courses on Microsoft technologies, wireless networking and security, and professional development skills such as project management, team leadership, and communication skills for technology professionals. Tom holds a CWNA, CWSP, and Wireless# certification with the CWNP program and is also a Microsoft Certified Partner. He and lovely wife, Tracy, live with their four children, Faith, Rachel, Thomas, and Sarah in Ohio.

About the Technical Editor

James Michael Stewart has been working with some form of IT since the early 1980s. Michael works with IMPACT Online d.b.a, a technology-focused writing and training organization. His work focuses on Windows 2003/ XP/2000, certification, wired and wireless networking, and general IT security. Recently, Michael has been teaching CISSP and CEH classes across the globe. Michael has coauthored over 75 books on a wide variety of subjects, including IT security certification and administration. He is also a regular instructor at Interop and COMDEX. Michael is married to an amazing woman, Cathy, and they live amidst their own private zoo of pets in Austin, Texas.

Contents at a Glance

Contents

Introduction

This *Wireless# Certification Official Study Guide* is intended to help you understand the basics of many wireless technologies and to prepare you to pass the Wireless# certification exam (PW0-050). The Wireless# certification is an entry-level certification that prepares the candidate to implement, troubleshoot, and maintain small and medium-sized wireless networks. The certification covers the following major wireless technologies:

- Wi-Fi
- WiMAX
- Bluetooth
- Infrared
- ZigBee
- RFID
- VoWLAN

If you are new to wireless networking, or to networking in general, this book is the place to start. When you accomplish the level of expertise needed for the Wireless# exam and certification, you'll find it much easier to move on to more advanced certifications such as the CWNA (Certified Wireless Network Administrator), CWSP (Certified Wireless Security Professional), and CWAP (Certified Wireless Analysis Professional). You'll also find it much easier to understand the material and concepts included in vendor-specific wireless certifications.

Who This Book Is For

This book focuses on the objectives for the Wireless# exam, but it's also a useful learning tool for anyone wanting to master the many domains of wireless. You'll learn about wireless technology basics such as radio frequency–based communications and infrared communications, and you'll learn about specific technologies such as RFID, ZigBee, and Voice over Wireless LANs. In addition, using step-by-step procedures, you will learn how to install, secure, and troubleshoot Wi-Fi or 802.11-based networks effectively. The Glossary provides you with a quick reference for definitions and basic knowledge of the many topics covered in this book.

As you prepare for the Wireless# certification, as with most other certifications, you need some hands-on experience with the technology to seal the information in your mind. In particular, be sure you have experience configuring consumer-grade Wi-Fi access points and Wi-Fi client devices. Linksys access points will provide all the features with which you should be familiar, and you can connect to them with most any client device. This makes for good testing and experience, but any vendor's access point should suffice as long as it provides most of the common features listed in Chapter 4 of this book. The main goal is to get your hands on some equipment and work through the configuration steps. However, because Wi-Fi is only a portion of the Wireless# exam, any equipment you can find related to Bluetooth, IrDA (infrared), or Voice over Wireless LAN will also be helpful.

The CWNP website (http://www.cwnp.com) lists official Wireless# training courses available in your area. These courses provide you with access to a certified instructor who can help answer any questions you may have related to the certification. You will also see demonstrations of equipment that may be more difficult to acquire on your own. I always recommend attending the official courses when time and budget allow.

Wireless Experts

Though the Wireless# exam is new and is an entry-level exam for wireless networking, many wireless experts might decide to gain this valuable certification because of the broad wireless topics that it covers. If you want a certification that shows you have a basic knowledge of RFID and/or ZigBee, and you already have the CWNA certification, you should strongly consider the Wireless# certification as an addition to your credentials.

In addition to the enhanced credentials, the process of studying these varied technologies makes you think differently about wireless technology and may bring greater value to your employer or customers. I work as an independent consultant and have been enriched greatly by going through the process of understanding these "alternate" uses of radio frequency–based technologies. My clients have benefited as well.

Wireless Beginners

There is no better place to start your educational journey into the world of wireless than the Wireless# certification. While you may choose to go on to a specialization in one or more of the wireless categories covered in Wireless#, this foundation sets the stage for your future success.

As I write this introduction, WiMAX hardware is being tested and certified by the WiMAX Forum and exciting discussions are under way that will hopefully lead to a full understanding of the potential return on investment of RFID technology. The 802.11n standard has just been approved and will likely result in newer Wi-Fi devices in the next few months. Plus, the new version of the CWSP certification is live! This is a great time to work in the wireless world.

How This Book Is Organized

The *Wireless# Certification Official Study Guide* is organized so you can start at the beginning and work your way through, or if you have mastered the information in the first few chapters, you can jump right to the chapter most relevant to your current needs. Each chapter begins with a list of exam objectives covered in that chapter and ends with review questions and answers to help you retain the important information covered. There are notes throughout the book that highlight interesting nuggets of information or warn you of common mistakes made with wireless technology.

Exam Objectives

The Wireless# certification exam certifies that successful candidates know the fundamentals of the following technologies:

- Wi-Fi, Bluetooth, WiMAX, ZigBee, Infrared, RFID, and VoWLAN
- Wireless organizations, standards, and protocols
- Wireless hardware, software, and installation
- Radio frequency (RF) technologies
- Applications, support, and security

The exam lasts 90 minutes and consists of 60 questions. You must answer 70 percent of the questions correctly to achieve a passing score. Practice exams are available at the CWNP website, and the objectives listed next might change, so you should consult the website frequently for the most current objectives. The following table breaks down the weight of each section of objectives on the exam.

xxii Wireless# Certification Official Study Guide

Subject Area	Approximate Percent of Exam
Wireless Technologies and Standards	32 percent
Hardware, Software, and Installation	28 percent
Radio Frequency (RF) Fundamentals	9 percent
Applications, Support, and Security	31 percent

Wireless Technologies and Standards—32 Percent

1.1 Define the roles of the following organizations in providing direction and accountability within the wireless networking industry:
- IEEE
- Wi-Fi Alliance
- ZigBee Alliance
- Bluetooth SIG
- WiMAX Forum
- Infrared Data Association (IrDA)

1.2 Define the characteristics of Wi-Fi technology:
- Range
- Frequencies/channels used
- Power saving modes
- Data rates and throughput
- Dynamic rate selection
- Roaming functionality
- Infrastructure and ad hoc modes
- SSID/network names

1.3 Summarize the basic attributes and advantages of the following wireless LAN standards, amendments, and product certifications:
- 802.11a
- 802.11b

- 802.11g
- Wi-Fi™ certification
- WMM™ certification
- WPA / WPA2™ certification

1.4 Summarize the characteristics, basic attributes, and advantages of ZigBee:

- Frequencies
- Power requirements
- Topology models
- Security features
- IEEE 802.15.4 standard
- ZigBee stack

1.5 Summarize the characteristics, basic attributes, and advantages of WiMAX:

- Fixed vs. mobile and frequencies used
- Data rates, throughput, range, and line-of-sight parameters
- Quality of Service (QoS) and security features
- Different wireless MAN standards—802.16-2004, 802.16e, ETSI HiperMAN, Wi-Bro

1.6 Summarize the characteristics, basic attributes, and advantages of Bluetooth:

- Frequencies used
- FHSS hop rates and adaptive frequency hopping support
- Data rates, throughput, and range
- Power classification
- Different wireless PAN standards—802.15.1, 802.15.2, 802.15.3, Bluetooth 1.2, Bluetooth 2.0+EDR

1.7 Summarize the characteristics, basic attributes, and advantages of infrared technology:

- Frequencies used
- Data rates, range, and line-of-site parameters
- Protocol types

- Interfering sources
- Different wireless PAN specifications—Serial Infrared (SIR), medium infrared (MIR), fast infrared (FIR), ultra fast infrared (UFIR), Infrared Simple (IrSMP), Infrared Financial Messaging (IrFM), Infrared Transfer Protocol (IrTRAN-P)

1.8   Summarize the characteristics, basic attributes, and advantages of VoWLAN:
- Wireless VoIP phones characteristics
- Wireless VoIP SOHO router characteristics
- Wireless VoIP SOHO router operation

1.9   Summarize the characteristics, basic attributes, and advantages of RFID
- RFID system requirements
- RFID tag types
- RFID hardware components

Hardware, Software, and Installation—28 Percent

2.1   Identify the purpose, features, and functions of the following wireless network components. Choose the appropriate installation or configuration steps in a given scenario.
- Access points
- Wireless LAN routers
- Wireless bridges
- Wireless repeaters
- WLAN switch
- Wireless VoIP gateway
- Wireless media gateway
- Power over Ethernet devices

2.2   Identify the purpose, features, and functions of the following client devices. Choose the appropriate installation or configuration steps in a given scenario.
- CardBus PC cards
- US /USB2 devices

- Compact Flash devices
- SDIO devices
- PCI devices
- Mini-PCI devices
- Client utility software and drivers
- Bluetooth connectivity devices
- Wireless IP phone
- Wireless gaming adapter
- Wireless print server
- Wireless IP camera
- Wireless hotspot gateway
- Wireless presentation gateway

2.3 Identify the purpose, features, and functions of the following types of antennas. Choose the appropriate installation or configuration steps in a given scenario.

- Omni-directional/dipole
- Semidirectional

Radio Frequency (RF) Fundamentals—9 Percent

3.1 Define the basic units of RF measurements:

- Milliwatt
- Decibel (dB)
- dBm
- dBi

3.2 Identify factors that affect the range and speed of RF transmissions:

- Line-of-sight requirements
- Interference (baby monitors, spread spectrum phones, microwave ovens, bright sunlight)
- Environmental factors

3.3 Define and differentiate between the following wireless technologies:

- DSSS
- OFDM

- FHSS
- Infrared
- MIMO

3.4 Define the concepts that make up the functionality of RF and spread spectrum technology:

- OFDM/DSSS channels
- Colocation of DSSS and OFDM systems
- Adjacent channel and cochannel interference
- WLAN/WPAN coexistence

Applications, Support, and Security—31 Percent

4.1 Identify proper procedures for installing and configuring common WLAN applications:

- Small Office, Home Office
- Extension of existing networks into remote locations
- Building-to-building connectivity
- Flexibility for mobile users
- Public wireless hotspots
- Mobile office, classroom, industrial, and healthcare
- Short-distance device connectivity
- Municipal connectivity
- VoWLAN
- RFID

4.2 Identify and describe common ZigBee applications:

- Building automation and residential/light commercial control
- Industrial control
- Personal healthcare
- PC and peripherals
- Consumer electronics

4.3 Identify and describe common WiMAX applications:

- Campus and wireless ISP broadband wireless access (point-to-multipoint)
- Wireless voice and data backhaul (point-to-point)

- Security/surveillance
- Enterprise private networks

4.4 Identify and describe common Bluetooth applications:

- Computer peripherals (GPS receivers, printers, keyboards, mice, digital cameras)
- Mobile audio (cell phones, MP3 players, headsets)
- Mobile data devices (PDAs)
- Unique devices (automotive diagnostics, wireless sensor links, gaming devices)

4.5 Identify and describe common Infrared applications:

- PDA data communication and synchronization
- Point-of-sale systems
- Laptop computer data communication
- Financial Messaging (IrFM)

4.6 Identify and describe the following wireless LAN security techniques. Describe the installation and configuration of each.

- SSID hiding
- WEP
- WPA-Personal
- WPA2-Personal
- RADIUS
- 802.1X/EAP
- Passphrases
- MAC Filtering
- Push-button wireless security
- Virtual private networking (VPN)

4.7 Identify procedures to optimize wireless networks in specific situations:

- Hardware placement
- Hardware selection
- Identifying sources of interference
- Network utilization
- Appropriate security protocols

4.8 Recognize common problems associated with wireless networks and their symptoms, and identify steps to isolate and troubleshoot the problem. Given a problem situation, interpret the symptoms and the most likely cause. Problems may include:

- Decreased throughput
- No connectivity
- Intermittent connectivity
- Weak signal strength

Tips for Succeeding on the Wireless# Exam

Here are some general tips that will help you become a successful Wireless# examinee:

- Take advantage of the Wireless# practice tests available through the CWNP website at http://www.cwnp.com.
- Arrive a few minutes before your exam is scheduled to start. This gives you time to review your notes and relax before entering the exam center.
- Read each question carefully to be sure you understand it (I always read each question at least twice even if I'm "sure" I know the answer).
- Do not leave any unanswered questions as these count against your score.

You are provided with instant notification of passing in the Examination Score Report. These scores are also sent to Planet3 Wireless, Inc. within ten working days. After you pass the exam, you receive a Wireless# Certificate and a welcome email with your CWNP ID number within three weeks.

Feel free to email me with any questions you have about the technologies covered in this book. My email address is carpenter@sysedco.com, and I love helping people learn technology and success skills so don't hesitate to ask your questions. Happy studying and good luck on your certification journey!

The Wireless World

Wireless# Exam Objectives Covered:

❖ Define the roles of the following organizations in providing direction and accountability within the wireless networking industry:

- IEEE
- Wi-Fi Alliance
- ZigBee Alliance
- Bluetooth SIG
- WiMAX Forum
- Infrared Data Association (IrDA)

❖ Summarize the basic attributes and advantages of the following wireless LAN standards, amendments, and product certifications:

- 802.11a
- 802.11b
- 802.11g
- Wi-Fi™ certification
- WMM™ certification
- WPA / WPA2™ certification

❖ Identify proper procedures for installing and configuring common WLAN applications:

- Small Office, Home Office
- Extension of existing networks into remote locations
- Building-to-building connectivity
- Flexibility for mobile users
- Public wireless hotspots
- Mobile office, classroom, industrial, and healthcare
- Short distance device connectivity
- Municipal connectivity
- VoWLAN
- RFID

We're living the dream. The ability to communicate electronically with people around the globe, without the need for cables and attachments, has freed us to experiment with new business models and social structures. Wireless networking and longer battery life (particularly in PDAs and mobile phones) mean more on-the-go computing than ever before. If you haven't been swept up by the waves yet, you are sure to be soon. Wireless networking is now practically ubiquitous and it's here to stay.

As I travel the country teaching technical programs to IT professionals, I've noticed this growth in wireless availability. You can connect to wireless networks in nearly every major city. These city-provided networks are often called "muni" networks because they are provided by municipalities. Many private organizations are providing wireless access as well, and with the introduction of WiMAX technology, many municipalities are considering the provision of wireless Internet for their citizens and businesses. With the mobile WiMAX specification finalized, the near future will likely see an ever greater focus on wireless technology.

In recent times, many have started to question the job security provided by an IT career, but with infrastructure-based technologies—such as wireless—you can rest assured that people skilled in the wireless craft will continue to be needed. Wireless networking is popular and growing, so now the question becomes, "How did we get here?"

In this chapter, I begin by providing the answer to this question through a discussion of the history of wireless communications in brief. Then you will learn about the common uses of wireless technologies today and the various wireless organizations and standards. Finally, you will review the networking basics needed to understand and make use of the ideas covered in the rest of this book.

History of Wireless Communications

You might be tempted to think the journey to mass wireless network usage has been a short one, but the reality is that it has been a long journey covering many milestones and centuries of time. To understand where we are today, it is helpful to discover the historical developments that have led to modern wireless networks. Today's wireless networks use light or radio waves to carry data through the apparently invisible medium of air. For this reason, we begin by investigating the relevant discoveries related to infrared light and radio waves.

Infrared Discovery

Sir William Herschel was a musician and an astronomer, but his most influential discovery related to wireless technology was made in 1800 when he discovered what is now call *infrared* and the *concept of light,* which is invisible to the human eye. Today, infrared light is used to create one form of wireless communications and is included in PDAs, laptop computers, remote controls, and many other implementations supporting specifications put forth by the Infrared Data Association (IrDA).

Sir William's discovery was even greater than he realized because he had actually discovered another portion of the electromagnetic spectrum beyond that of visible light—a fact that remained unknown for another 30 years. Infrared light includes the portion of the electromagnetic spectrum that reaches from just below the visible red light range to the microwave range. This infrared range is used by so many wireless technologies that it was included as a possible physical layer (PHY) technology in the IEEE's 802.11 standard.

Electromagnetic Waves

The next big discovery leading to wireless capabilities was that of electromagnetic wave theory. Any time you listen to the radio, cook your dinner in a microwave oven, watch broadcast TV, or communicate on a Wi-Fi network, you are using electromagnetic waves. Electromagnetic waves carry information without wires and are used in most major wireless communications today. These waves were explored in depth by James Maxwell.

While living a short life, by today's standards, of just 48 years, James Clerk Maxwell had a tremendous impact on the scientific world. His discoveries and theories related to astronomy, mathematics, and physics. Born in 1831, Maxwell took the concepts of Faraday, and Herschel to a lesser degree, to the next level. He codified electromagnetism as a series of mathematical formulas, theorized that these electromagnetic waves traveled at roughly the speed of light, and proposed that light itself was a form of electromagnetic disturbance, which proved to be correct. Today, the electromagnetic spectrum includes visible light, infrared light, radio waves, and more.

If you have ever seen a wave in the ocean or a ripple effect in a pond, you've seen the concept of disturbance-based wave forms. In much the same way, electric and magnetic fields join to create a disturbance known as an *electromagnetic wave.* Maxwell's discoveries related to electromagnetism, founded on the research of Faraday and Ampere coming before him, evolved in much the same way into another important concept.

Heinrich Hertz, a German physicist destined to an even briefer life than Maxwell of just 37 years, would build on the discoveries of Maxwell by proving that electromagnetic waves actually travel at approximately the speed of light and that electricity can be carried on these waves. Because of his discoveries, he was honored by having the term used to measure radio and electrical frequencies named after him, hence such terms as kilo*hertz* and mega*hertz*.

In Chapter 2, you'll learn more about electromagnetic waves and the discoveries of Heinrich Hertz as you read about radio frequency fundamentals and behavior. For now, just remember that you could not use the wireless communications you do today without these exceptional discoveries. Sir William showed us that there are invisible forces around us; Maxwell revealed that these invisible forces can be calculated and theorized; and Hertz empowered us to develop radio technologies by discovering that electromagnetic waves could carry electricity.

Military Use

Throughout the 1900s, wireless communications were of great interest to the military and there was very little focus on it in the private sector. The advantages to the military were many, including carrying messages to the front lines and using satellite or long distance communications for global coordination. In these early days, security was ensured by the lack of available hardware needed to interpret the radio frequency signals. Unique encoding techniques could also be used, but the cost of the wireless equipment was prohibitive in and of itself, which prevented feasible use outside the military for many years. As the hardware became more readily available in the 1970s, the price decreased, but more important, the private sector began to discover wireless technologies' many benefits.

Today's Wireless Applications

There are many benefits of wireless technology for small and large organizations today. When you can reduce hardware or time requirements, you can almost always reduce costs. This cost reduction is an excellent benefit of wireless networks.

A second area of benefit is mobility. The ability to be mobile and remain connected to the network is an efficiency gain as well as a convenience for those who must move around to do their jobs. In the early days, moving often meant losing your wireless connection and having to reassociate, but newer technologies make roaming seamless and accurate.

While early wireless technologies were very feature limited, this is changing rapidly. Inexpensive wireless devices now include the latest security capabilities and radios that are as powerful and stable as those in the most expensive devices of the past. As the price of wireless hardware has decreased, the number of features has increased, giving most organizations an excellent return on investment.

Popular areas of wireless use today include the following:

- Small Office, Home Office
- Network extension
- Building-to-building
- Mobile computing
- Personal area networks
- Municipal connectivity
- Voice over wireless LAN
- Radio Frequency Identification
- Sensor networks

Small Office, Home Office

One of the most beneficial uses of wireless networking technology, and certainly an early adoption group, is in the *Small Office, Home Office (SOHO)* area. SOHOs have limited budgets and, more important, limited space and technical capability. Because of this, tremendous benefits come from implementing wireless networking in these environments. For this reason, the SOHO market has led the way in wireless implementations. The benefits of wireless include the following:

- Reduced implementation costs
- Shorter implementation times
- Less space required for equipment and cabling

Implementation costs are reduced because it doesn't take as much time to implement a wireless network. Most SOHO companies have no technical professionals on staff, which means they must pay moderate to high consulting fees to install and use most technologies. By reducing the implementation time, costs are greatly reduced as well.

When you install standard networking, you must also install cabling in the walls, ceilings, and/or floors. You have to install hubs or switches in the closets or in work areas. This hardware requires space, which is a valuable commodity to the average SOHO. If current wireless standards provide you with the needed bandwidth and response times, all of this hassle is eliminated.

Network Extension

Many organizations have existing wired networks, and these networks serve their needs exceptionally well. However, if a company's current facilities are expanded, the cost of running cables and power can be expensive. To prevent this cost explosion, wireless networking may be utilized in these scenarios. By installing one or more wireless access points in the new area, you may be able to provide adequate coverage to the systems in this area.

Another situation demanding network extension is that of implementing new technology. Imagine the scenario where an organization built a warehouse on their property more than 30 years ago. They have no cables running throughout the building as networking was not expected at the time of construction. Now, they want to use PDAs and Tablet PCs to perform inventory management and tracking, but they need to extend their existing network throughout the warehouse. Wireless networking will provide an exceptional solution to this situation.

Depending on the needed coverage, you could place access points in strategic locations with omni-directional antennas to provide complete coverage for the warehouse, or you could install semi-directional antennas aimed down corridors, if coverage is adequate when using this model. Either way, wireless networking will prevent you from accruing the additional costs of running cables and power to the point of access. You will also get the added bonus of mobility for the inventory-management workers as they roam throughout the warehouse with their PDAs or Table PCs.

Building-to-Building

Another expensive networking connection point is the connection between buildings. If the cable is not placed during initial construction, you have to run the cable at a later time, usually at a greater expense. If the buildings are far apart, leased lines might be required, incurring ongoing monthly costs for the organization. In either case, costs or maintenance will be a continuing burden.

With wireless networking, an organization can install equipment to bridge the networks quickly and easily. In order to use this solution, wireless line-of-sight (LOS) must exist and communication frequencies must be available. These connections can reach across the street or across the town, depending on the technology used.

Point-to-Point

There are two ways to implement building-to-building connections. The first type is call *point-to-point (PTP)*. In this scenario, antennas aimed toward each other are installed on each building. This provides a connection between the two buildings, but does not provide connections among more than two buildings or locations. When creating a PTP connection, you need to use semidirectional or highly directional antennas. Figure 1.1 demonstrates a PTP connection.

Point-to-Multipoint

The second choice in building-to-building connectivity is *point-to-multipoint (PTMP)*. When implementing PTMP connections, you use one omni-directional antenna with multiple semidirectional or highly directional antennas. PTMP implementation is similar to that of a star topology on a wired network with the omni-directional antenna acting as the hub or central point of communication similar to that depicted in Figure 1.1.

Although there are many possible implementations of building-to-building wireless connections, they fall into one of these two categories. In a scenario where you have a PTP connection from a first building to a second building and then another PTP connection from the second building to a third building, you still have a structure consisting of multiple PTP connections. This is true regardless of how you might route the data on the network. For example, you may configure the routing tables to allow systems at the first building to communicate with systems at the third

FIGURE 1.1   Point-to-point and Point-to-multipoint connections

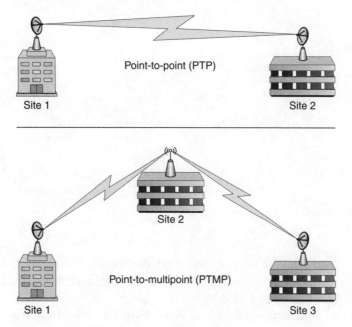

building; however, this does not mean you have a PTMP building-to-building configuration because you do not have a single omni-directional antenna receiving communications from each of the other buildings.

Mobile Computing

The speed of wired networking technologies have increased over the past two decades to the point where having gigabits of bandwidth is not unusual. Wireless LANs still have a long way to go to catch up to the speed of wired LANs; however, they provide an exceptional advantage in mobility. Can you imagine moving around your facility and plugging a cable into a port every time you need to access the network? This would be both frustrating and time consuming.

There are many scenarios in which the mobility provided by wireless networking is advantageous. In the world of healthcare, wireless abilities provide tremendous opportunities. A nurse can report on a patient's condition from his or her room to a centralized database without having to physically connect to the network. A doctor can prescribe medicines

FIGURE 1.2   Wireless mobility in an inventory-management scenario

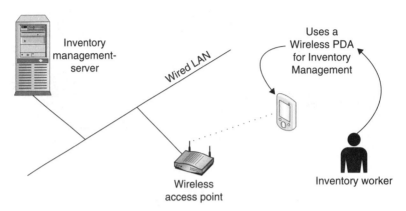

and send the hospital pharmacy instant notification of that prescription. These capabilities not only improve efficiency, but they also improve the healthcare provided by the hospital.

Imagine being able to enter items into inventory from any location in a warehouse facility. Of equal importance, you can make provisions to remove items from inventory in an automated fashion such that no human need be involved. These advancements allow for reduced costs and greater accuracy in inventory management. Figure 1.2 demonstrates the benefit of wireless mobility in an inventory-management scenario.

Have you ever been in a meeting and wished you could connect to the network and retrieve that file you forgot to bring along? With a wireless network, you can move your laptop from your office to a conference room—no cables needed. You can roam throughout the building with full network capabilities from any location, assuming proper wireless coverage has been provided. These are just a few of the many mobility benefits introduced with wireless networking.

Personal Area Networks

Short distance devices, usually referred to as *personal area network (PAN)* devices, allow for communications between PDAs and computers as well as various other devices. Among the PAN standards are Bluetooth, 802.15, and Infrared.

A PAN is a computer network consisting of various computers and devices generally used by one individual. When using Bluetooth, this PAN is called a piconet. A piconet is limited to eight devices, including the master device, which is the first device in the piconet.

The distance of most PANs is only a few meters so the applicability is limited to personal devices, hence the concept of personal area networks. These devices include PDAs, headsets, speakers, joysticks, MP3 players, and other generally small and locally used devices. While you could, theoretically, create a peer-to-peer network using Bluetooth, this would be beyond the intention of the designers.

While long distance connections of more than a half mile have been demonstrated, this is not the common implementation or suggested use of Bluetooth technology. For long distance connections such as this, highly directional antennas utilizing the appropriate 802.11 standards are more effective by today's standards.

Municipal Connectivity

When a local city or town decides to provide wireless connectivity to their citizenry, this is called *municipal connectivity*. In many cases, the infrastructure is already in place for providing such connectivity and, therefore, costs are greatly reduced. In some areas, this diminished barrier to entry has caused heated debate over allowing municipalities to provide wireless Internet access. Many telephone companies suggest that it is too difficult to compete in these circumstances; the future will tell how this debate is resolved.

Voice over WLAN

Today, people can collaborate no matter where they happen to be because of the merging of two modern technologies: Voice over IP (VoIP) and wireless networking. With the introduction of VoIP, the ability to communicate internally with anyone was made possible. The creation of wireless networks combines with VoIP to create what is being called *Voice over Wireless LAN* or *VoWLAN,* which gives you the ability to communicate internationally with anyone from anywhere.

Some organizations are referring to this as *wVoIP* for *wireless Voice over IP* instead of VoWLAN. In both cases, the same concept is being implemented. You should also know that VoIP is often called *IP telephony* or *Voice and Data Convergence.*

The 802.11e standard provides the much needed *Quality of Service (QoS)* specifications that allow for packet prioritization and, therefore, improved quality for VoWLAN. While many users have become accustomed to lesser quality voice communications because of cellular technology, VoWLAN quality can degrade rapidly when many people are using the service at the same time. The degradation can exceed that of cellular technology so QoS management is a must-have feature in VoWLAN implementations.

Another problem with VoIP in wireless networks is that of roaming. The handoff from one access point to another must happen quickly to avoid interrupting communications. The 802.11r working groups is responsible for standardizing *Fast Transitions,* which will allow for smooth roaming around a wireless network.

You will learn more about VoWLAN in Chapter 4. This emerging wireless capability is providing a lot of excitement and generating a lot of interest in the wireless community.

Radio Frequency Identification

Radio Frequency Identification (RFID) is an extremely useful technology that is positioned to replace barcodes as an identification system and provide other benefits as well. RFID uses wireless technology to inventory, monitor, and identify unique items in many environments.

This technology provides an excellent solution to shoplifting problems through inventory tracking. Stores place RFID tags in or on items, boxes, or packages so that, if the package has not first been cleared, signals an alert as the package passes through a scanning zone. At a few cents each, RFID tags save retail stores thousands of dollars in theft costs per year.

Another benefit of RFID is that of process tracking. RFID tags can be attached to items as they start through a manufacturing process and then the item can be tracked through the entire process. This can be used to provide quality improvement analysis and calculate manufacturing times or costs at each stage of the process. A similar scenario would be the tracking of items as they move around within a facility such as a construction yard. Knowing where the half-inch drywall sheets are at any time can be useful.

RFID systems work based on two major components: the RFID reader and the RFID tags. RFID tags can be either active or passive. Active tags have their own battery to provide energy for operations and usually provide greater processing capabilities. Passive tags contain no battery and receive their energy through electromagnetic waves. These passive tags usually contain less processing capabilities than their active counterparts.

These RFID tags, both active and passive, contain an Electronic Product Code (EPC) that is used to track the RFID tags, which allows for the tracking of millions of items in inventories and processes. This tag is comparable to the Universal Product Code (UPC) used in bar-coding systems. Rather than type codes into a tracking system to monitor inventory or rely on a user to scan the barcodes, the RFID reader reads the information from the RFID tags within the reading zone automatically. This process reduces the need for human intervention and, therefore, lowers the likelihood and severity of human-related errors.

Sensor Networks

When you want to monitor changes in the environment, track storms, track inventory, manage environmental lighting, or just play with a toy, you might consider using ZigBee. *ZigBee* is a standard that allows for the creation of low power wireless devices with low data rates, high security, and reliability. These devices can be used to create mesh, peer-to-peer, and cluster tree network topologies. Chapter 9 will provide in-depth coverage of the ZigBee standard.

Wireless Organizations

Organization provides the logical structure to get things done. It is fitting, then, that there should be a number of organizations aimed at improving, standardizing, and forwarding the use of wireless technologies. Some of these organizations are governmental operations, some are in the private sector, and others combine various organizations public and private. These organizations include

- FCC
- IEEE
- Wi-Fi Alliance

- ZigBee Alliance
- Bluetooth SIG
- WiMAX Forum
- Infrared Data Association

FCC

The Federal Communications Commission (FCC) is a government body within the U.S. that is responsible for overseeing and regulating the use of communications technology. According to their website at www.FCC.gov:

> The Federal Communications Commission is an independent United States government agency, directly responsible to Congress. The FCC was established by the Communications Act of 1934 and is charged with regulating interstate and international communications by radio, television, wire, satellite, and cable. The FCC's jurisdiction covers the 50 states, the District of Columbia, and U.S. possessions.

What this means, in a nutshell, is simple: When implementing a wireless technology in the U.S., because it will be a *communication by radio,* you must abide by the regulations set forth by the FCC.

 While you will not be tested on your knowledge of the FCC as an organization as part of the Wireless# examination, you should be familiar with the regulations and limitations imposed when you implement any wireless technology.

The FCC regulates where on the radio frequency spectrum wireless LANS can operate, what power level they can utilize, the transmission technologies they can use, and how and in what locations different wireless LAN hardware can be implemented. They have identified two basic license-free bands that are identified as the Industrial Scientific Medical (ISM) band (915 MHz, 2.4 GHz, and 5.8 GHz) and the Unlicensed National Information Infrastructure (UNII, pronounced *you-nee*) band (5 GHz, Lower, Middle, and Upper).

The need for an organization such as the FCC becomes obvious when you consider two factors: shared air space and limited frequencies. We all share the same air space, and there are indeed a limited number of frequencies. To guarantee certain frequencies for governmental and emergency services usage, an organization such as the FCC disallows the use of certain frequencies without a license (legal and official allowance for use). The unlicensed space is, just as its name implies, wide open for use by anyone, which means we have to work with other networks close to us to ensure there are no conflicts preventing effective operations as no official governing body licenses this space.

IEEE

The *Institute of Electrical and Electronics Engineers* (IEEE, pronounced *eye-triple-e*) creates standards for many technologies to operate within the regulatory guidelines of the countries in which the standards will be applied. The IEEE creates and manages the popular 802.11 specification for wireless networking. They divide a given technology into many working groups. These working groups are commissioned to develop operational standards for effective use of the technology under consideration. For example, the 802.11e working group is focused on implementing QoS features needed in certain wireless networking technologies such as VoWLAN and streaming multimedia.

The constitution of the IEEE defines the purpose of the organization as scientific and educational, directed toward the advancement of the theory and practice of electrical, electronics, communications, and computer engineering, as well as computer science, the allied branches of engineering, and the related arts and sciences. The IEEE produces approximately 30 percent of the world's literature in the electrical and electronics and computer science fields, and they have developed more than 900 active standards utilized in these areas of study. In the U.S., they define the technology you will utilize to build a wireless network based on FCC regulations or rules. Remember, the IEEE does not define the rules; this is the realm of the FCC. The IEEE defined the standards that help you work within the rules set by the FCC.

Wi-Fi Alliance

Because the IEEE defines standards, but does not evaluate hardware or software to verify compliance with the standards, various organizations have been created to do just that. The Wi-Fi Alliance, formerly known as the Wireless Ethernet Compatibility Alliance, was formed to promote and test for the interoperability of 802.11b, 802.11a, and 802.11g devices. Products meeting certain interoperability requirements set forth by the Wi-Fi Alliance may place a logo on their packaging indicating such.

The term *Wi-Fi* itself is short for *wireless fidelity*. The Wi-Fi Alliance promotes the freedom of networking without wires and the confidence of doing it by purchasing equipment with the Wi-Fi logo. The Wi-Fi Alliance formally states their purpose as being threefold: (1) to promote Wi-Fi worldwide by encouraging manufacturers to use standardized 802.11 technologies in their wireless networking products; (2) to promote and market these technologies to consumers in the home, SOHO, and enterprise markets; and last but certainly not least, (3) to test and certify Wi-Fi product interoperability.

Wi-Fi should not be considered a catch-all term for all things wireless. The intention of the Wi-Fi Alliance is to support and promote 802.11-based technologies. *Wi-Fi,* as a term, should be used to reference 802.11-based systems only and not other technologies such as WiMAX, Bluetooth, or IrDA.

ZigBee Alliance

The ZigBee Alliance is an association of companies working together to enable reliable, cost-effective, low-power, wirelessly networked monitoring and control products based on an open global standard. They state their goal as providing consumers with flexibility by embedding wireless intelligence into everyday devices. The focus of the ZigBee Alliance is to

- Define the network, security, and application software layers
- Provide interoperability and conformance testing procedures
- Promote the ZigBee brand globally to build market awareness
- Manage the evolution of the technology

In Chapter 9, you will learn more about the ZigBee standard and the ZigBee Alliance as well as the 802.15.4 specification put forth by the IEEE, which provides the physical and MAC layer specifications upon which ZigBee is based.

Bluetooth SIG

The Bluetooth Special Interest Group (SIG) is a trade association comprised of leaders in the telecommunications, computing, automotive, industrial automation, and networking industries that is driving the development of Bluetooth wireless technology, a low-cost, short-range wireless specification for connecting mobile devices and bringing them to market. Because of their intent to unify the various technology vendors and consumers around a standardized wireless technology, the Bluetooth SIG's name was inspired by the Danish King Harald "Bluetooth" Blatand, known for unifying Denmark and Norway in the 10th century. Bluetooth technologies are mostly used in PANs because of their limited distance capabilities.

WiMAX Forum

The WiMAX Forum was created to promote and certify compatibility and interoperability of broadband wireless products. They are an industry-led nonprofit corporation. Their main goals are to provide equipment interoperability among vendors and faster and cheaper access that is more readily available. The primary standard supported and certified by the WiMAX Forum is the 802.16 standard.

As part of their vision, they see WiMAX as an alternative to cable or DSL Internet connectivity with the ability to serve hundreds of businesses in an area with T1-like speeds and thousands of residences with DSL-like speeds. The technology is intended to support fixed, nomadic, portable and eventually mobile wireless connectivity. A major goal is to provide *last mile* access for homes and businesses out of reach of the wired infrastructures.

Infrared Data Association

In the month of June, 1993, in Walnut Creek, California, 50 companies met to officially create the Infrared Data Association (IrDA) as a nonprofit organization. The organization exists to provide a forum for discussion and standardization of infrared specifications. Since that time, many specifications have been released and maintained and infrared technologies are in wide use. In Chapter 8, you will learn more about the IrDA and the technical details of this technology.

Wireless Standards and Product Certifications

Without question, the most important collection of standards is the 802.11 specification put forth by the IEEE. However, there are many other standards you must be familiar with if you are to be an effective wireless network technician. At a minimum, you will want to know about the following standards:

- 802.11
- Wi-Fi
- WMM
- WPA/WPA2

802.11

While the *802.11* base standard is seldom seen in newer hardware, it is the foundation on which the various 802.11 working groups or substandards are based. This original 802.11 standard described direct sequence spread spectrum (DSSS) or frequency hopping spread spectrum (FHSS) systems that operated at 1 Mbps or 2 Mbps only. Sometimes the DSSS systems are called clause 15 systems because this is the clause, in the 802.11 standard, that refers to them. This original 802.11 standard also included specifications for infrared physical layers.

A DSSS system is said to be 802.11-compliant if it can operate according to the 802.11 standard at 1 or 2 Mbps. This is true even if the system can communicate at higher speeds such as 11 Mbps or 54 Mbps. It is important to remember that these systems can either run in 802.11-compliant mode or not. When in 802.11-compliant mode, they are operating at 1 or 2 Mbps. When operating at any other speed, they are not in 802.11-compliant mode.

FHSS systems are similar in that hardware vendors have created FHSS-based systems that communicate at more than 1 or 2 Mbps, but these systems should not be expected to operate well with standards-based FHSS systems. These FHSS systems are known as clause 14 systems for the same reason DSSS is known as clause 15—it is the clause in the standard that refers to the FHSS systems.

There are many substandards or working groups for the 802.11 standards. The most important of these to small- and medium-size businesses include

- 802.11b
- 802.11a
- 802.11g
- 802.11e
- 802.11i

802.11b

The *802.11b* supplement was ratified in 1999 and provides for data rates up to 11 Mbps using DSSS. The original 802.11 standard specified the use of a collision management technique known as Carrier Sense Multiple Access with Collision Avoidance (CSMA/CA), and 802.11b still uses the same method. Because CSMA/CA generates overhead communications, the actual throughput is generally somewhere around 6 Mbps for an 802.11b device. In noisy environments, data rates may lower to 5.5, 2, or 1 Mbps.

802.11b devices came to market quickly and saturated the wireless space. Because of this, many environments still support, or require, 802.11b today. Most newer wireless devices (such as those based on the 802.11g supplement detailed later) provide backward compatibility with the 802.11b standard, and they fall back to this functionality in situations that demand it.

Most 802.11b implementations are access-based in that there is a centralized antenna that connects and bridges multiple client devices within a confined space to a wired LAN or the Internet. With high-gain antennas, however, it is possible to use the 802.11b standard to implement point-to-point or point-to-multipoint building-to-building networks.

802.11a

Like 802.11b, *802.11a* was completed in 1999. This supplement to the 802.11 standard provides for up to 54 Mbps data rates, but it uses the 5 GHz UNII band frequency as opposed to the 2.4 GHz ISM band frequency shared by 802.11b and 802.11g. The problem with this decision is the lack of backward compatibility with 802.11b. In other words, 802.11b/g devices cannot communicate directly with 802.11a devices. However, many access points can run two radios to provide both 802.11a and 802.11b/g support, thereby supporting both client types. Many client devices also support multiple standards such as 802.11b/g or 802.11a in one device. You should realize that these clients cannot talk with each other directly, but they might be able to communicate through some bridging technique. The benefit of this difference in frequency is that you can actually operate two wireless networks in the same air space. The 802.11b/g network will use the 2.4 GHz frequency, and the 802.11a network will use the 5 GHz frequency.

Also similar to 802.11b is the fact that 802.11a networks have communications overhead, which means that actual throughput is in the mid 20s. Whereas 802.11b uses DSSS, 802.11a uses Orthogonal

Frequency Division Multiplexing (OFDM). Data rates can then be reduced to accommodate noisy environments or distance communications. The data rates specified by the 802.11a standard are 54, 48, 36, 24, 18, 9, and 6 Mbps.

802.11a devices did not begin shipping until 2001, which caused resistance to implementation based on the fact that many environments were already utilizing 802.11b equipment and the two are not compatible. This was not necessarily a fault of the standard or capabilities of 802.11a as there was an extended delay in the production of 5 GHz components needed to build the products.

802.11g

June of 2003 brought the ratification of the *802.11g* supplement to the 802.11 standard. Like 802.11a, 802.11g supports a 54 Mbps data rate with actual throughput being about half that or around the mid 20s. 802.11g also uses OFDM instead of the DSSS used by 802.11b or the FHSS used by 802.11. This provides the higher throughput due, in large part, to better interference handling. Unlike 802.11a, 802.11g uses the 2.4 GHz frequency and, therefore, is backward compatible with 802.11b. Because of this backward compatibility, 802.11g has become much more popular than 802.11a in general use.

You will learn more about DSSS and OFDM in Chapter 2; however, it is important that you also understand the basic differences between these three core supplements to the 802.11 specification: 802.11b, 802.11a, and 802.11g.

802.11e

As a draft standard, *802.11e* specifies techniques for providing Quality of Service (QoS) in LANs. The standard is specifically aimed at 802.11 Wi-Fi networks and is intended to provide greater support for time-sensitive applications such as streaming media and VoWLAN. This QoS is provided through the definition of traffic classes (TCs), which are used to give priority to specific data types. For example, you might configure FTP access as a low priority class and streaming media as a high priority class.

802.11i

June 24th is an important day for two reasons. The first reason is that it is my birthday, and the second, and most likely more important to you, is that on this day in 2004 the *802.11i* draft standard was ratified by the IEEE, making it official. The intent of this supplement is to provide security standards to the 802.11 Wi-Fi worlds. This is an extremely important supplement because it provides a standard that can be followed going forward instead of having every vendor implement security in a different way. This new standard is intended to replace the weak Wired Equivalent Privacy (WEP) security protocol.

Because of the great need for security solutions in wireless networks, the Wi-Fi Alliance released the Wi-Fi Protected Access (WPA) standard before 802.11i was completed. WPA is a subset of the 802.11i specification. In order to reduce confusion, the Wi-Fi Alliance refers to the full implementation of 802.11i, in their certifications, as WPA2.

Wi-Fi Certification

Wi-Fi certified hardware or software is certified to meet the specifications set forth by IEEE standards. A device can be Wi-Fi certified for one standard or for many. The Wi-Fi Alliance is responsible for certifying products in this way.

WMM Certification

WMM or Wi-Fi Multimedia is a certification using a subset of the 802.11e draft standard. If a product has this certification, it means that it provides QoS features in line with the 802.11e standard for VoIP or multimedia streaming services.

Remember, a draft standard is a proposed standard that has not yet been ratified. To be *ratified* means to be *approved.* In the case of IEEE standards, ratification is performed by the standard governing body.

WPA/WPA2 Certification

Another certification managed by the Wi-Fi Alliance is the WPA/WPA2 certification. The WPA certification verifies that a device or software meets the demands of the Wi-Fi Alliance WPA certification, which is based on a subset of the 802.11i standard and provides for encryption on wireless networks. The WPA2 certification is a verification of compliance with the 802.11i standard. The IEEE does not refer to 802.11i as WPA2; this is a term trademarked by the Wi-Fi Alliance only.

This difference in terms between the standards and the certifications often leads to confusion in the marketplace. A perfect example of this is the WPA-Personal and WPA-Enterprise technologies. WPA-Personal is a subset of the WPA certification that uses a passphrase or shared key to secure communications. WPA-Enterprise is the subset that requires an authentication server. Many vendors implement this in a way that does not clearly differentiate between the two subsets of the WPA certification, leading to a confused perspective in the marketplace that says all WPA implementations are the same. Nothing could be further from reality. WPA-Personal, in most cases, uses the same passphrase until it is changed manually. WPA-Enterprise can use certificates and other more secure authentication and encryption mechanisms, making it easier to manage centrally and, when implemented properly, more secure.

Important Foundational Networking Concepts

To fully understand wireless LAN technologies, you need to have a basic understanding of general networking concepts. Among these concepts, several important items stand out, including networking terminology, networking communications, and networking models. If you are already familiar with basic networking terms and concepts, you may choose to skip ahead to the summary section of this chapter. However, a review might be helpful even for those savvy in basic networking, and if you are new to the networking world, this section will be very beneficial.

Networking Terminology

As you learn about wireless networking technologies, you have to understand some basic networking terms:

- Packet
- Bandwidth
- Throughput
- Latency
- Authentication

- Broadcast
- Node
- Host
- Server
- Client/Workstation
- Protocol
- Network
- LAN
- WAN

A *packet* or *datagram* is the basic unit of information used in modern computer networks. Packets usually include sending and receiving device information, error-control data, and the message being sent from the source to the destination device. When sending large data files across the network, the data is split into multiple packets and then sent.

Bandwidth refers to the information carrying capacity of a network. Bandwidth is usually measured in kilobits per second (KBPS) or megabits per second (MBPS). It is also important to understand *throughput* and how it differs from *bandwidth*. Throughput is generally used to reference the actual amount of "real" data that can be sent across the network. All networks consume a certain amount of the available bandwidth because of overhead issues such as error-control, broadcasts, and collisions. Because of this, throughput is generally somewhat lower—and sometimes much lower—than the stated bandwidth of the network. This—the extra overhead—is why an 11 Mbps wireless connection provides only 5–6 Mbps of actual throughput.

Sometimes communications between devices on a network are delayed because of the distance from one device to the other or the speed of the connecting devices, such as routers. This delay is known as *latency*. Latency can have a significant impact on network communications because the actual speed of communications is dependent on the combined bandwidth and latency.

When a device connects to a secure network, it must be validated. This validation is called *authentication*. Both people and devices can be authenticated and, in the most secure environments, both are authenticated using a secure mechanism. In wireless networks, the default authentication type is an open authentication model, and you should use additional security measures. These might include WPA/WPA2 or VPN tunnels to encrypt the wireless traffic and EAP-type authentication mechanisms. These security measures are covered in more detail in Chapter 11.

A particular type of packet used in network discovery and communications is a *broadcast*. Broadcasts are used to discover network services such as DHCP servers and devices such as wireless access points. Broadcasts can cause decreased performance on wired networks as each *node* (device connected or point of connection to the network) must evaluate the packet because no specific node is identified in the broadcast message.

A *host* is a type of node connected to the network. This node can be a server, client, or any device hosting services, peripherals, or data. The *server* is a specific kind of host that is intended for data storage, service provision, and various centralized computing purposes. Examples of servers include email servers, telnet servers, file and print servers, and Internet access servers. A *client* or *workstation* is a host that utilizes the services of the network. Sometimes the term *workstation* is used to refer to a powerful desktop computer whether it is connected to a network or not.

For all the hosts on a network to communicate with one another, they must speak a common language. These standard methods of digital communication are known as *protocols*. In most cases, the term *protocol* refers to higher-level communications such as TCP/IP (from the Internet world) or IPX/SPX (from the Novell world), however, you could apply the term *protocol* to Ethernet or token-ring technologies that operate at a much lower level. In its most basic sense, a protocol is a standardized set of instructions for communications between nodes on a network, and the instructions can apply to the physical level or the application level of the communications process.

I have used the term *network* throughout the previous section many times and through this use have, in effect, defined the term. A computer network is an arrangement of interconnected devices utilizing a shared protocol (or a set of shared protocols) for communications.

There are two other terms you should know that are used frequently in the networking world: *LAN* and *WAN*. A LAN is a local area network and a WAN is a wide area network. A LAN is usually defined as a network confined to a single location; this location can be a single building or a campus with multiple buildings. A WAN is usually the combination of two or more LANs separate by some significant distance; a WAN can span a city or the globe. When using wireless networking technology, these terms—LAN and WAN—are usually combined with a *W* to represent wireless and thus you have a WLAN or WWAN.

Networking Communications

To fully understand any form of computer networking, you must understand the basics of computer operations and data communications. Computers work with data, and from the perspective of the computers, all data is numeric. In effect, a text document or a picture is just a bunch of 1s and 0s to your computer. Knowing this is of fundamental importance if you are to truly understand everything else about computers. Trying to learn how wireless networking operates without knowing how computers and networks work in general is like trying to learn calculus without first learning addition and subtraction. True understanding comes through constructive techniques or layers of knowledge.

When I say that all data is a bunch of 1s and 0s to a computer, this may seem odd or confusing, however, this is exactly true. Consider that a computer processor is, at its most basic, a conglomerate of many on-and-off switches or toggles. There are billions of possible state combinations resulting in all the capabilities of the processor. Digital data is much the same. You could, for example, say the following:

- 00 = Blue
- 01 = Red
- 11 = Green
- 10 = Orange

Now, when your application sees 00, it knows to use blue, and when it sees 10, it knows to use orange. The point is that your application determines the meaning of the data and the computer just stores a bunch of 1s and 0s. Because this is the case, at the most basic level, you need to be able to represent only two things to communicate across wires on a network. You need a signal to represent a 1 and a signal to represent a 0. While modern networks are more complicated than this, this ability is the basic minimum requirement for communications to take place. This data communications model could be called binary communications as it uses *binary data* (1s and 0s).

These signals are sent on the wire in the form of packets. Each device connected to the wire looks at each packet to determine if the packet is intended for itself or another device. If the packet is intended for another device, it simply ignores the packet internally. This works much the same way mail processing works at my house. My wife, Tracy, goes out to the mail box and gets all the mail. She then looks to see what is for her, the children, and me. She takes hers and leaves ours on the counter. Then I come to the counter and take my mail, leaving the rest. This process continues until the last person on the "house wire" gets to inspect the mail.

Wireless networking works similarly, only the information is in the air instead of on the wire, and the wireless client listens for specific messages from the network telling it when it can communicate. The greater complexities of communications in the wireless world will be introduced in Chapter 2 and detailed throughout the remaining chapters.

Networking Models

A networking model provides a mechanism for consistent communications between individuals and technologies. Having a shared mental construct and language, which is what a networking model provides, allows for simpler communications and standards development. The fundamental networking model is the Open Systems Interconnection (OSI) model. If you have read much in the field of computers or networking, you have encountered statements such as, "L2TP is a layer two protocol providing for tunneled communications between two devices on a public network." The phrase *layer two* is a reference to the OSI model.

The OSI Model

The OSI model came too late. This is the reality, and yet the OSI model is the most referenced model in networking. There is good reason for this. The OSI model provides a great theoretical tool for learning how networking works. Because few, if any, networking systems use it to exactness—that is exactly how you should think of it—theoretically. Due to frequent references to the OSI model in networking books, white papers, and RFCs, a basic understanding is a must.

The model provided by the OSI is a seven-layer model, as depicted in Figure 1.3. Communications travel down the model on the sending computer and up the model on the receiving computer. Each layer represents different networking functions and responsibilities.

The *Application layer* represents the level at which applications access various network services, daemons, or subprotocols, and is often called *layer 7*. This layer represents the services that directly support applications such as FTP for file transfer or SMTP for email.

FIGURE 1.3   The OSI model

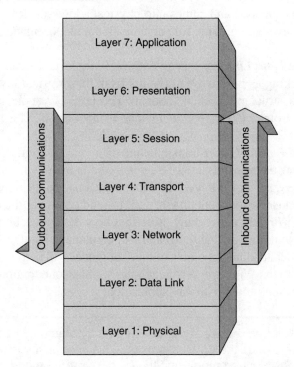

The *Presentation layer* translates data from the Application layer into an intermediary format and is *layer 6.* This layer often manages security issues by providing services such as data encryption and compression. However, these services can also take place at layers 3, 4, and 5, and even by user software before data is sent to the protocol for transmission.

The *Session layer* allows two applications on different computers to establish, use, and end a session. An example of this would be the management of a session when a user visits a website on the Internet. This layer is *layer 5.*

The *Transport layer,* also known as *layer 4,* handles error recognition and recovery, if it is provided. This layer also breaks long messages when necessary into small packets for transmission and then rebuilds the packets into the original message on the receiving end. The receiving Transport layer also sends receipt acknowledgments, if using TCP. You should know that UDP operates at this layer, and it is a connectionless protocol.

Layer 3 is the *Network layer* and it addresses messages and translates logical addresses and names into physical addresses. Routers function at this level and provide for segmentation and QoS management when applicable.

The *Data Link layer* is an extremely important layer in wireless networking as it packages raw bits from the Physical layer into *frames* (logical, structured packets for data). This layer is responsible for transferring frames from one computer to another, without errors. This layer is referenced as *layer 2.*

The *Physical layer* transmits bits from one computer to another and regulates the transmission of a stream of bits over a physical medium. This layer, *layer 1,* defines how the cable is attached to the network adapter and what transmission technique is used to send data over the cable, or in the case of wireless networking, it defines how the connection to the network occurs and how the medium (air) will be managed and utilized.

Understanding the basics of the OSI model will help you in your studies related to the Wireless# certification as well as your continued education for certifications and day-to-day applications.

You will not be required to understand and communicate the OSI model in order to pass the Wireless# exam. This information is provided to give you a basic understanding of the model's purpose and use in network-related education. You can find more in-depth information about the OSI model in McGraw-Hill's book entitled *Network+ Certification Study Guide, Third Edition,* by Glen E. Clarke.

Summary

You can now chart the path that led us to where we are today in the field of wireless communications, including the discovery of infrared by Herschel and the codification and understanding of electromagnetic waves by Maxwell and Hertz. You should also have an awareness of the different organizations supporting standards and certifications related to wireless networking, such as IEEE and the Wi-Fi Alliance, and the benefits that they provide. Understanding the various 802.11 standards and supplements, you are on your way to selecting the best technologies for any given situation, and the foundational networking information provided in this chapter will help you understand and master the information in succeeding chapters.

Key Terms

- ☐ **802.11**
- ☐ **802.11a**
- ☐ **802.11b**
- ☐ **802.11g**
- ☐ **electromagnetic**
- ☐ **infrared**
- ☐ **IEEE**
- ☐ **last mile**
- ☐ **point-to-point**
- ☐ **point-to-multipoint**
- ☐ **SOHO**

Review Questions

1. The waves known as visible light, infrared, and radio are the combination of what two fields?

   A. Electric and radio

   B. Electric and magnetic

   C. Magnetic and radio

   D. Radio and frequency

2. What kind of light is often used for remote controls or data transfer between PDAs?

   A. White light

   B. Visible light

   C. Infrared light

   D. Black light

3. From among the following list, select the benefits to SOHO organizations provided by wireless networking over wired networking.

   A. Reduced implementation costs

   B. Increased security

   C. Reduced implementation times

   D. Reduced bandwidth

4. You have implemented a building-to-building connection configuration for your organization. You are using an omni-directional antenna on one building and a semidirectional antenna at each of two other buildings. The semidirectional antennas are each aimed at the one omni-directional antenna. What type of building-to-building configuration do you have?

   A. Point-to-point

   B. Point-to-multipoint

   C.   Multipoint-to-point

   D.   Centralized

5.   What organization is responsible for defining the standards upon
which wireless and other technologies are based?

   A.   Wi-Fi Alliance

   B.   FCC

   C.   IEEE

   D.   Intel

6.   Why is the 802.11a standard not backwardly compatible with the
802.11b standard?

   A.   802.11a uses the 5 GHz UNII band

   B.   802.11a uses OFDM instead of DSSS

   C.   802.11b was a proprietary standard

   D.   802.11g causes interference

7.   Which of the following wireless technologies cannot be used in the
same place at the same time, assuming each technology is implemented
using all available nonoverlapping channels and they are implemented
with separate access points?

   A.   802.11a

   B.   802.11g

   C.   802.11b

   D.   IrDA

Review Answers

1. **B.** The correct answer is electric and magnetic. These two fields combine to create an electromagnetic wave. These waves, when propagated through the air, are referred to as radio frequency waves in wireless technologies.

2. **C.** The correct answer is infrared light. Infrared light is invisible to the human eye, but can be used as a carrier of information in electronic communications.

3. **A, C.** The correct answers are reduced implementation costs and reduced implementation times. Because you do not need to run cables, the cost and time for implementation is greatly reduced. Security is not enhanced when using wireless networking instead of wired networking, and bandwidth may or may not be reduced depending on the comparative technology.

4. **B.** The correct answer is point-to-multipoint (PTMP).

5. **C.** The IEEE does not create rules, the IEEE creates standards that conform to the rules in the countries where the technology will be used. The FCC defines rules (regulations) for the U.S.

6. **A.** 802.11a uses the 5 GHz UNII band for communications. 802.11b uses the 2.4 GHz frequency.

7. **B, C.** 802.11g and 802.11b. You cannot use 802.11b and 802.11g in the same space at the same time using all channels with each technology and implementing them with separate access points. This is because they use the same frequency (2.4 GHz). However, you could implement 802.11b/g access points and then use a mix of 802.11b and 802.11g clients.

Radio Frequency Basics

Wireless# Exam Objectives Covered:

❖ Define the basic units of RF measurements

- Milliwatt
- Decibel (dB)
- dBm
- dBi

❖ Identify factors that affect the range and speed of RF transmissions

- Line-of-sight requirements
- Interference (baby monitors, spread spectrum phones, microwave ovens, bright sunlight)
- Environmental factors

❖ Define and differentiate between the following wireless technologies

- DSSS
- OFDM
- FHSS
- Infrared
- MIMO

Every communication's technology must have a medium to travel along in order to pass information between two devices. Ethernet networks pass this information along coaxial or some other cable such as UTP. Telephone networks use wiring. Wireless networks, specifically Wi-Fi, RFID, Bluetooth, and WiMAX, use radio frequency (RF) waves as the medium, and IrDA-based communications use another electromagnetic technology known as infrared.

In this chapter, you will learn about RF, including its behavior and functionality. You will learn about the methods used to measure RF waves and the various languages spoken on an RF-based network. When you are finished, you will also understand the environmental impact on RF capabilities and communications.

RF Defined

It should be immediately clear that there are at least two important words related to RF that need to be defined; however, there is a third word that also needs to be defined to fully understand RF. These three words are

- Radio
- Frequency
- Signal

The *radio* is the device that generates and receives the signal known as an RF signal, and this signal is transmitted on a specific frequency. The *frequency* is what distinguishes one RF signal from another. Technically, the number of times per second the signal cycles or repeats a particular waveform is the source of the frequency identification. This means that a signal operating at the 2.4 GHz frequency is cycling 2,400,000,000 times per second (1 GHz = 1 billion cycles per second and 1 MHz = 1 million cycles per second).

Electric energy can be made to vary over time. This variance in electrical energy is known as a *signal*. There are two general categories of signals: *digital* and *analog*. The sine wave is an example of an analog signal.

Figure 2.1 illustrates a sine wave. As time passes, the sine wave's intensity increases to some maximum point (point A) and then returns to the baseline (point 0). The wave's intensity decreases to some minimum point (point B) and then returns to the baseline again. This process continues over time.

FIGURE 2.1   The sine wave

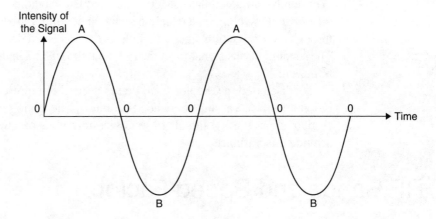

By adjusting the number of cycles (going from point 0 to A to 0 to B to 0) in a given window of time, you adjust the frequency. Figure 2.1 represents two cycles of the wave.

Digital signals differ from analog signals in that the digital signal varies abruptly between two electrical values as depicted in Figure 2.2, and the analog signal varies gradually, as was demonstrated in Figure 2.1. Digital signals are used to communicate and relay information within computer networks, but are not used as carriers of information in RF networks. Only analog signals are used as carriers of information. The information being carried by the RF waves might be digital or analog, but it is encoded (carried) on analog signals in an RF-based network connection.

An analog carrier signal can carry data represented by analog or digital techniques. This carrying of an information signal on a carrier signal is known as *modulation*. Modulation has been utilized for decades; one well-known

FIGURE 2.2   Digital signal

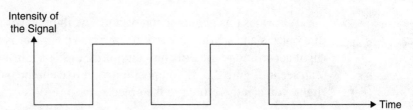

example is the modem. The *mod* in modem stands for modulator, and the *dem* stands for demodulator. Much like a modem modulates and demodulates information traveling on a telephone wire, an RF *radio* modulates data to send through the RF medium and demodulates data received through the medium. The sending of this signal from the radio out through the antenna is known as *radiation*.

As discussed in Chapter 1, all that is needed to represent digital data is some form of variance between two states. The analog or digital signals carried across the RF signals from device-to-device on a wireless network provide this variance.

RF Range and Speed Factors

To effectively implement an RF-based network, such as Wi-Fi or WiMAX, you need to understand the factors that impact the distance or range RF signals can travel and the bandwidth available for communications. In this case, *bandwidth* refers to the speed of the communications. Issues such as line-of-sight, Fresnel Zone clearance, interference devices, and standard RF behavior become very important when setting up a wireless network.

Line-of-Sight

Line-of-sight (LOS) is the seemingly straight line from the object in view (the transmitter) to the observer's eye (the receiver). This is also called the *visual* line-of-sight. The LOS is a *seemingly* straight line because, in fact, light waves travel in a similar fashion to RF waves.

Light waves can bounce off objects and be redirected. A mirror demonstrates this well. Stand directly in front of a mirror and note what you can see in the mirror. Now take a step to your right or left and note what you can see. You should be able to see more objects or information opposite to the direction of your move. For example, if you step to your right, you'll now see more items that are actually located to your left and vice versa.

Why does this phenomenon occur? The light waves are bouncing off the objects and soaring toward the mirror. The mirror is then reflecting the light according to the directionality of the strike against the mirror, as you can see in Figure 2.3. If you position your eyes in the path of this reflected light, you can therefore see the objects.

FIGURE 2.3   Line-of-sight and reflection

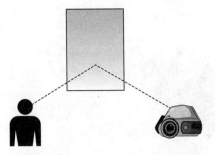

   In this same way, RF devices must have LOS with each other in order to communicate. As this example demonstrates, they do not necessarily need to have direct visual LOS as the RF waves can pass through some objects and reflect, refract, and diffract, around others. This is particularly true for indoor communications and is the reason LOS concerns are more relevant to outside connections than they are to inside communications.

   When creating building-to-building connections, visual LOS must be in place. While you might not be able to see the receiver you are transmitting to, the space between the transmitter and the receiver (or two transceivers) must be mostly clear. This space is referred to as the *Fresnel Zone*.

Fresnel Zone

The Fresnel (pronounced *fra-nel*) Zone is an area centered on the visible LOS between the transmitting and receiving antenna and was discovered by Augustin Jean Fresnel of France. It is not a square area, but rather is ellipse shaped. As Figure 2.4 shows, the Fresnel Zone is narrower toward the antennas and widest in the middle. This Fresnel Zone comes about because an antenna does not transmit RF waves in a laser-type beam, but rather the RF waves propagate (or spread) as they travel through the air.

FIGURE 2.4   The Fresnel Zone

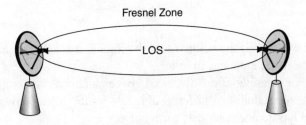

FIGURE 2.5 Fresnel Zone blockage

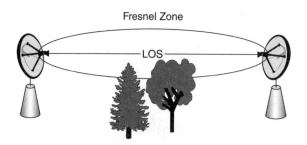

For effective RF communications, 60 percent of the Fresnel Zone should remain unblocked by objects such as trees and buildings. To be safe, you should err on the side of caution and make sure no more than 20 percent of the Fresnel Zone is blocked—or that at least 80 percent is clear. Trees and buildings in the Fresnel Zone will absorb some of the RF energy (see Figure 2.5) or reflect it off the intended path. When this occurs too much, while you might still have visual LOS, RF LOS is unavailable or blocked. When setting up building-to-building links, review the environment between them periodically. It is better to discover that a tree is growing or that a new building is being constructed in the Fresnel Zone before blockage occurs so you can deal with it effectively.

For very long-distance links, the earth itself may intrude upon the Fresnel Zone. This is because the earth is round and the center LOS within the Fresnel Zone is a straight line. Also, the longer the link, the larger the Fresnel Zone becomes. When and if this blockage occurs depends on the height of the antennas being used to radiate the RF signals. Generally, when creating building-to-building links, you will not have to worry about earth-based interference (usually called *earth bulge*) unless the distance between the communicating antennas is greater than seven miles.

When the distance is greater than seven miles, you can calculate the additional antenna height needed using the following formula:

$$H = \frac{D^2}{8}$$

where *H* equals the height of earth bulge in feet and *D* equals the distance between the antennas in miles.

For example, if the distance between antennas is 10 miles, you should plan on an additional 12.5 feet of height for the antenna towers, or mounting locations, to accommodate earth bulge.

While there are formulas available for calculating the Freznel Zone clearance, you will not need to know them for the Wireless# exam or for basic wireless installation and support. You will not be tested on the concept of earth bulge either, but you should be aware of its impact as a wireless technician or sales professional. To learn more, see the *CWNA Certified Wireless Network Administrator Official Study Guide* by Planet3 Wireless and published by McGraw-Hill/Osborne (2005).

Interference Devices

In addition to the interference caused by objects in the environment where RF communications are taking place, devices can cause interference by generating RF noise or signals. Many objects use RF technology as a form of communications and others use RF energy for alternative purposes. The most common of these include the following:

- Microwave ovens
- Elevators
- Baby monitors
- Spread spectrum phones
- Bright sunlight

Microwave ovens and elevators generate what is called RF noise, as they are not designed with the intention of transmitting information. However, this noise can prevent you from transmitting information you hope to deliver. Think of it like this: If you are in a room talking with a friend and suddenly 50 people come into the room and start yelling at each other, will you still be able to hear your friend? You'll probably miss all or part of what your friend is saying. This same problem is faced by the RF receiver, for example, a baby monitor in the kitchen, that is trying to "hear" what the RF transmitter (the monitor in the baby's room) is sending to it while a microwave oven is screaming (transmitting unintentional RF waves) in the background.

By the way, if you have ever wondered how a microwave oven heats food, you are about to find out. When RF energy is absorbed into an object, it is converted to heat. Water is a great absorber of RF energy, and this is why liquid objects get hot when placed in the microwave. Try placing a dry piece of paper in the microwave; it won't heat up. This is because the dry paper is not a good absorber of RF energy like a bowl of soup is. This is the same reason you must use the right cabling and connectors when building a wireless network. Use the wrong devices in the wrong places and you could get a meltdown—seriously.

Baby monitors and spread spectrum phones, such as a 2.4 GHz cordless phones, can also cause interference as they are generating RF signals intentionally in the environment. You can often resolve interference issues by changing channels on your wireless networking devices.

A final source of interference is the weather. Bright sunlight (remember, light is part of the complete electromagnetic spectrum) can cause reduced bandwidth or communications capabilities and severe stormy weather can also cause problems. Just as the RF energy is absorbed into water in a microwave oven, RF energy can be absorbed by raindrops falling through the communication path. Rain can reduce the signal strength at the receiver and possibly lower it enough to disrupt communications, though this scenario is an extreme one, likely requiring more than five to six inches of rainfall per hour for links of less than two to three miles.

Interference types, like those mentioned previously, could be categorized as *narrowband* interference or *all-band* interference. Narrowband interference, as the name implies, interferes with a small part of the spectrum and you can usually solve the problem by changing channels within the wireless devices. *All-band interference,* on the other hand, requires using more extreme measures such as changing wireless technologies. For example, you might need to switch to an 802.11a device instead of an 802.11b/g device, if the entire 2.4 GHz spectrum is being used by others. This scenario occurs commonly in shared office spaces such as malls and leased office buildings.

Gains and Losses

Radio frequency communications occur within many different environments, and these various environments introduce problems and advantages for the RF signals. What is generally considered an advantage in RF communications is called *gain* and that which is usually seen as a problem is called *loss*. It is important to understand these two concepts if you are to appreciate the full impact of the RF behavior in any given environment.

Gain

Amplitude is a measurement of the change in RF energy caused by a passing RF wave. This is much like the voltage level in an electrical signal. A higher amplitude signal is more likely to have a strong signal strength at the receiver. An increase in amplitude of the RF signal is known as *gain*.

Gain is either active or passive. Active gain is achieved by adding an amplifier (you will learn about these devices in Chapter 4) in-line between the RF signal generator, such as a wireless access point, and the propagating antenna. Adding an amplifier increases the signal strength in a literal way in that the signal is actually stronger. Passive gain does not actually increase the signal strength, but directs it. Passive gain is achieved by using semidirectional or highly directional antennas to focus the energy of the signal in a more specific direction.

To understand passive gain, think of water spraying out of a water hose. Imagine the water volume is equivalent to the RF signal strength. If you let the water flow out of the end of the hose without focusing it, it may spray for a few feet; however, if you focus the volume of water by putting your thumb over a portion of the hose end, the water will spray many times farther. Note that you have not increased the volume (understood as RF energy in this analogy), but you have increased the distance that same volume is traveling. A directional antenna focuses the beamwidth toward a specific location in the same way.

All devices, including connectors and cabling, in the path of the RF signal leading up to the antenna have the potential to either increase the strength (amplify) or decrease the strength (attenuate) of the signal. Once the signal leaves the antenna and is propagated through the air in the form of RF waves, it will experience only a weakening in strength until it arrives at the receiving antenna because of various environmental behavior factors discussed shortly in "RF Behavior."

Loss

When a signal's strength is weakened, we refer to it as *loss*. Loss is a decrease in the signal's amplitude. This signal loss can occur within the cabling of the wireless devices and infrastructure and when the antenna sends the signal through the air as RF waves.

Cables and connectors can cause loss because of the resistance they impose. When this loss occurs in the cabling and connectors, the temperature of the cables will increase generally. The AC electrical signal is absorbed as it travels on the wire (the signal travels the wire as an AC electrical signal and is converted to an RF wave by the antenna) because of resistance.

If the impedance of the cables and connectors do not match, you have an impedance mismatch that causes power to be reflected back toward the source. Less energy can be transmitted forward, as some has been reflected backward, and this creates a loss in signal amplitude. In worse case scenarios, this reflection can even damage equipment.

As the RF wave travels through the environment, walls, humans, animals, and even the air, some of its energy will be lost because of absorption and other RF behaviors. The most damaging environmental objects are generally those with high moisture levels—water is an excellent absorbent of RF energy.

Loss can also occur intentionally. Because the FCC regulates the power output of RF signals from your antenna, you might need to reduce the signal strength intentionally before it leaves the antenna using an RF attenuator.

Because receivers have a sensitivity threshold, you must account for gains and losses. A signal leaving an antenna without the needed strength demanded by the receiver, the distance, and the environment will not be sufficient to reach its destination.

RF Behavior

After RF waves leave the antenna and begin to travel through the environment in which communications must occur, many behavioral factors influence the results achieved. Understanding the behavior of RF waves is essential to configuring a working wireless network in small or large environments.

Most of these behaviors will be easy for you to understand as they are similar to what you have learned through experience with light. Remembering that light is part of the electromagnetic spectrum and has a similar behavior to RF will help you understand these behaviors.

 Remember that light and infrared do not behave exactly like RF in that they are more easily absorbed into objects; however, they do reflect and refract and even scatter in similar ways.

Reflection

Reflection, as the name indicates, occurs when an RF wave strikes an object with large dimensions in comparison to the wavelength of the propagating

FIGURE 2.6   Reflection

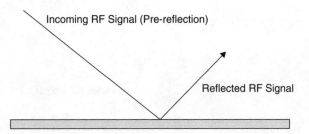

wave and is represented in Figure 2.6. Objects that cause reflections include the earth's surface, large buildings, walls, and other obstacles in the RF wave path. As Figure 2.6 suggests, reflection usually occurs in a direction related to the pre-reflection direction of the RF signal. In other words, the signal will be reflected or bounced back from the reflecting object much like a beam of light reflects off a mirror.

The amount of reflection, as opposed to absorption, that occurs depends on two basic things: the frequency of the RF signal and the material of the object. As materials go, metal reflects more than concrete and water absorbs more than concrete. If an object is smoother, like metal, more of the RF signal will remain intact as it is reflected.

In a wireless LAN, reflection can cause a problem known as *multipath*. Multipath occurs when the main signal is reflected off many objects in the area of the transmission. Multipath can degrade or even cancel out a signal, and this can cause gaps in the RF coverage you achieve. Watch out for metal roofs, metal blinds, and metal doors in the environment, as they can cause reflection and multipath to occur.

Refraction

Refraction, depicted in Figure 2.7, describes what happens when part of the RF signal is reflected and another portion bends through an object. Cold air is an example of an "object" that might cause refraction. Refraction causes problems for long-distance RF links because changes in the weather or atmosphere can cause a significant portion of the RF signal to be redirected away from the intended target and so much energy may be lost that the receiver cannot detect the signal. A pane of glass can also cause refraction.

Diffraction

Diffraction describes a wave bending around an obstacle, as indicated in Figure 2.8. To understand diffraction, it might be helpful to think of a rock

FIGURE 2.7   Refraction

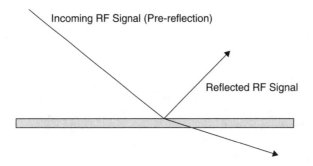

dropping into a pool of water and the ripples created by this action. Think of the ripples as propagating RF waves. Now imagine placing a stick in the water in a perpendicular fashion in the path of the waves. Notice how the waves diffract around the stick. This action is similar to what happens with RF waves that are diffracted around an object.

FIGURE 2.8   Diffraction

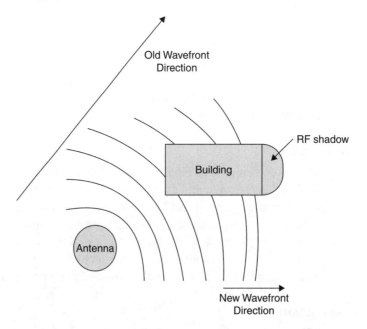

This analogy also helps you to understand that diffraction cannot occur if the impeding object is too large. Imagine placing a large piece of plywood in front the ripples propagating out from the entry point of the rock into the water. Now the waves are not strong enough to diffract around the object and they are simply blocked by the plywood—the energy of the waves is absorbed. In much the same way, RF waves might not be able to diffract around large obstructions.

One final reality revealed by this analogy is the concept of *RF shadow.* Imagine placing a 2 × 4 in the water instead of the stick or plywood. When you place the stick in the water, you cannot see the shadow created, but the 2 × 4 is large enough to reveal the shadow, but not too large—as the plywood is—to block the wave. Look closely behind the 2 × 4 (or the building shown in Figure 2.8) and you will notice a space where no waves exist. This space is the wave shadow, or on wireless networks, the RF shadow. You will not get wireless reception in this space.

Scattering

Scattering is what happens when the medium the RF wave is traveling through contains objects with dimensions that are small in comparison to the wavelength of the RF signal. Scattering is produced by rough surfaces, small objects, or irregularities in the signal path. Figure 2.9 shows that scattering is a lot like many little reflections. When referred to as *reflection,* the vast majority of the signal is reflected in the same direction, and when referred to as *scattering,* many portions of the signal are reflected (scattered) in different directions.

FIGURE 2.9   Scattering

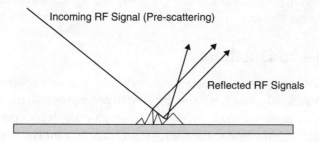

Incoming RF Signal (Pre-scattering)

Reflected RF Signals

Absorption

The final important RF behavior that you must understand is absorption. As noted earlier, absorption is what makes microwaves work and your wireless signal degrade. RF signals can be absorbed by many different objects, including the air through which the signals pass, causing a reduction in signal strength until, eventually, the signal is lost. Water is an excellent signal absorber above the 2 GHz range. This is why the 2.4 GHz range is generally used by microwave ovens. While the RF waves can move through food well, water molecules cannot vibrate fast enough to keep up with the RF waves and so they absorb the energy instead.

It is important to remember that humans are basically moving food (not a pleasant thought, huh?) because we are mostly water. Therefore, the more humans in a space, the more of the RF signal that will be absorbed. Keep this in mind for large convention spaces with low ceilings and large rooms. For this same reason, it is important to remember that most living things have a large saturation of water, including plants and animals, and therefore, heavily forested areas are prime spots for weakened signals in the 2.4 GHz spectrum.

RF Mathematics

To successfully implement and manage an RF-based network, you must understand the power levels of the RF signal. RF math provides us with a standardized way to communicate the strength, or weakness, of an RF signal at the point of radiation as well as the point of reception.

To come to grips with RF math, you must understand *milliwatts* and *decibels* and then move on to learn about *dBm* and *dBi*. Finally, you can't work with wireless technology for very long without encountering the phrase *signal-to-noise ratio,* so you will learn about this as well.

Milliwatts and Decibels

In much the same way that our ears need a certain volume level to hear sounds, RF antennas require a certain power level to receive signals. In order to ensure the power levels are high enough for operations, you must employ a method to measure the power. The *watt* is a standard measure of power used in most engineering applications; however, in wireless networking because lower power levels are used, another measurement is needed in addition to the watt.

A watt is technically defined as one ampere (A) of current at one volt (V). This is also said as "one watt is equal to an ampere multiplied by a volt." As an analogy, think of the water hose with water passing through it. The pressure on the water line can be compared to the voltage in an electric circuit and the flow of the water can be compared to the amperes (or current). In perspective, a common nightlight uses about 7 watts of power.

You may be wondering why wireless networks use such low power levels and, therefore, require a different measurement method than a watt. To answer that question, think of that 7-watt nightlight. On a clear night, this light could be seen up to 50 miles in all directions. This is why the FCC limits RF signal output in the 2.4 GHz band to just 4 watts. As with that 7-watt nightlight, a 4-watt signal can be sent for miles.

Because a small amount of power is required, we use the term *milliwatt* to measure most wireless communication power levels. Standard access points, wireless clients, and wireless network devices have output power levels that are commonly between 1 and 100 milliwatts. A milliwatt (represented by "mW") is 1/1000 of a watt. So 100 mW of output is the same as 1/10 of a watt of output. When you document the power levels needed to provide the required communication signal strength, you use milliwatts or decibels in most cases.

A *decibel* is used to represent extremely small numbers in a manageable way. Some receivers are sensitive enough to RF signals that they can receive a signal as small as 0.000000001 watts. Because of the difficulty in grasping such small numbers, the decibel is used to measure these levels of strength.

Decibels are used to measure increases and decreases in signal strength in a manner that is easy to grasp for administrators, technicians, and users alike.

Decibels (dB) are based on a logarithmic relationship to the literal or linear power measurement of a watt. This is a complex way of saying that decibels allow you to represent large (and small) numbers with numbers you can wrap your mind around. The most important thing for you to remember is the rule of 10s and 3s in RF math. Here's how it works:

−3 dB = half the power in mW

+3 dB = double the power in mW

−10 dB = one tenth the power in mW

+10 dB = ten times the power in mW

Using creative combinations of 10s and 3s, you can usually calculate the output or input power levels of any wireless system. You use this most frequently when calculating gains and losses based on equipment used to form an *intentional radiator* (all of the equipment, cables, and connectors leading up to, but not including, the output antenna in an RF system) or when determining the actual Equivalent Isotropically Radiated Power (EIRP) power output, which is the actual output from an antenna including calculations of the intentional radiator and any antenna gains or losses.

As an example, imagine you have a wireless access point with 30 mW of output power connected to a cable with 3 dB of loss and feeding into an amplifier with 9 dB of gain and then into another cable with 3 dB of loss and finally output through an antenna with 7 dB of gain. What is the actual output power (EIRP) of this system? The answer can be found by using the 10s and 3s of RF math as follows:

30 mW − 3 dB for the cable = 15 mW

15 mW + 9 dB for the amplifier = 120 mW

120 mW − 3 dB for the second cable = 60 mW

60 mW + 7 dB for the antenna = 300 mW

This is where the creative use of the 10s and 3s comes into play. The last calculation of 60 mW + 7 dB might have seemed impossible. However, by multiplying the 60 mW times 10 (60 mW + 10 db), you arrive at 600 mW. What is 7 from 10? The answer is 3. You now subtract 3 dB from the 600 mW and arrive at 300 mW of EIRP. In other words, because dB calculations are additive, +7 dB is the same as +10 dB/−3dB. This trick allows you to calculate more complex power level scenarios more easily.

dBm vs. dBi

Other common measurements you will see in the area of wireless technology include *dBm* and *dBi*. The reference point that relates the logarithmic dB scale to the linear watt scale is 1 mW = 0 dBm. Because dBm is linked to the linear milliwatts scale, it is an absolute reference of power. The *m* in dBm simply stands for *milliwatts*. This means that when wireless product packaging states that a device provides up to 20 dBm of output power, it is promising a specific level of output power (in this case, it is promising approximately 100 mW of output power).

Remember that 1 mW is equal to 0 dBm, so a 20 dBm product would be equal to 1 mW $\times$ 10 $\times$ 10, or 100 mW. Likewise, a 9 dBm product would be equal to 1 mW $\times$ 2 $\times$ 2 $\times$ 2, or 8 mW. dBm is a reference to the relationship between decibels and linear watts.

The second term, dBi, is used to reference the increase in power in a certain direction by an antenna. The *i* in dBi stands for *isotropic*. This simply means that the change in power provided by the antenna is calculated against what an isotropic radiator would produce. An isotropic radiator is a theoretical transmitter that propagates RF energy exactly equally in all directions. No such antenna exists as all antennas propagate more of their energy in one or more directions than in others, which results in a gain in the output power according to the directionality of the antenna. Think of this, again, as placing your thumb over a portion of the opening of a water hose. The same pressure is being applied but the possible "direction" of the pressure is reduced causing the water to spray farther.

If an antenna is referenced as a 6 dBi antenna, it means that it quadruples (remember, +3 dB +3 dB = $\times$ 2 $\times$ 2) the output power in the direction of the antenna. If 100 mW of power is fed into the antenna, the output power is estimated at 400 mW in the direction of the antenna.

SNR—Signal-to-Noise Ratio

One final measurement used to determine the strength and quality of an RF signal is the signal-to-noise ratio (SNR or S/N ratio). The SNR does not measure the power of the signal by itself in absolute or relative terms like dB or dBm does, but it is used to measure the signal power compared to the power of the noise in the environment. A higher SNR indicates a better signal, as the signal is much "louder" than the noise.

Returning to the human hearing analogy, if you are in a quiet room, another person could whisper to you and you could hear them easily. However, in a football stadium watching the Super Bowl, the person will have to shout so you can hear them over the noise. The same basic concepts apply to wireless networking.

The RF noise in the environment is often referred to as the *noise floor*. Many programs give you the ability to view the SNR in your environment. One of the most commonly used tools is NetStumbler, which is shown in Figure 2.10. Determining the SNR in areas of desired coverage is an important part of wireless network implementation.

FIGURE 2.10   Signal-to-noise ratio in NetStumbler

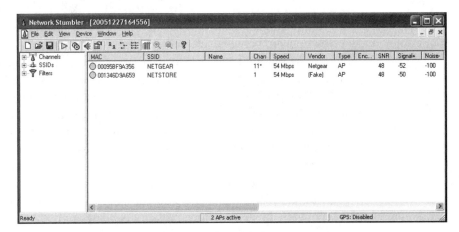

To calculate the signal-to-noise ratio, calculate the difference between the power levels of the signal and the power levels of the noise. For example, a signal power level of –55 dBm and a noise power level of –97 dBm gives you an SNR of 42. This is better than a SNR of 17, which is the result of the same noise level with a signal level of –80 dBm.

RF and Infrared Technologies

There are many different technologies that utilize RF communications. The major differences among them are the frequencies and encoding techniques they use. While more information about each technology is provided in the next chapter—specifically DSSS, OFDM, and FHSS—a brief overview will be helpful here. These technologies include the following:

- DSSS
- OFDM
- FHSS
- Infrared
- MIMO

DSSS

Direct sequence spread spectrum (DSSS) is the technology used in 802.11 and 802.11b devices, providing data rates of 1, 2, 5.5, and 11 Mbps. Because backward compatibility is provided, 802.11b devices operating at 5.5 or 11 Mbps can communicate with 802.11 devices running at 1 or 2 Mbps. Of course, these devices are limited to the speed of the slower device in the link. The 802.11 and 802.11b standards specify that DSSS is to be used in the 2.4 GHz spectrum of RF frequencies.

DSSS systems use assigned channels for communications. These channels are blocks of frequency space or frequency ranges. Unlike frequency hopping spread spectrum systems, DSSS systems are configured to use the same frequencies permanently, so frequencies do not change during communications.

OFDM

802.11a utilizes a different technology for communications known as Orthogonal Frequency Division Multiplexing, or OFDM to avoid the mouth full. OFDM is also used in 802.11g with modifications for backward compatibility with 802.11b's use of DSSS. Unlike DSSS, which uses the full channel as a single "pipe," OFDM divides a channel into subcarriers or subchannels and sends data streams on these "separate pipes." This provides for greater resistance to multipath interference and allows for greater bandwidth.

FHSS

Frequency hopping spread spectrum (FHSS) is another spread spectrum technology, such as DSSS, that is used by older 802.11 devices and Bluetooth devices as well as some RFID units. FHSS is limited to 1 or 2 Mbps in the 802.11 specification. As you might guess by the name, FHSS systems hop from one frequency to another during communications. This helps to avoid the problems caused by narrow-band interference.

Infrared

The 802.11 standard includes a PHY (physical layer) specification for infrared communications. However, because of lack of interest, this layer has not been implemented. You might question this if you have a laptop or PDA that uses an infrared port, but that port is most likely designed according to standards set forth by the Infrared Data Association (IrDA) and not the 802.11 PHY standard. Chapter 8 focuses on the IrDA specifications.

MIMO

Multiple input/Multiple output (MIMO, pronounced *my-moe*) devices allow the use of more than one antenna at the same time by using multiple data streams in the same channel via "smart antennas." MIMO-based networks can help in overcoming multipath problems (the result of the signal being reflected off different objects in the environment) and increasing the speed of communications. Many devices by such companies as Belkin, Cisco, and more provide this technology.

MIMO is expected to be part of the new 802.11n standard for high throughput communications. The 802.11n task group was formed in January 2004 aimed at creating a wireless standard with theoretical throughputs of up to 540 Mbps. 802.11n is expected to use a combination of MIMO and OFDM technologies.

Summary

Understanding RF is key to implementing and supporting a wireless network. In this chapter, you learned how RF signals are propagated throughout an environment, and you understand the fundamental behaviors of RF signals including reflection, refraction, diffraction, absorption, and scattering. The RF math skills gained helps you determine power levels needed and available in your wireless implementations, and the high-level understanding of various RF-based technologies prepares you for the more in-depth learning that lies ahead.

Key Terms

- ☐ **Radio frequency**
- ☐ **signals**
- ☐ **modulation**
- ☐ **line-of-sight**
- ☐ **Fresnel Zone**
- ☐ **gain**
- ☐ **loss**
- ☐ **reflection**
- ☐ **refraction**
- ☐ **scattering**
- ☐ **diffraction**
- ☐ **absorption**
- ☐ **milliwatt**
- ☐ **decibel**
- ☐ **dBm and dBi**
- ☐ **signal-to-noise ratio**
- ☐ **MIMO**

Review Questions

1. You are planning to implement a wireless network in a doctor's office. The network will be contained within the building and will require no outside links. Will you be concerned about line-of-sight issues?

   A. Yes. Line-of-sight is a concern inside a building just as it is outside of a building.

   B. No. Line-of-sight issues are generally resolved through the normal behavior of RF signals bouncing off and around objects indoors.

2. You are creating a link between two buildings on a campus. There are several pine trees between the antennas located on each building, but you can see the antenna on either building from the other. Should you be concerned about the pine trees since you have visual line-of-sight?

   A. Yes. The Fresnel Zone may be blocked and the antennas could be raised to avoid blockage from the pine trees.

   B. No. If you can see the antenna, the antennas can communicate.

3. When some of the RF signal is reflected and some passes through an object but is redirected, this is known as what?

   A. Scattering

   B. Reflection

   C. Refraction

   D. Diffraction

4. Which of these are absolute measurements of power? Select two.

   A. Milliwatt

   B. dBi

   C. decibel

   D. dBm

5. You have connected a wireless access point with 50 mW of output power to a cable with 3 dB of loss and then to an antenna with a rating of 6 dBi. What will be the actual output power of this configuration?

    A. 500 mW

    B. 100 mW

    C. 4 watts

    D. 400 mW

6. You have determined that you can accomplish a signal-to-noise ratio of 43 with one technology and 37 with another. All else being equal, which of these technologies would you prefer?

    A. The one with 37 SNR

    B. The one with 43 SNR

7. When RF signals move around an object in their path, what is this called?

    A. Reflection

    B. Scattering

    C. Refraction

    D. Diffraction

8. What encoding or modulation technology does 802.11a use?

    A. FHSS

    B. DSSS

    C. OFDM

    D. MIMO

9. Which of these wireless technologies uses hopping during the communications process?

   A. OFDM

   B. FHSS

   C. DSSS

   D. 802.11i

10. What standard is expected to incorporate MIMO technologies along with OFDM?

    A. 802.11n

    B. 802.11e

    C. 802.11g-FAST

    D. 802.11a-FAST

11. An increase in the RF signal strength is known as what?

    A. dB+

    B. gain

    C. impedance

    D. dBm

Review Answers

1. **B.** Line-of-sight problems do not usually exist indoors as reflection, refraction, scattering, and diffraction usually cause the signal to travel throughout the inside of the building without the need for direct line-of-sight.

2. **A.** Fresnel Zone blockage can prevent effective wireless communications. You will have to either clear the blockage or raise the antennas high enough to clear the Fresnel Zone for effective communications.

3. **C.** Refraction occurs when an RF signal is redirected as it passes through an object. When refraction occurs, some reflection might also occur.

4. **A, D.** The milliwatt and dBm measurements are used as absolute measurements of power. The decibel (dB) is used to measure power gains and losses, and dBi is used to refer to the gains or losses of an antenna specifically.

5. **B.** With 50 mW of output divided by 2 (3 dB of loss), you have 25 mW. When you add 6 dBi of gain (25 mW × 2 × 2), you have 100 mW of output power at the antenna. Remember, 3 dB is a factor of 2, while 10 dB is a factor of 10.

6. **B.** The one with 43 SNR would be better as it has a higher SNR and higher is better. Of course, the technology alone does not determine the SNR; you must also factor the environment into the equation. The point here is to remember that a higher SNR is generally better.

7. **D.** Diffraction is the moving or bending of the RF wave around an obstacle, such as a building.

8. **C.** 802.11a uses Orthogonal Frequency Division Multiplexing (OFDM) for communications. 802.11 and 802.11b utilize direct sequence spread spectrum (DSSS), and 802.11 may use frequency hopping spread spectrum (FHSS). MIMO (multiple input/multiple output) is a newer use of multiple antennas that takes advantage of multipath for greater throughput. MIMO runs in conjunction with other modulation schemes.

9. **B.** FHSS (frequency hopping spread spectrum) uses pseudo-random hopping sequences to communicate information across radio frequencies.

10. **A.** 802.11n is a standard expected to be ratified in late 2006 or early 2007, providing the combination of MIMO and OFDM technologies and theoretical throughputs of up to 540 Mbps. This is roughly 10 times that of 802.11g.

11. **B.** *Gain* is the term used to refer to an increase in RF signal strength. *Loss* refers to a decrease in RF signal strength.

Wi-Fi Features and Functionality

Wireless# Exam Objectives Covered:

❖ Define the characteristics of Wi-Fi technology

- Range
- Frequencies
- Power saving modes
- Data rates and throughput
- Dynamic rate selection
- Roaming functionality
- Infrastructure and ad hoc modes
- SSID/Network names

❖ Define the concepts that make up the functionality of RF and spread spectrum technology

- OFDM/DSSS channels
- Colocation of DSSS and OFDM systems
- Adjacent-channel and cochannel interference
- WLAN/WPAN coexistence

Once you understand basic RF behaviors and functionality, you can begin to understand the various technologies that utilize RF. Without question, the major RF-based technology in production today is Wi-Fi. *Wi-Fi,* short for *Wireless Fidelity,* is both an organization and a certification. The Wi-Fi Alliance certifies wireless equipment to operate according to IEEE standards such as 802.11a, 802.11b, and 802.11g. This equipment will then be assigned the appropriate Wi-Fi certification logo, like the one shown in Figure 3.1, indicating the standards with which the equipment is in compliance.

As for Wi-Fi equipment, that will be covered in detail in Chapters 4 and 5. In this chapter, you will learn about the different Wi-Fi standards in greater detail than in previous chapters. You will discover the range (or distance covered) of wireless technologies and the methods used for large and small areas alike. You will also gain an in-depth understanding of the real issues surrounding communication speeds (bandwidth and throughput) and how to get the most out of your wireless network. Finally, you'll study roaming and wireless infrastructures so you can support the mobile workforce effectively.

Range and Coverage

Just as Ethernet cabling is limited by the length of various cable types, wireless networks cannot pass a signal to infinity. Many factors impact the real distance an RF signal can be transmitted and the actual throughput for data on that signal. Products often list a wireless range that cannot be realized in true environments because the range estimate assumes completely open space with no weather interference. For this reason, you must test products in actual implementations to determine the true range (understood as *distance*) and coverage (understood as *availability* and *usability* within the true range) provided by the device.

FIGURE 3.1   Wi-Fi certification logo for a B/G compliant device

As you learned in Chapter 2, because of diffraction and other RF behaviors, an area may be "within range" of the wireless device and still lack coverage if the area is in RF shadow. If you are a *Lord of the Rings* fan, you might remember when Gandalf fell into shadow. During this time, the others in the Fellowship of the Ring did not know where he was; it was as if he wasn't there. This is also what happens when your wireless client is in an RF shadow area even though the area is within the stated range of the wireless server (access point, router, and so on). In Chapter 12, you will learn the basic techniques used to overcome RF shadow and other common wireless networking problems.

Range and coverage issues are important to the success of your wireless implementation. If you attempt to install a wireless network using PDAs throughout a warehouse for inventory management, you wouldn't want there to be areas without proper RF coverage. Users would have to move from one place to another just to enter data, and in addition to this, reassociation procedures would slow down the entire process.

The range of your wireless network depends on the frequencies used and, therefore, the 802.11 standard you choose. While one 802.11 standard might provide greater bandwidth capabilities, it might not provide the needed range. Choosing the appropriate technology for each scenario is essential.

Assuring coverage in all areas of your building or wireless network campus can usually be accomplished through the creative use of wireless channels and the strategic positioning of wireless base stations or access points and routers.

Frequencies and Channels

For a device to determine the difference between RF noise and intentional RF signals, you must configure the device so it knows which signal to monitor. You do this using frequencies and channels. The *frequency* is what distinguishes one RF signal from another, and a *channel* is generally a portion of the entire frequency assigned to a specific technology such as 802.11b or 802.11a.

Most modern devices hide the frequency information from you in two ways. First, 802.11b devices can communicate with other 802.11b devices because they all use the same total frequency range, which is discussed shortly in this chapter in the "Frequencies" section. You don't have to know the frequencies used—necessarily—as long as you know you're using all 802.11b devices.

The second method of hiding the frequency information is through the use of simple channel assignments. Most access points, for example, provide an easy-to-use drop-down box that lists the available channels. Often, these access points make no reference to the actual frequencies used by these channels. Of course, enterprise-class wireless devices from Cisco and other venders reveal this information frequently though it is seldom needed for effective operation.

The concept is similar to the way the domain name system (DNS) works on the Internet. DNS provides a simple naming system for Internet locations, so you don't have to memorize the IP address. For example, the IP address for SYSEDCO.com is 204.14.106.29. Would you rather remember hundreds of numbers like this or domain names that actually have meaning? If you're like me, you opted for the second choice. This is what frequency hiding does for you. It's easier to remember that all your devices should be communicating on channel 11 and using 802.11b than to remember that all devices should use the frequency of 2.462 GHz within the total 2.4 GHz frequency spectrum.

Frequencies

Two major frequencies are used in Wi-Fi networks at this time: the 2.4 GHz ISM (Industrial, Scientific, and Medical) band and the 5 GHz UNII (Unlicensed National Information Infrastructure, pronounced *you-nee*) band. The ISM band includes a 900 MHz band (starting at 902 MHz and going to 928 MHz), a 2.4 GHz band (starting at 2.4000 GHz and going to 2.5000 GHz), and a 5.8 GHz band (starting at 5.725 GHz and going to 5.875 GHz).

The 2.4 GHz band is used for 802.11, 802.11b, and 802.11g devices. While the full range from 2.4000 GHz to 2.5000 GHz is included in the designated band, wireless networks use only the range from 2.4000 to 2.4835 GHz because the FCC has provided power output specifications for this range of frequencies only.

The 5 GHz band is used for 802.11a devices and is divided into three bands known as the lower, middle, and upper bands. These bands use a frequency range 100 MHz wide and each contain four nonoverlapping channels. Where the 2.4 GHz devices use FHSS or DSSS, the 5 GHz 802.11a devices use OFDM.

The lower UNII band goes from 5.15 GHz to 5.25 GHz (this is sometimes referenced as 5.150 to 5.250 or as 5150 to 5250, though you will not need to know this for the Wireless# certification exam) and has an FCC-imposed limit of 50 mW of maximum output power. The middle UNII band goes from 5.25 GHz to 5.35 GHz and is limited to 250 mW of output power. The final band, known as the upper band, goes from 5.725 GHz to 5.825 GHz with a total allowed output power of 1 watt.

Channels

The frequency ranges used in the various 802.11 standards and assigned by the FCC are further divided into smaller frequency ranges by the IEEE. These frequency ranges form channels that are used for actual communications. You do not generally use all channels, or the entire frequency range, for a single link between two devices; instead, you choose a single channel to use for communications.

The channels available differ depending on the technology used. These technologies include OFDM, DSSS, and FHSS.

OFDM Channels

Each of the three UNII bands (lower, upper, and middle) provides four channels for communications in an 802.11a network. In most cases, the lower and middle bands are used indoors and the upper band is used outdoors. For this reason, indoor coverage is usually provided by a maximum of eight different channels. Because these channels are separated with no overlapping, they should not interfere with each other.

To better understand channel interference, think back to the early days of 900 MHz cordless phones. Remember turning on the phone only to hear your neighbor's conversation? You would press the channel button on the phone to change to a different channel and then you'd be listening to the other neighbor's conversation. Well, maybe it wasn't that bad, but you understand the point. In much the same way, you cannot operate two wireless networks in the same general area using the same channel— remember, a channel is nothing more than a range of frequencies.

Table 3.1 provides a quick reference of the channels used by 802.11a and OFDM in wireless networks in the Americas on the lower and middle UNII bands. These bands are used by consumer-grade and indoor wireless technologies. Each channel is 20 MHz wide surrounding the center frequency.

TABLE 3.1   802.11a OFDM Channels

Channel	Center Frequency	Lower (L)/Middle (M)
36	5.18 GHz	L
40	5.20 GHz	L
44	5.22 GHz	L
48	5.24 GHz	L
52	5.26 GHz	M
56	5.28 GHz	M
60	5.30 GHz	M
64	5.32 GHz	M

DSSS Channels

The DSSS-based technologies, such as 802.11b, provide 11 channels in the U.S. and up to 14 channels in other countries, as listed in Table 3.2. Unlike 802.11a OFDM channels, 802.11 b/g channels do overlap. This overlap can cause what is sometimes called *channel fading* or *cochannel interference*. For example, you would not want to use in the same general area two access points on channels 1 and 2; however, using channels 1 and 11 would be fine.

As you can see from Table 3.2, different locations have different rules. In the U.S., you can use only channels 1–11, while Japan allows the use of all 14 channels. These rules are important to consider when creating and implementing wireless networks.

It is also important to remember that the frequencies listed in Table 3.2 are center frequencies. This means the channel uses the center frequency +/−11 MHz. In the end, each channel uses a 22 MHz wide frequency range. For example, channel 1 uses the range from 2.401 to 2.423 and is centered on 2.412.

FHSS Hopping Sequences

A frequency hopping spread spectrum system does not use channels in the same way as DSSS and OFDM. Instead, FHSS systems hop from frequency-to-frequency using a pseudorandom hopping sequence. This hopping sequence—or *pattern*—is defined as the channel. During communications, the radios in each device change from one frequency to another in a pseudorandomly generated pattern and then they loop back

TABLE 3.2   802.11/802.11b/802.11g DSSS Channels

Channel Identifier	Frequency in GHz	Regulatory Domains				
		Americas	EMEA	Israel	China	Japan
1	2.412	X	X	—	X	X
2	2.417	X	X	—	X	X
3	2.422	X	X	X	X	X
4	2.427	X	X	X	X	X
5	2.432	X	X	X	X	X
6	2.437	X	X	X	X	X
7	2.442	X	X	X	X	X
8	2.447	X	X	X	X	X
9	2.452	X	X	X	X	X
10	2.457	X	X	—	X	X
11	2.462	X	X	—	X	X
12	2.467	—	X	—	—	X
13	2.472	—	X	—	—	X
14	2.484	—	—	—	—	X

through that pattern continually. The amount of time spent on a particular frequency is known as *dwell time,* and the amount of time it takes to move from one frequency to the next is known as *hop time.*

The FCC regulates FHSS systems in areas of dwell time, frequencies used, and output power. These regulations restrict the available bandwidth because of dwell time limits and the number of channels because of frequency limits. However, 79 total channels (frequency hop patterns) are available and provide for many colocated systems. However, FHSS equipment is becoming more and more difficult to find and, therefore, is not covered in extensive detail on the exam. You are unlikely to encounter it frequently as you support and implement wireless networks.

There is, of course, one major exception to the ever-decreasing use of FHSS and that is Bluetooth. Bluetooth devices are extremely popular today in PDAs, cell phones, and laptop computers. These devices use FHSS, as you will learn in Chapter 7.

Facility Coverage

By this time, you may be wondering why you need to know all this information about frequencies and channels. The answer is simple: By using channels effectively, you can provide the needed coverage in most facilities. The concept of colocation allows for the strategic placement of wireless access points, bridges, and routers based on channels within frequencies, different standards (802.11g vs. 802.11a), or both. In order to implement colocated systems effectively, you must also understand channel interference and the potential problems created by personal area network devices.

Colocation

To provide proper coverage in any facility, you need to strike a balance between bandwidth and range. While an access point might be able to provide service to a client that is 100 feet away, it might not provide sufficient speeds for the needs of the user. Table 3.3 provides a listing of the various wireless LAN standards and advertised ranges. Remember, these are *advertised* ranges and will seldom be seen in production environments. For example, it is not uncommon to lose 20 feet (or more) of distance for every internal wall the signal has to pass through.

Imagine you are installing a wireless network in a facility with the dimensions represented in Figure 3.2. In this scenario, we'll assume you are using 802.11g devices. While the advertised range is 300 feet, the real range will probably be closer to 120–200 feet indoors with walls, filing cabinets, and other objects in the RF space. Let's also assume you have tested the signal ranges within the building and determined that you can achieve an average range of between 100–150 feet.

TABLE 3.3   Standards and Advertised Ranges

	802.11	802.11a	802.11b	802.11g
Frequency	2.4 GHz	5 GHz	2.4 GHz	2.4 GHz
Data Rate(s)	1, 2 Mbps	5, 9, 12, 18, 24, 36, 48, 54 Mbps	1, 2, 5.5, 11 Mbps	6, 9, 12, 15, 24, 36, 48, 54 Mbps
Modulation	FHSS, DSSS	OFDM	DSSS	OFDM
Advertised Range	300 feet	225 feet	300 feet	300 feet

FIGURE 3.2   Facility dimensions

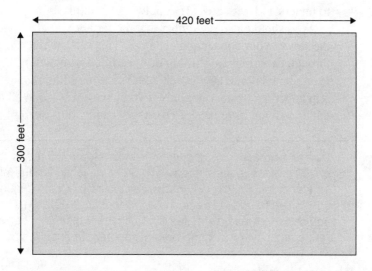

Based on this information, you could provide adequate coverage in the facility using six access points located, as shown in Figure 3.3. Note the channels used by the different access points. Using these channels, you can accomplish the needed coverage through colocation without much

FIGURE 3.3   Facility coverage

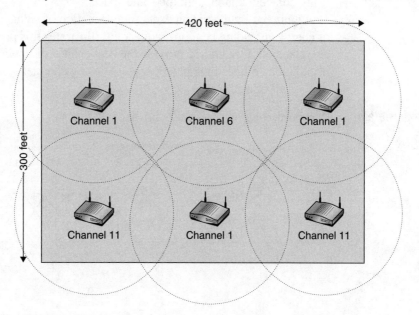

channel interference. However, channel interference is an important concept to understand with 802.11b/g networks and this topic will be discussed next.

You should also remember that the farther you get from the access point, the slower your connection becomes. This is a general rule and is applied through dynamic rate shifting or dynamic rate selection, which you will learn about later in the "Bandwidth" section of this chapter. For now, just remember to consider not only if you have coverage in all necessary areas, but also if you have needed coverage (bandwidth) in all of those areas.

Range estimates vary greatly by vendor. Some will tell you to use the figure of 100 feet for your estimates with 802.11b, while others will tell you to use 75 feet or less in your estimates. For example, Cisco suggests a range of 20–75 feet for 802.11a and 100–150 feet for 802.11b/g. In the real world, you can use these estimates for preliminary planning, but you must test range and coverage in the live environment to ensure accurate results.

Channel Interference

The fact that DSSS channels are centered on frequencies separated by 5 MHz, while the channel is 22 MHz wide, results in overlapping channels. This overlap means that adjacent channels actually use some of the same frequency space for communications. Throughput can suffer greatly and possibly disappear altogether if you attempt to build a wireless network using adjacent channels in the same space.

Figure 3.4, while not an exact representation of signal overlap because of energy spreading beyond frequencies, illustrates this problem. As you can see, channels 1, 6, and 11 provide the best chance of having no overlap in an installation. While some have suggested using channels 1, 4, 8, and 11, tests

FIGURE 3.4 Channel overlap with DSSS/802.11b and 802.11g

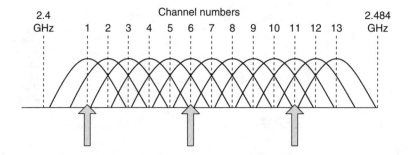

by various organizations show a loss in throughput of as much as 50 percent when using this latter configuration. For this reason, using channels 1, 6, and 11 is considered a best practice.

This best practice assumes you need three channels. If you are installing a wireless network that will be serviced exceptionally well with two access points, consider using channels 1 and 11. The main thing is to separate the channels by a total of 5 channels or more, which means a channel arrangement of 3 and 8 or 5 and 10 would also be acceptable. Using these channels is helpful if another network is using Wi-Fi technology on channels 1 or 11 at some distance away so the interference is minimal on these close channels. Instances such as these are about the only time you would want to break the "5 channels of separation" rule.

If client devices are not in need of roaming capabilities (the ability to move around and transfer from one access point to another automatically), another colocation solution is to use both 802.11b/g and 802.11a devices in the same space. Because they communicate on different frequencies, they do not interfere with each other.

Here is a great analogy to help you understand this. Imagine you are sitting in a room talking with a friend. Two other friends are sitting behind you as well, but you are not interrupted by them at all. In fact, it seems as if they are not talking as you do not hear a conversation. When you turn and look at them, you discover they are using sign language to converse. Think of your verbal conversation like 802.11b/g and their sign language conversation like 802.11a. While these two wireless standard do not differ as much as verbal and sign language, this analogy illustrates the fact that 802.11a networks cause no interference to 802.11b/g networks, and they are not interfered upon by the 802.11b/g networks either.

Personal Area Network Integration

Up to this point, the focus has been on wireless networks known as wireless LANs or WLANs; however, wireless PANs (WPANs) also use similar technologies. For example, Bluetooth devices utilize FHSS for communications and their existence on the network is an important thing to know about.

When considering the impact of Bluetooth devices, remember that they transmit at a very low power and they hop across differing frequencies. As you will learn in Chapter 7, newer Bluetooth standards also implement algorithms to provide resistance to interference and the creation of interference.

Because FHSS systems operate in the 2.4 GHz ISM band, you should not experience interference problems if you use 802.11a devices for the WLAN, as they use the 5 GHz UNII band.

Bandwidth

In the world of networking, bandwidth has become synonymous with speed. In other words, the phrase "I've got a lot of bandwidth" is taken to mean you can transfer information very quickly. In the world of Wi-Fi, bandwidth can have a twofold meaning. In one sense, bandwidth can refer to the width of the RF band (such as 22 MHz for DSSS channels); in another sense, it can refer to the available bandwidth or data rates supported by the technology.

If it ended here, the concept would be complex enough, but the reality is that data rates can be a bit misleading if you don't understand the difference between data rates and throughput. Most packaging states the supported data rates of the device, but provides no details about how much useful information can pass through the device. For this reason, you must understand the following essential concepts:

- Data rates
- Throughput
- Dynamic rate selection

Data Rates

The data rate of a device refers to the *total* data transfer rate the device can handle. It is important to distinguish this from the *actual* data throughput discussed momentarily. The data rate bandwidth will be consumed partially by overhead operations.

Table 3.4 provides a list of the data rates supported by the different Wi-Fi standards and will be a helpful reference as you plan and design wireless networks.

TABLE 3.4   Wi-Fi Standards—Data Rates

	802.11	802.11a	802.11b	802.11g
Data Rate(s)	1, 2 Mbps	5, 9, 12, 18, 24, 36, 48, 54 Mbps	1, 2, 5.5, 11 Mbps	6, 9, 12, 15, 24, 36, 48, 54 Mbps

Actual Throughput

Testing has revealed that you can usually estimate that approximately half the stated data rate will be available for data transfer or throughput. *Throughput* refers to the amount of actual data you can transfer across the network in a given amount of time.

Think of it like this: Imagine you have a big rig (also known as a tractor trailer, semi-truck, or 18 wheeler) with a carrying capacity of 37 units of a certain product. However, you are required to use 10 percent of your available space for documentation related to the product and another 10 percent for security devices to protect the product during transit. As you can see, your actual carrying capacity is only 29–30 units of the product. The 37-unit capacity is similar to a wireless device's data rate and the 29–30–unit capacity is similar to the device's throughput. As you can see, more than 20 percent (closer to 50 percent) of the data rate is consumed by overhead data related to association, power save mode information, encryption, and other management-type data. While some technologies have been created that allow for as much as 80 percent throughput, these technologies are usually nonstandard and may not operate with the equipment of other vendors.

Dynamic Rate Selection

Dynamic rate selection (DRS) is the term used to refer to a method of dynamically adjusting the speed of wireless LAN client devices. Some vendors may use differing terms such as *dynamic rate shifting,* but they are referring to the same thing. DRS works by adjusting the speed of the connection as the wireless LAN client moves farther away from the access point. It will also dynamically adjust the speed if increased interference occurs. Generally speaking, to achieve a higher data rate, you must shorten the distance between you and the access point.

As you plan your wireless LAN, you must consider the impact of DRS on your wireless clients. For example, if you determine that you need a minimum data rate of 36 Mbps for an estimated throughput of 18 Mbps, you must ensure that the clients are close enough to the access points and interference is low enough to allow for this. In the end, you can ensure this only through testing.

When a client moves farther away from the access point, data is more likely to be corrupted at higher data rates. This is the reason for lowering the data rate. Theoretically, you can achieve greater throughput at a lower data rate because there are fewer retransmissions of data (retransmissions are caused by data corruption). This will, in the end, provide greater throughput to those clients closer to the access point as well. Not only can they communicate at a higher data rate but also lowering the retransmissions of data from clients who are farther away "frees the air waves" for the closer clients.

Figure 3.5 represents the functionality of DRS. Though the concentric circles are not meant to represent absolute distances in this diagram, you can use these estimates to perform preliminary planning. For example, you can estimate that DRS will shift from 54 Mbps to 48 Mbps at approximately 80 feet. The next shift is likely to occur at around 100 feet when DRS shifts the rate to 36 Mbps. Table 3.5 provides estimates of rate-adjustment ranges based on differing frequencies and power levels. The figures in Table 3.5 are intended to represent *ideal* situations and cannot be assumed true in every implementation.

FIGURE 3.5   Dynamic rate selection

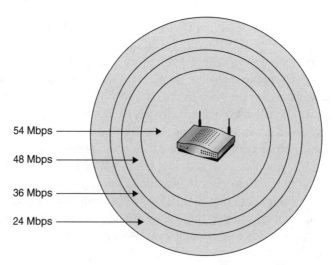

TABLE 3.5   DRS Rate Adjustment Estimates

Rate	Distance (in feet)	Frequency	Power
54 Mbps	60	5 GHz	40 mW
48 Mbps	80	5 GHz	40 mW
36 Mbps	100	5 GHz	40 mW
24 Mbps	120	5 GHz	40 mW
18 Mbps	130	5 GHz	40 mW
12 Mbps	140	5 GHz	40 mW
9 Mbps	150	5 GHz	40 mW
6 Mbps	170	5 GHz	40 mW
11 Mbps	140	2.4 GHz	100 mW
5.5 Mbps	180	2.4 GHz	100 mW
2 Mbps	250	2.4 GHz	100 mW
1 Mbps	350	2.4 GHz	100 mW

Operational Modes

Wireless networks can function in one of two basic modes: *ad hoc* or *infrastructure*. Understanding these operational modes and their benefits will help in your decision making during installations and provide you with the knowledge you need to troubleshoot existing wireless implementations.

Ad Hoc

As with peer-to-peer networking in the traditional wired networking world, when operating in ad hoc mode, wireless devices communicate with each other directly. There is no central server. There are no routers. Each device is a node on the network, and they can all communicate with each other. Figure 3.6 illustrates ad hoc mode.

Benefits of ad hoc mode include

- No access point needed
- Can be formed dynamically
- Supported by most wireless hardware
- Simple to set up and operate

FIGURE 3.6   Ad hoc mode

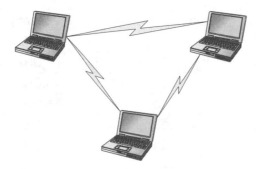

Problems with ad hoc mode include

- No access to the Internet or network infrastructures
- No centralization of management
- More difficult to secure (WEP keys can be used, but are difficult to manage among many clients)
- Limited in size because of bandwidth consumption just as in Ethernet peer-to-peer networks

Infrastructure

Infrastructure mode provides centralized control and is more like the client-server model used in traditional networks. In this case, the access point is as the server and the wireless client devices are the clients. Using infrastructure mode generally costs more because of the need for access points, but you can manage it more easily and provide access to the Internet or your existing network infrastructure. Figure 3.7 depicts infrastructure mode.

FIGURE 3.7   Infrastructure mode

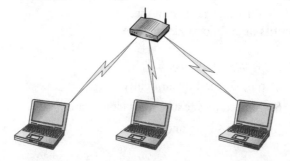

Benefits of infrastructure mode include

- Centralized management
- Greater security control
- Access to the Internet or network infrastructures
- High bandwidth availability with proper implementation

Problems with infrastructure mode include

- Greater cost
- Longer and more complex implementations
- Less dynamic than ad hoc mode
- Requires one or more access points

Naming the Network—the SSID

The network your device participates on is determined by the name of the network. If your device has the same name as other devices, and all the devices use the same networking technology (802.11b/g or 802.11a) and are within range of each other through some communication's channel, then these devices are said to form a network.

Most access points come with a default name. For example, older Cisco access points used the name *tsunami,* and Netgear devices generally use the name *Netgear*. It is generally considered a best practice to change the name to something other than the default. If you are broadcasting the name, clients will still be able to see it, but too many "netgear" names in an area make things confusing. For this reason, you should make it standard practice to change these names.

You are probably beginning to wonder what this name does for your network. The answer is that it determines your service set's SSID. An SSID is a *service set identifier,* or the name (identity) of the service set. A *service set* is a group of devices (access points, routers, etc.) sharing the same name (SSID) and technology. There are three types of service sets:

- Independent Basic Service Set
- Basic Service Set
- Extended Service Set

IBSS

The *Independent Basic Service Set* (IBSS) is also known as an ad hoc network. An IBSS has no access point and is created dynamically based on all the connecting client devices sharing a consistent SSID. For the IBSS or ad hoc network to function, all the devices must be in earshot of each other so they can communicate since there is no access point. Because of this restriction, IBSS networks are useful only for smaller networks in confined spaces.

There are, however, multiple instances where this configuration could prove helpful. One primary example is the small group meeting. If you are meeting with five other individuals, and you all have laptop computers with wireless devices supporting ad hoc mode, you can create a temporary IBSS for data exchange during your meeting. This ability is particularly useful if the meeting takes place outside your facility in a rented conference space or library. Though you do not have control of the infrastructure in this remote facility, you can create an IBSS for temporary communications.

You can also create an ad hoc network for personal or family gatherings. At a recent meeting, a friend and I both pulled out our laptops, and configuring them with the same SSID, placed them in ad hoc mode (this is how an IBSS is referenced in most configuration interfaces). We then configured our IP addresses to the same network and enabled sharing on the folders with data in them that we wanted to share. In less than five minutes, we were live and transferring information between our machines. The best part of this scenario is the fact that we were in a place us West Virginians call "the middle of nowhere." That's the beauty of ad hoc networks and battery powered laptops.

While IBSS networks work great in these kinds of scenarios, the reality is that they are not the best configuration for small and large business networks that must exist on a more permanent basis. Certain consistency problems with Windows clients and ad hoc networks can wreak havoc on a business network. For this reason, another network type is needed; you will learn about it next.

BSS

The *Basic Service Set* (BSS) is also known as an Infrastructure Basic Service Set. Because we have already used the acronym *IBSS* for an Independent Basic Service Set, we simply call the infrastructure service set a BSS, which is much more common than the IBSS and therefore it makes sense to grant the base acronym to this mode.

A BSS does utilize an access point. The access point acts as the connection point to the infrastructure or forms the infrastructure itself, which is why it is called an infrastructure BSS. In this mode, client devices do not communicate with each other directly. Instead, they communicate with the access point in a hub-and-spoke fashion, as depicted previously in Figure 3.7.

When an access point connects to a physical network infrastructure, such as Ethernet, it forwards frames (information or data) from the wireless clients to the wired devices and back. When an access point does not connect to a physical network infrastructure, it forwards frames from one wireless client device to another and back. In the first scenario, an existing infrastructure is extended, and in the second, an infrastructure is created.

When you connect a physical patch cable to an Ethernet network, you are connected to the network. Since cables aren't used in wireless networks, something else is needed. In a wireless network, both IBSS and BSS, the concept of association is analogous to plugging in the patch cable. *Association* means the wireless client requests and is then granted permission to join the service set. This is important because any given area can have multiple access points and the client must know with which access point to communicate. This is determined by the SSID configured on the client and the access point.

ESS

You might guess that an ESS is another kind of service set and you are right. An *Extended Service Set,* or ESS, is two or more BSSs that share the same network name or SSID. The concept of the ESS allows user to roam around (physically) on the network and still connect to the same network with the same name.

Ignoring possible security hindrances, when a user moves from an area (sometimes called a *cell*) covered by one access point to an area covered by another, they should be able to roam. The reality is that roaming is not perfect, and some vendors' access points will not properly pass the user off to other vendors' access points. If you want the best odds of implementing functional roaming capabilities, make sure you buy the same access point for each cell coverage area.

Roaming Around the Network

This concept of roaming is important to understand as you work with medium and large WLANs. In order to be called "true" roaming, the user should be able to move seamlessly from one BSS to another without losing their network connection. The access points hand the client off from one to another, and the client should be oblivious to the background details. The client determines if the received signals are getting too weak in relation to an access point the user is moving away from and requests reassociation with another closer and stronger access point in the same ESS. In the end, the client requests reassociation with a different access point, and the two access points perform the hand-off.

Certain standards define the basics of communications on 802.11 networks, and there are even standards that define how a client communicates to an access point to which it is roaming. In 802.11, however, there are no standards dictating how the access points communicate the hand-off of the user from the old access point to the new one. This is why different vendor's devices do not always work with other vendors devices when it comes to roaming transfers. A new recommendation known as 802.11F addresses this issue by suggesting a standard process or protocol for communicating between the access points.

Reassociation

Client devices use various parameters to determine when they should attempt to reassociate with a different access point than the one they are currently associated with. Depending on the access point and client devices, these can include

- Data rate
- Number of connected stations
- Average throughput

Whatever parameters they use, a client device that has determined it needs to reassociate begins what appears to be a two-step process to the client, but is actually a four-step process in total. The four-step process includes the following:

1. The wireless client sends a reassociation request to the new access point with which it desires to connect.

2. The new access point notifies the old access point that a reassociation request has been made.

3. The old access point acknowledges that this reassociation is about to occur.

4. The new access point sends a reassociation response frame to the wireless client.

Notice that the client does not have to disassociate with the old access point. Disassociation is handled by the access points themselves. You might be wondering, if you have more than two access points, how the new access point knows which of the other access points holds the current client association. The answer to this is found in the initial reassociation frame sent from the client to the new access point. Remember that each BSS has one access point and a BSSID, which is the MAC address of the access point). Every network interface has a unique address or identity known as a MAC address. The initial reassociation request sent to the new access point contains the BSSID of the old access point, and this is how the new access point discovers the old access point for reassociation notification.

The protocols used by the access point to communicate during steps 1 and 2 may be proprietary to the vender and require that you use the same vendor's equipment for all access points. However, the IEEE has ratified a new recommendation that many newer access points are using. This recommendation is known as 802.11F and may provide for cross-vender reassociations.

It is important to note that reassociation can also fail because the new access point was unable to communicate with the old access point. This could happen because of a failed device between the two access points or some other unforeseen issue. In these scenarios, the client receives a rejection from the new access point and continues using its association with the old access point.

If this occurs (you are receiving phone calls from users complaining that they can no longer roam to a certain area known to be covered by a particular access point), check the connections between the access points. In most cases, you will discover other problems as well because the access points generally have to be on the same IP subnet for users to roam between them.

802.11F

IEEE's 802.11F recommendation will allow roaming from one access point to another regardless of the vendor. Of course, all access points in the ESS must implement the 802.11F recommendation. 802.11F is a definition of the Inter-Access-Point Protocol (IAPP). IAPP describes three protocol sequences:

- Adding a station's information after it associates
- Moving a station's information after reassociation
- Caching actions that improve performance when a station reassociates

The first process of adding a station's information after association deals with a common problem in multiple access point networks. The problem is that, though the clients are supposed to disassociate when they leave a BSS, they do not always do so. For this reason, an access point supporting 802.11F sends out a packet that will be understood only by other access points running IAPP, notifying them that they can remove the client from their association tables if it exists. This is important because a client can only be associated with one access point at a time.

The second process of moving a station's information occurs when a client sends a reassociation request to an access point. The 802.11F recommendation not only provides for this mechanism, but also adds some security measures to help prevent an attacker from spoofing a roaming event and causing problems for your wireless clients.

The caching action is not a requirement of the 802.11F recommendation and, therefore, is not covered here. All access points supporting IAPP or 802.11F will implement the first two, but not all will implement the latter.

Fault-Tolerance and Load Balancing

Installing multiple access points in the same coverage area can provide fault-tolerance and load balancing. This concept is similar to roaming, but in this case, the goal is not to provide mobility as a user roams; the goal with fault-tolerance or load balancing is to provide availability as the user remains stationary.

For various reasons, access points can become unavailable. If you have more than one access point in a given area, the client can move to another

FIGURE 3.8   Load balancing

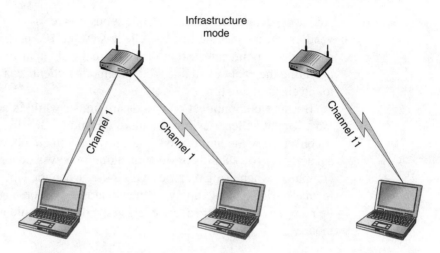

available access point when one fails. This can be accomplished manually in smaller environments or automatically in large enterprise environments. This concept is known as *fault-tolerance* or *fail-over response*.

In other situations, you may need to increase the bandwidth available to users. If you place two wireless access points in the same coverage area and configure one to channel 1 and the other to channel 11, you can provide greater bandwidth to the average user in that coverage area. You will, of course, need to configure some of the clients to use the access point on channel 1 and the other half to use the access point on channel 11. Just remember to use different SSIDs in this scenario because your goal is not to provide roaming or fault-tolerance, but rather to provide increased bandwidth. Figure 3.8 illustrates this concept.

Power Saving Modes

If you have many wireless client devices, you have probably noticed that most of them are powered by battery. Laptops, PDAs, Bluetooth devices, and more require batteries. For this reason, the IEEE has specified power management standards for wireless devices. They have defined two modes of operation known as *active mode* and *power save mode*.

Active Mode

Active Mode, also known also Continuous Aware Mode (CAM) by some vendors, means that the wireless client is awake 100 percent of the time, so an access point can send information to the client any time. If you are operating the client in ad hoc mode, then other clients can send information to the client at any time.

Because communication speeds are higher while in active mode, most wireless client devices default to this mode. Because more power is consumed while in this mode—even when you are not connected to a network—you should consider changing to power save mode on laptop computers when using batteries. Of course, when the laptop is connected to an electrical power supply, or the client is a desktop machine, there is no reason to use power save mode and the device should remain in active mode.

Power Save Mode

When a wireless device is in power save mode, it alternates between dozing and awake based on its need to send and receive frames. Because the client cannot receive frame when it is dozing, the normal communications process must be altered. This new communications process differs, depending on whether the machine is part of an ad hoc or infrastructure network.

Ad hoc Power Save Mode

When in an ad hoc network, the wireless clients all calculate when a particular window of time, known as the ATIM (ad hoc traffic indication message) window, will occur. During this window, all wireless clients are awake and any client that needs to send information to another client will notify that client while the window is open. The machines that need to communicate will stay awake for data transfer and will remain awake until the next ATIM window. The clients that do not need to transfer any data will return to dozing mode until the next ATIM window.

When clients are transmitting data between ATIM windows, they communicate as if they were in active mode. In other words, they simply communicate as standard wireless clients in an ad hoc network. If the data to be transferred requires more multiple ATIM windows of time, the sending client sends another data notification message to the receiving client during each ATIM window. As you can imagine, this causes extra management traffic and can reduce the total throughput of your network. For this reason, power save mode should be used only when it is truly beneficial for power management purposes.

Infrastructure Power Save Mode

An infrastructure network is impacted in the same way as to bandwidth, but the methods used for power management are very different. Unlike ad hoc mode, where there is no access point, in infrastructure mode, the access point plays a large role in power management.

In every frame they send to the access point, client devices inform the access point whether they are in active mode or power save mode. One bit in this frame determines the mode the client is in. Some client devices can switch modes dynamically and others must be configured through the client utilities, though this is not relevant to the access point as it just needs to know if it should *buffer* (temporarily hold) frames for the client or transmit them to the client. When the access point receives a frame from a client indicating that it is in power save mode, it will treat that client as a power save client regardless of what previous frames had indicated. Likewise, when an access point receives a frame indicating that the client is in active mode, it will treat the client as being fully awake regardless of what previous frames indicated.

Each client has a unique identifier that the access point tracks, known as an *association identifier* (AID). Access points handle power save mode clients through their beacon frames. A *beacon frame* is a periodic frame sent out from the access point containing management information. This information includes a traffic indication map (TIM) that contains the AIDs of any clients with data waiting at the access point. When the client comes out of dozing state, it sees that there is data waiting at the access point based on this information in the TIM of the beacon frames, and the client then sends a special request to the access point asking it to send the data.

If the data at the access point consists of more than one frame, the access point notifies the client of this in the initially sent data frame, so the client knows to stay awake until it has received all the data frames. The last data frame contains information informing the client that all the data has been delivered and then the client can return to a dozing state.

The difference between ad hoc and infrastructure power management functions is very important. When in infrastructure mode, the access point can be impacted tremendously by too many clients running in power save mode. For this reason, you might consider it a best practice to avoid power save mode as much as possible in business networks where throughput is valuable.

Summary

With the knowledge provided in this chapter, you are prepared to plan and implement real-world wireless networks. Understanding the channel structure of the various wireless technologies and colocation issues allows you to provide the needed coverage in areas both large and small. Knowing the different ranges of communications you can expect from 802.11a and 802.11b/g devices helps you determine the right technology for the right situation.

The Independent Basic Service Set, or IBSS, provides an exceptional solution for small dynamic networks where centralized administration is not required. An infrastructure Basic Service Set, or BSS, allows for centralized administration and greater control over who can access your network. Extended Service Sets, also known as ESSs, give you the ability to allow roaming on your network without the loss of network connection as long as client hand-off is handled effectively. The 802.11F recommended implementation of IAPP handles this for you.

Finally, understanding the difference between active mode and power save mode for power management allows you to make the right decision when it comes to battery-powered devices on your network. Remember that power save mode reduces throughput, but active mode reduces battery life. When you know which of these two is the most important, you'll be able to make the right choice in any situation.

Key Terms

- [ ] **802.11F**
- [ ] **active mode**
- [ ] **ad hoc mode**
- [ ] **BSS**
- [ ] **channels**
- [ ] **colocation**
- [ ] **data rates**
- [ ] **ESS**
- [ ] **IBSS**
- [ ] **infrastructure mode**
- [ ] **power save mode**
- [ ] **range**
- [ ] **roaming**
- [ ] **throughput**

Review Questions

1. When an area is within the range of the RF signal but does not receive coverage, which is known as what?

   A. RF oversight

   B. RF shadow

   C. Invisibility

   D. Noncoverage

2. 802.11b networks have a longer range than 802.11a networks.

   A. True

   B. False

3. How many channels are supported for use in the U.S. with an 802.11g network?

   A. 14

   B. 13

   C. 11

   D. 3

4. How many nonoverlapping channels are generally available for 802.11a networks for indoor use?

   A. 8

   B. 4

   C. 12

   D. 3

5. You have installed an 802.11g network with five access points. All access points are configured to use channel 6 and are approximately 50 feet from each other. You notice that throughput is suffering and you cannot seem to accomplish more than 1–2 Mbps. What should you do to resolve this issue?

    A. Make every other access point an 802.11a access point

    B. Make the three middle access points 802.11 access points using FHSS technology

    C. Enable channel overlap algorithms on all access points to resolve channel conflicts automatically.

    D. Set the access points to alternating channels so that no access point is on a channel within five channels of the access points next to it. Use channels 1, 6, and 11 to accomplish this.

6. When a device advertises that it supports data rates of up to 54 Mbps, this means you will be able to transfer 54 Mbps of data on the network.

    A. True

    B. False

7. You have been monitoring your wireless connection as you move your laptop around to different locations in your building. As you move, you've noticed that the declared rate is sometimes 54, sometimes 36, and sometimes other numbers. What is the name of the technology that handles this rate adjustment for you?

    A. Dynamic rate adjustment

    B. Dynamic rate selection

    C. Performance rate adjustment

    D. Dynamic performance selection

8. 802.11g networks use which modulation technique?

    A. OFDM

    B. DSSS

    C. FHSS

    D. QSPK

9. What are the advantages of ad hoc mode wireless networks? Select two.

    A. Centralized management

    B. No access point needed

    C. Provides enhanced security

    D. Can be formed dynamically

10. What is the IEEE recommendation for standardizing roaming client hand-off in wireless networks?

    A. 802.11e

    B. 802.11q

    C. 802.11b/g-roaming

    D. 802.11F

11. Select the two power management modes available in most wireless client devices.

    A. Power save mode

    B. Power management mode

    C. Awake mode

    D. Active mode

12. In relation to the IEEE 802.11F recommendation, what does the acronym IAPP stand for?

    A. Internet Access Proxy Protocol

    B. Internal Awake Power Protocol

    C. Inter-Access-Point Protocol

    D. Inter-Awake-Point Protocol

13. The network name, on a wireless network, is also called what?

    A. Service set identifier

    B. System set identifier

    C. Security set identifier

    D. Basic Service Set

Review Answers

1. **B.** RF shadow is the term used to refer to a space that is not receiving RF signals even though it may be in range of the wireless access point or communicating device.

2. **A.** It is true that 802.11b networks have a longer range than 802.11a networks. This is due in part to the frequencies used by the differing technologies.

3. **C.** According to FCC regulations, 802.11g networks can use any of 11 channels in the U.S. These are channels 1–11 and are each 22 MHz wide with a separation of 5 MHz between the center frequencies of each channel.

4. **A.** The 802.11a lower and middle bands provide four channels each for communications, allowing a total of eight channels for use indoors. While there is no real restriction in place preventing the use of the four channels from the upper band, most installations use the upper band channels for outdoor site-to-site (point-to-point) links.

5. **D.** By using channels 1, 6, and 11 and making sure that no access point is in close proximity to other access points using a channel within 5 channels of it, conflicts will decrease and throughput should increase greatly.

6. **B.** There is a difference between the data rate and the actual throughput. You will generally be able to achieve a throughput of roughly half the advertised data rates because of overhead bandwidth consumption and the management data used by the networking devices.

7. **B.** Dynamic rate selection handles the automatic adjusting of data rates to reduce retransmissions caused by data corruption as the distance increases between the device and the access point or as interference increases.

8. **A.** To allow for backward compatibility with 802.11b devices that use DSSS, 802.11g networks use OFDM with some modifications. 802.11a networks also use OFDM, which stands for Orthogonal Frequency Division Multiplexing.

9. **B, D.** Ad hoc networks do not require an access point, are simple to set up, can be created dynamically, and are supported by most wireless client devices. However, they do not provide centralized management or enhanced security, as the security features are more difficult to manage or are nonexistent.

10. **D.** The 802.11F recommendation of the IEEE specifies how access points should handle roaming clients and is supported by many newer access points and wireless infrastructure devices.

11. **A, D.** The two power management modes supported by wireless networking clients are power save mode and active mode. Awake is a state a wireless client can be in when power save mode is enabled or it is the client's permanent state when in active mode. The nonawake state is known as dozing and is only available when the client is in power save mode.

12. **C.** The acronym IAPP stands for Inter-Access-Point Protocol and is a standard way for access points to handle the communications between access points and clients and between access points themselves during roaming.

13. **A.** A service set identifier (SSID) is also known as the network name and uniquely identifies the network so client devices can determine to which network they should connect.

Wireless Networking Devices

Wireless# Exam Objectives Covered:

❖ Summarize the characteristics, basic attributes, and advantages of VoWLAN

- Wireless VoIP SOHO router characteristics

- Wireless VoIP SOHO router operation

❖ Identify the purpose, features, and functions of the following wireless network components. Choose the appropriate installation or configuration steps in a given scenario.

- Access points

- Wireless LAN routers

- Wireless bridges

- Wireless repeaters

- WLAN switch

- Wireless VoIP gateway

- Wireless media gateway

- Power over Ethernet devices

❖ Identify the purpose, features, and functions of the following types of antennas. Choose the appropriate installation or configuration steps in a given scenario.

- Omni-directional/dipole

- Semidirectional

The most basic wireless network contains wireless network client devices communicating in ad hoc mode and nothing more. However, these simple networks will not provide the necessary functionality for many business purposes. For this reason, you need to understand the many different types of wireless networking devices available.

A perfect example of the disadvantages of using only wireless client devices is in an inventory management application. Using only client devices, a scenario such as the following occurs. A worker goes to the receiving area and inventories all the new shipments on a wireless device such as a laptop PC, tablet PC, or PDA. After entering all the items into the device, the worker returns to her work area and synchronizes the data with a centralized server. If she used a PDA, she has to synchronize with an application running on her desktop PC. Using a laptop or tablet PC, she has to plug in the Ethernet cable and then import the data into the server-based system. She has to take all these extra steps because the wireless network uses client devices exclusively.

The problems with this scenario are many. First, the worker's time is being consumed by extra tasks such as synchronizing data and taking multiple steps to complete a process. Second, because a human is involved in more than just data entry, there are more opportunities for errors or forgetfulness. Imagine the worker returns to her office only to find her manager waiting with a list of tasks to perform. She becomes sidetracked and forgets about synchronizing the data. In another part of the company, a sales representative checks inventory through the server-based system for the items received that day and shows no items in inventory. The result is the loss of a sale even though the products had been received in the shipping department.

All of these problems can be resolved by implementing an infrastructure-based (infrastructure mode) network that provides immediate wireless access to the central server while the worker is in the shipping and receiving area. As she enters the data in her PDA or laptop, it is entered into the server automatically and is available to the sales representatives immediately. The worker's time is being used more effectively, and there is less opportunity for human error. By placing access points in the warehouse that are connected to the server-based system through the wired (or wireless) network infrastructure, you have simplified the entire inventory management process.

The simplest infrastructure mode network contains one or more access points and some number of client devices. More complex configurations require other wireless devices. In this chapter, you will learn about the most important infrastructure devices, including

- Access points
- Routers
- Bridges
- Repeaters
- Switches
- VoIP gateways
- Media gateways
- Power over Ethernet devices

I also provide a brief overview of enterprise class wireless devices. Although the Wireless# exam does not cover these devices and they will not be discussed in detail here, it is important that you know they are available and where you can get more information about enterprise class hardware when you need it.

Finally, you will learn about antennas, including the basic functions of an antenna in a wireless network, the various types and uses of antennas, and strategies for determining the best location for antennas in different installation configurations.

Access Points

The access point (AP) is the fundamental building block of an infrastructure mode network. One or more APs working together can form an entire network infrastructure for inside use with just one connection to the outside world (such as the Internet), if desired. Because of stability and throughput issues, you seldom see this kind of implementation. Most of the time, you still implement a wired infrastructure, connecting all infrastructure devices such as routers, bridges, switches, and gateways to the wired network. You usually connect servers and printers directly to the wired network as well, though wireless print servers are becoming more common. You then use APs to connect wireless clients to this wired infrastructure.

 Sometimes APs are referred to as *wireless access points (WAPs)*, however, I recommend avoiding this term as it's easily confused with the Wireless Application Protocol (WAP) used for wireless phones and other mobile devices.

FIGURE 4.1   Wireless network storage device with built-in AP

Access points can be stand-alone devices or they can be built in to other devices. The D-Link DSM-G600 is a perfect example of a non-AP wireless device with AP functionality built in. This device, shown in Figure 4.1, provides access to one IDE hard drive and two external USB hard drives at the same time. I run one on my network with a 400GB IDE hard drive and two 300GB external USB drives providing a terabyte of storage to my network. This device includes a built-in AP so you can access it through the Ethernet port or by using an 802.11b/g device. Figure 4.2 shows the configuration interface for enabling the wireless radio in either the AP mode or client mode.

With so many kinds of APs available on the market, things can get confusing very quickly. For this reason, I cover their common features and then some of the more advanced features of a select few. I'll discuss the different applications or uses of APs, and finally the different configuration interfaces and methods provided.

Common Features

Most APs share certain features in common. These common features include

- Compatibility
- Upgradeability
- Security features

FIGURE 4.2   The DSM-G600 AP-enabling interface

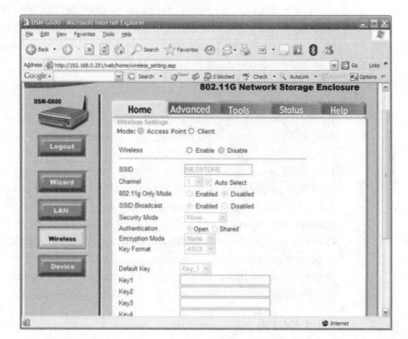

Compatibility

To increase sales and customer buy-in, most APs are compatible with industry standards. You should select APs that are compatible with the wireless standard you need to support. Some devices support only 802.11b, others support 802.11g and 802.11b, while others support 802.11a and still others support 802.11a/b/g. Be cautious, however—not all devices advertised as supporting 802.11a/b/g can support all three at the same time. It is not uncommon for the device to support either 802.11a or 802.11b/g, but not both consecutively. If you need a single device that does support both standards simultaneously, be sure to read the vendor's data sheet closely.

Because vendors sometimes want to move more quickly than the standards groups are moving, some APs implement nonstandard capabilities to increase throughput or provide QoS and security features. In some cases, you can upgrade the AP to support the actual standards when they are finalized. However, it is important to remember the lessons learned with the 802.11i standard. (This is the newer IEEE standard for implementing a secure wireless network using what the Wi-Fi Alliance calls WPA2.)

Many older APs cannot be upgraded to support it because the newer standards require more processor power than the old APs provide. Keep this in mind when you purchase equipment that has implemented a standard that is "not yet a standard" because it has not been ratified. At a minimum, make sure the nonstandard feature can be disabled.

Upgradeability

Be sure you can upgrade your AP. While I don't know of any devices released that cannot be upgraded, it is still important to make sure the vendor supports this. Upgrading the AP is usually done by applying new firmware. Firmware is just the software that the device runs to do its job. This software is stored in the device's memory whether the power is on or off. While I don't know of any nonupgradeable devices, this doesn't mean vendors release new firmware regularly. Some vendors, such as Cisco, release firmware upgrades frequently and others only once or twice after the device is placed on the market. You generally find that enterprise class equipment is upgraded more frequently than SOHO and personal equipment.

To upgrade the firmware for your APs, follow these steps:

1. Go to the vendor's website and download the most recent firmware.
2. Access the configuration interface of your AP (this is usually browser-based).
3. Look for the place to apply the firmware.
4. Select the firmware file you downloaded and apply it.

It is best to apply firmware upgrades through the Ethernet port of the AP and not across the wireless connection. Attempting to upgrade the firmware of an AP across the wireless network can corrupt the APs software, according to some vendors. It can, theoretically, also pose a security concern. Firmware upgrades are easy to do if you have a computer on the Ethernet cable that does not utilize wireless. (Sometimes this cable may need to be a crossover cable, though in most cases, a standard patch cable should work just fine.) If you don't, you'll have to take the AP offline to perform the upgrade. Just unplug the Ethernet cable from the back of the AP and then plug a patch cable into the AP that is connected to a laptop (be sure to disable wireless on this laptop and that you have downloaded the firmware to this machine). Check that your IP configuration is set properly so you can access the AP, and then launch your web browser and point it to the AP's IP address to begin the upgrade.

Security Features

One of the most important feature sets in any AP is the security capabilities it provides. If the AP can provide the throughput needed and the technology standards you demand, but does not provide security, you risk exposing your data. If you want to be sure the device supports the most recent standards, look for 802.11i or WPA2 support. Some devices only support WEP, and WEP is not as secure as WPA or WPA2 because hacking tools have been created that break the security in short order. Even WPA is susceptible to fast cracks in certain configurations.

MAC filtering should also be a consideration. There are readily available tools that will allow an attacker to spoof (impersonate) a valid MAC address, but MAC filtering makes the attacker's job that much more difficult, though it is not a complete solution by itself. If you do not want to set up RADIUS servers (these are centralized authentication, authorization, and accounting or auditing servers), VPN servers, and other advanced security mechanisms, combining WPA-Personal and MAC address filtering can give you a level of comfort in a smaller environment without much security risk.

This last statement should not be taken to mean that all small environments are at a low risk of attack. Some small businesses are at higher risk than some large multinational organizations. One reason is that they may provide an entry point to other larger organizations because of the services they provide to those organizations. Another is that a small company may work in an expertise that other groups do not like. Finally, they might be seen as an easier target because of their size.

When using older security technologies, remember to layer them. For example, hide the SSID, enable WEP or WPA, and use MAC filtering. Using them all together deters casual attackers because they get through one layer only to find there is yet another barrier to overcome.

Another security feature to consider is VPN pass-through functionality. This functionality allows a client to connect to the AP and then create a VPN connection to the network for even greater security than that provided by authentication alone and disabling SSID broadcast. While disabling the SSID broadcast feature does not secure your environment against an attacker, it hides your network from casual browsers who are looking for an easy way to get onto the Internet.

If the AP supports remote management through telnet, you should ensure that it either supports SSH telnet or provides a client to configure the device that does not send data as clear text on the network. Telnet, by default, sends information "in-the-clear," which means an attacker can monitor the data being transmitted and possibly intercept passwords or other sensitive information.

These security features and more will be covered in greater detail in Chapter 11, and they are extremely important to understand for the Wireless# exam. However, it is even more important that you understand how they work for real-world implementations; an unsecured wireless network can lead to disastrous outcomes.

Adjustable Power Levels

APs that offer the ability to adjust power output levels give you greater control over cell size. The term *cell size* is used to reference the size of the area covered by wireless RF signals. Adjusting the power levels to lower settings reduces cell size, while raising them to higher power levels increases cell size.

You might also need to increase or decrease the power level to ensure that you are getting the coverage needed beyond walls and other barriers. For example, if you need to provide wireless coverage to an area that is only 50 feet away, but has three walls between it and the AP, you might need to increase power levels. In this case, you are not really focused on increasing the literal cell size (physical area covered), but you are increasing the signal strength in the outer regions of the cell and will effectively increase the cell size as well in this situation.

Quality of Service Features

Quality of Service (QoS) features such as WMM (Wi-Fi Multimedia) for streaming video or VoIP applications are often available in APs. These applications allow you to define specific types of traffic that should be given higher priority. To maintain needed quality, you might have to give higher priority to streaming video traffic. Alternatively, you might need to grant higher priority to Voice over IP traffic to maintain connections with acceptable quality. According to the Wi-Fi Alliance, which is the organization that certifies WMM-compatible equipment, more than 200 devices have been certified since 2004.

Antenna Types

APs come with two basic types of antennas: *attached* and *detachable*. Attached antennas are nonreplaceable, which means you can use only the antenna that comes with the AP unless you want to solder a different antenna connection that could damage the equipment.

Other devices support detachable antennas that allow you to replace the factory-installed antennas with more powerful alternatives. It's not uncommon to upgrade antennas to stronger gain antennas such as 7 dBi or 10 dBi. It is important, however, to ensure that an upgrade antenna kit provides the correct connector type for your AP.

Power over Ethernet Support

Devices that support Power over Ethernet (PoE) to power the AP when no local power outlet is available provide great flexibility. You can install an AP in an area with no power outlet and then power the AP through the Ethernet cable that is connected to a power injector somewhere down the line. This feature allows you to place APs in ceilings, closets, or outdoors where it may be difficult or impractical to install power outlets.

Access Point Form Factors

APs come in many form factors, as depicted in Figure 4.3 and Figure 4.4. Figure 4.3 shows a "pocket" or portable AP, called such because they can literally fit in your pocket. This particular model from D-Link supports

FIGURE 4.3   D-Link DWL-G730AP

FIGURE 4.4   Linksys WAP54G

WPA-PSK (also known as WPA-Personal) and WPA2-PSK with a firmware upgrade that is free at the website. As you can see, this device comes with a carrying case and can even be powered through USB. Figure 4.4 shows a more common form factor for an AP, in this case with dual antennas.

Mounting Options

APs often come with simple mounting kits that work for basic installations, and pocket APs are usually placed flat on a desk or even on the floor. Because pocket APs are intended for temporary use, they do not provide even the most basic mounting options in most cases. The DWL-G730, for example, doesn't even have holes to connect any kind of mounting device. For this reason, the only real mounting option is to use ties wrapped around the device.

Permanent APs usually provide a mounting plate that you can fasten to a wall or beam with screws or ties. You can then attach the AP to the mounting plate for secure and stable positioning. By fastening the AP with ties at a minimum, you reduce the likelihood of device theft. While the ties or screws do not guarantee the device won't be stolen, it does make it more time-consuming to steal and therefore deters the random thief.

If you are planning to use a mounting kit fastened with screws, you might consider using zip-ties first to test the positioning of the AP. You can do this during your site survey, but it's not uncommon to obtain different results at the time of implementation because of changes in the environment. A quick test of the AP fastened using zip-ties can verify that the location is still appropriate, and then you can fasten the device using the more permanent and aesthetically pleasing mounting kit.

Common Applications

Wireless APs are used most frequently in one of three ways:

- Single AP serving clients
- Multiple APs serving different locations
- Multiple APs serving the same location

As a single AP serving clients, the AP serves as a connection point to a network infrastructure or as a hub for all the wireless clients. In a small SOHO implementation, it is not uncommon to see a single wireless AP and multiple wireless clients. Figure 4.5 illustrates such a situation. In this case, the wireless AP is connected to a router that is connected to the Internet. The AP allows for communications between the clients as well as with the Internet.

When you have a medium or large existing wired network, it is more common to implement multiple APs serving different locations. You can use the APs in addition to wired networking or to provide network access

FIGURE 4.5   Single AP serving clients

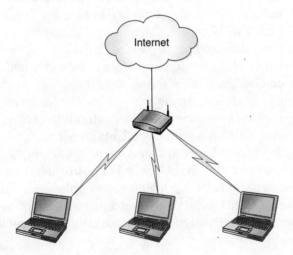

FIGURE 4.6   Multiple APs serving different locations

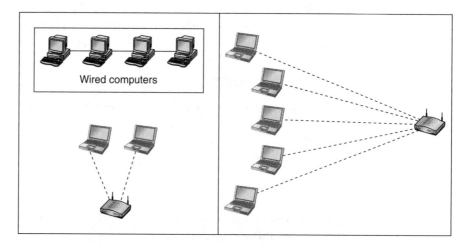

in areas of the building without wired networking. Figure 4.6 demonstrates both of these scenarios in one building. On the left, you see an installation in which an existing wired infrastructure is available, but it does not provide the roaming capabilities needed by users. On the right, a wireless AP provides networking access to a remote portion of the building where no Ethernet wires are available.

As pointed out in Chapter 3, APs are commonly used to provide load-balancing or fault tolerance. You can install multiple APs in the same coverage areas, providing greater total throughput (load-balancing) or high uptime rates (fault tolerance). In Figure 4.7, you can see how this is done. The AP labeled "marketing" is running on channel 1 and is an 802.11b/g device. The AP labeled "sales" is running on channel 11 and is also an 802.11b/g device. Notice that a portion of the clients have been configured to associate with the device on channel 1 and the remaining clients are associating with the device on channel 11. This implementation is accomplished by configuring each AP with a different channel and SSID to ensure that clients do not roam.

Routing of data between clients on the marketing AP and the sales AP will be handled by the existing wired infrastructure. There is no need for the users to be limited to communications with wireless devices. A client associated with the sales AP can communicate through that AP to the router to the marketing AP and finally to a marketing AP client device.

FIGURE 4.7   Multiple APs serving the same location

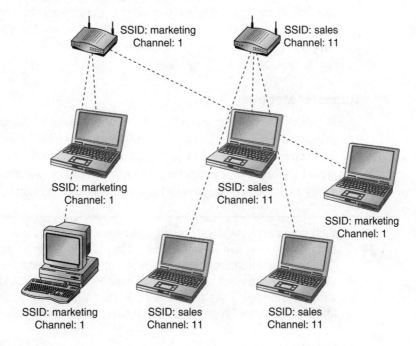

Operational Modes

All three of the scenarios discussed in the previous section represent one of the three major modes (root mode) in which an AP can operate. These three modes are

- Root mode
- Repeater mode
- Bridge mode

While the IEEE has not defined modes of operation for APs, root node matches the default operations demanded by the IEEE standards. The other two modes represent functionality that has been added by the vendors.

Root Mode

Root mode is used typically when an AP is connected to some kind of wired infrastructure through its wired interface, usually an Ethernet network with printers, servers, and other networking devices attached. Root mode is also the default mode used when the AP is not connected to any wired network but is serving wireless clients in a "hub-type" mode. Although many APs support repeater and bridge modes, they are configured to root mode as the default.

Repeater Mode

An application of wireless APs that was not covered by the three examples discussed earlier in "Common Applications" would be using the AP as a repeater. This mode can be useful when you need to extend the wireless signal farther. For a temporary extension, mini or pocket APs can work wonders. Repeaters are covered in the "Repeaters" section later in this chapter.

With some wireless APs, you can achieve similar results as repeater mode through the creative use of AP client mode (not covered here in detail). This mode is intended to connect a remote wired LAN to a local centralized LAN, but with the right configuration, it can effectively extend the wireless signal distance. While not covered on the Wireless# exam, it's useful knowledge for those urgent situations that arise.

Bridge Mode

Bridge mode performs the exact function its name implies. It creates a bridge between two networks. To create a wireless bridge link, you need a minimum of two wireless APs or bridges. Wireless APs can perform the functions of a wireless bridge and this is a useful extra capability. Bridging is covered in more detail in the "Bridges" section of this chapter. Figure 4.8 shows the configuration screen of a Linksys WAP54G AP, which supports AP, client, repeater, and bridge modes. You select the AP mode on this screen.

Configuration Methods

APs are configured through various methods, including

- Telnet
- Console
- Browser based
- Client applications
- SNMP

FIGURE 4.8   Linksys AP mode selection screen

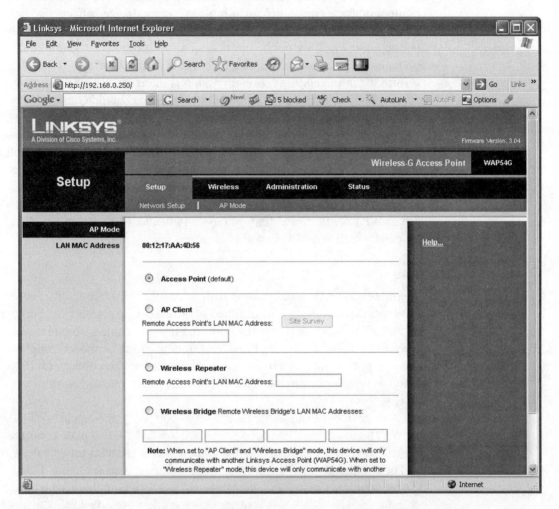

If you decide to use telnet connections to configure your AP, be sure to encrypt the channel using IPSec VPN tunnels or SSH. If your AP does not support encrypted telnet, you should consider one of the other connection types. Most APs block the telnet port, and it must be enabled if it is supported. In the past, only enterprise class systems have had support for telnet. Modern SOHO and home devices, however, are becoming more powerful, so make sure your devices have telnet disabled—particularly if you are connected to the Internet.

The most important recommendation I can make is to ensure that your common practice is to configure all infrastructure devices offline. Do not connect them to the production network and then configure them through "public interfaces." By public interface, I mean browser-based or client applications. If the device supports a console connection, you usually perform the initial configuration through this interface. When the device supports only an Ethernet or wireless interface, you should configure the device in a secure area using the provided browser-based interface.

The reason for this precaution is simple. Most APs, even those from enterprise device vendors, come with open network settings as the default. This gives hackers an open window of opportunity to attack your network if you place the AP on the infrastructure before configuring it. While this window may be small, it is not worth the risk. Configure security parameters such as WPA *before* connecting the device to the network infrastructure and you greatly reduce the likelihood of an attack getting through.

Console

Enterprise class APs usually come with a console connection port. These console ports often look like an Ethernet or token-ring connection, but you need a serial connector to use the port. You also need client software such as HyperTerminal, Procomm Plus, or QModem Pro to connect through the serial port. HyperTerminal usually works fine, and it comes with the Windows operating systems. You will be using a command-line interface (CLI) in this mode.

Other devices use a standard 9-pin serial port, such as Netgear's WG302 AP. With these devices, you need a standard RS-232C DB-9 male connector. You still use HyperTerminal or some other terminal program for connectivity.

The commands used differ depending on the AP you are using. Cisco APs use standard Cisco IOS commands and should be familiar if you have configured Cisco switches or routers. Other vendors provide documentation for the command-line interface that their devices support. The CLI will usually look like some variant of Unix or Linux and generally contains fewer commands than a full operating system.

Browser Based

Browser-based configuration interfaces are useful once an AP is in production. At this point, all communications with the AP should be secured (encrypted) so it's safe to configure various settings through the simpler interface. You can usually configure the majority of the AP's settings through this interface:

- DHCP settings
- VPN settings
- Radios
- Power levels
- Data rates
- LAN IP address
- AP mode (root, bridge, client, repeater)
- SSID and SSID broadcasting
- MAC filtering
- Authentication types
- Administration passwords

You can often view logs and connection status in this interface as well. For example, you can view the association tables or the status of the AP's interfaces using this graphical view. Figure 4.9 shows the browser-based (HTTP) interface to a Cisco 1200 series AP.

Client Applications

A common trend occurring with SOHO and personal-use wireless devices of all kinds is the inclusion of custom configuration applications allowing localized secure setup for initial installation. These applications vary, but it is common for these tools to launch from an autorun menu on the driver CD that comes with the device. These interfaces are common on devices from wireless network storage devices to wireless APs. Figure 4.10 shows the custom client application for configuring a Linksys AP.

Simple Network Management Protocol

The Simple Network Management Protocol (SNMP) is a common management standard for managing networked devices from client computers to infrastructure devices such as APs. When using SNMP, you can manage multiple APs with single points of configuration centrally. Many SNMP management tools allow you to create a policy or configuration set and then push that one set down to hundreds of devices. This reduces administration time and overhead in large complex environments.

FIGURE 4.9   Cisco browser-based configuration interface

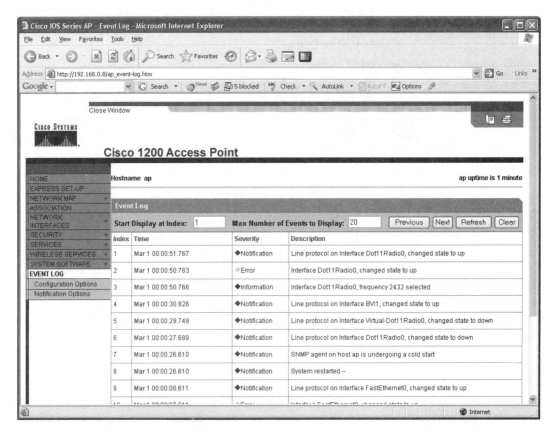

You should note, however, that many security vulnerabilities have been discovered in SNMPv1 and there are some inherent issues in SNMPv2. SNMPv3 provides for authenticated and secure management of devices, but is not yet implemented in as many devices. Many vendors have released patches to help with security issues in older implementations of SNMP.

Access Point Summary

The AP provides the most basic functionality needed in an infrastructure mode wireless LAN. There are many options available with the many different APs, but you can be sure to spend more money on devices with more features. In the past, SOHO APs included only WEP and basic WPA-personal (WPA-PSK) for secure implementations, but a few now support

FIGURE 4.10   Linksys custom configuration utility

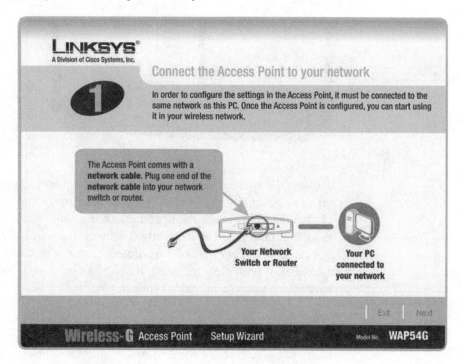

WPA-enterprise. Some vendors, such as Linksys, even provide backend authentication with paid access to their RADIUS servers across the Internet (known as Linksys Wireless Guard).

When it comes to choosing an AP, you must determine the demands of your environment and then select the appropriate device. The main items to consider include mounting options, security features, management interfaces, and technologies supported. Discover your needs in all these areas and then selecting the right AP is much easier.

Routers

A wireless AP is basically a bridging device in that the clients generally have IP addresses that are on the same network as the wired side of the AP. A wireless router is a device with a LAN connection on one network (IP subnet) and a wireless radio providing access to wireless clients on a different network (again, IP subnet). The wireless router routes data

FIGURE 4.11   A Netgear wireless router

between the two networks. Figure 4.11 shows a wireless router; you can see that, externally, the device looks just like an AP.

Wireless clients use the IP address of the "wireless side" of the router as their default gateway generally. This way, the wireless clients can access devices on the other side of the wireless router, which can be very useful in a number of scenarios, including routing through to the Internet or adding wireless clients to a full wired subnet.

Common Features

Many of the features of wireless routers are the same as those found in APs, however, unique features available in routers include

- Built-in switches or hubs
- Firewalls
- Port forwarding
- Port triggering
- Route definition

Built-in Switches or Hubs

If you are installing a small network with only four to eight devices, a single wireless router may serve your needs. Wireless routers usually support a range of four to eight Ethernet ports. With eight Ethernet ports and a WAN link for the Internet, you can build a network with one printer, seven wired clients, and multiple wireless clients through just one device. Figure 4.12 illustrates the port configuration of a four-port wireless router with uplink capabilities.

FIGURE 4.12   Wireless router port configuration

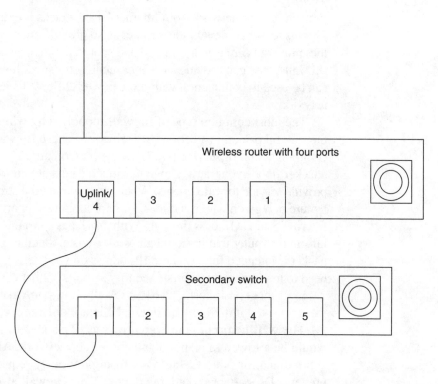

When building single-point networks like this, remember that you have also created a single point of failure. If the wireless router fails, your entire network is unavailable. In situations where you need fault-tolerance, you can achieve this easily in a small network with multiple wireless routers going through a single point of access to the Internet.

It is also important to give proper attention to the specifications of the wireless router you select. Some devices have one WAN port for connecting to the Internet, four switch ports, and an uplink port. These types of devices are often purchased for their expansion abilities through the uplink port. For instance, connecting a larger switch to this port provides access to a greater number of Ethernet devices. The reason for paying extra attention to the vendor specifications is that many devices disable one of the built-in switch ports when the uplink port is used. In other words, you can't use the uplink port and all four switch ports at the same time.

Firewalls

Protecting your network from Internet-based attacks is extremely important. For this reason, many wireless routers also provide built-in firewalls. While these firewalls are usually limited and should not replace more powerful firewalls, they can provide sufficient security for small home networks and can be used in conjunction with more powerful firewalls in small business networks.

The most common type of firewall supported by wireless routers is the stateful packet inspection (SPI) firewall. These firewalls help prevent common denial of service (DoS) attacks. A DoS attack occurs when an attacker floods your network with so much data that your device is unable to provide service to valid clients. When investigating the strength of the SPI feature of a given wireless router, look for logging support, advanced packet filtering, and DMZ pass through. With DMZ pass through, you can actually inform the router that it should allow all packets (data) to pass through if the packet is intended for a specific IP address on your network. You will then need to implement appropriate security settings on that device.

In its most basic form, an SPI firewall allows only data through that was requested initially by an internal client. For example, if you type **www .McGrawHill.com** in your web browser, IP packets from that location would be allowed to respond and enter your network. Allowing only communications into the network from previously requested locations prevents DoS attacks to a large degree. This firewall also helps prevent other types of attacks from nonrequested machines on the Internet.

Port Forwarding

If you are using Network Address Translation (NAT) to provide private addresses on your internal network, you can use port forwarding to direct incoming requests to a specific device. Figure 4.13 demonstrates this concept. In the diagram, a client computer on the Internet (at address 201.12.13.85) requests to view a web page (port 80 by default) at the IP address of 71.144.8.45. In actuality, this is the IP address of a port forwarding router. The router sees that the client is trying to access port 80 and forwards the communication to the internal IP address of 10.10.10.75. When the actual web server responds to the router, it forwards the response to the client device at 201.12.13.85.

This kind of configuration allows the use of private addresses (10.*x.x.x*; 172.16-31.*x.x*; 192.168.*x.x*) on your internal network. You can still allow

FIGURE 4.13   Port forwarding

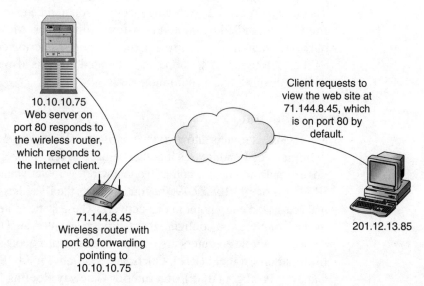

10.10.10.75
Web server on
port 80 responds to
the wireless router,
which responds to
the Internet client.

Client requests to
view the web site at
71.144.8.45, which
is on port 80 by
default.

71.144.8.45
Wireless router with
port 80 forwarding
pointing to
10.10.10.75

201.12.13.85

clients to access public addresses on the Internet by using a NAT router. The NAT router lets clients browse the Internet and its port forwarding feature lets Internet clients access internal services.

Port Triggering

Port triggering works a little differently than port forwarding. In this case, the port is allowed by the router because of an internal request by a client. Once port triggering is configured, it operates as follows:

1. A client device makes an outgoing connection using a port number that is defined in the port triggering table.

2. The wireless router records this connection, opens the incoming port or ports associated with this entry in the port triggering table, and associates them with the client device.

3. The remote system receives the client device's request and then responds using a different port number.

4. The router matches the response to the previous request and forwards the response to the client device.

If port triggering were not used, the final response from the remote system would be treated as a new connection and be disallowed by the SPI firewall or handled by default port-forwarding rules. Most routers allow only one client device to use a particular port triggering configuration at a time. Before a new session can be created, there is also a wait time after a client device finishes communicating.

Route Definition

Most wireless routers allow you to configure *static routes*. Static routes are definitions of IP addresses that can be used to reach specified locations. For example, if a device connected to a wireless router wanted to reach an IP address of 192.168.27.49, the router knows the IP address of the device that acts as the entry point to that network. These static routers are defined manually unless you configure them through an automated tool such as SNMP.

Many wireless routers also support routing protocols such as Router Information Protocol (RIP), Open Shortest Path First (OSPF), Border Gateway Protocol (BGP), and Interior Gateway Routing Protocol (IGRP). These protocols make announcements related to known routes so routers can self-configure. This prevents you, as the administrator, from having to configure static routes manually. You can also configure the direction of the routing protocol. For example, you can set the direction to "in only" when you want the wireless router to receive routes but not communicate its routes. This feature is useful if the wireless router is the single point of connection to the Internet.

Common Applications

Wireless routers are used for two main applications: connecting an internal network to the Internet and connecting a wireless network to an existing network infrastructure.

Connecting to the Internet

Figure 4.14 illustrates a configuration in which the wireless router connects a wireless network to the Internet. This configuration allows for browsing of web pages and hosting of web services internally.

When creating connections such as this, firewalls become very important. Automated attacks from worms and attack scripts try to attack any network they can find, which means an attack does not have to be directed at you

FIGURE 4.14   Connecting to the Internet with a wireless router

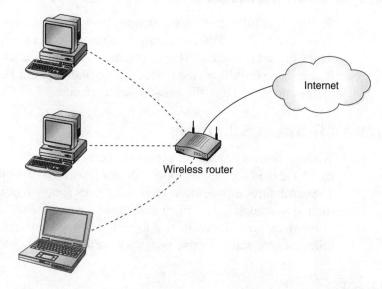

intentionally for it to damage your network. Firewalls help prevent worm attacks, script attacks, and even intended attacks by skilled crackers.

Connecting to an Existing Network Infrastructure

Sometimes you just need to connect some wireless clients to a wired network. In many cases, an AP works perfectly, and in others, a wireless router is needed. Scenarios in which you should use a wireless router instead of an AP include the following:

- Situations in which an insufficient supply of IP addresses are available on the existing wired subnet
- Situations in which you want to place special limits on the wireless clients that are not usually available in wireless APs, such as a firewall

Perhaps you want to provide access to wireless clients visiting your organization, but you can't control these client devices and the security they have configured on their systems. For this reason, you might choose to provide limited access to network resources at the router in order to provide protection from these unknown clients.

Configuration Methods

The configuration interfaces supported by wireless routers are the same as those used by APs. You can configure a router with a console connection, telnet, browser-based interface, custom vendor applications, or SNMP. Remember to configure the device offline with baseline security settings *before* connecting it to the network infrastructure.

Wireless Routers Summary

Wireless routers provide an excellent alternative to wireless APs because they have the functionality of a built-in AP plus the capabilities of a router. The capabilities of wireless routers range from simple routing to full-featured routing functions in enterprise-class units. Features such as firewalls, port forwarding, port triggering, and logging allow you to implement a solid infrastructure with effective security measures.

Bridges

Wireless bridges connect two wired or wireless networks that would otherwise be unable to communicate with each other. Wireless bridges can connect a remote building to a main building on a campus or to separate locations in a small town. You can configure them as single connections (*point-to-point*) or multiple connections in a hub-and-spoke fashion (*point-to-multipoint*). Either way, understanding the features, applications, and configuration options is essential.

Common Features

Bridges are basically APs configured to operate primarily in bridging mode. Consumer, or SOHO, bridges are usually APs that you run in bridge mode. Enterprise class bridges, however, are generally sold as bridges and configured to operate as such by default. However, you can configure even enterprise class bridges to act as standard APs. So what is the difference between them? In most cases, the only difference is the intended use.

Features are unique or important to wireless bridges include

- Antenna alignment utilities
- Detachable antennas

Antenna Alignment Utilities

A wireless bridge connects two otherwise disconnected networks. The greater the distance between these two networks, the more difficult it is to align the antennas. For this reason, many wireless bridges provide antenna alignment utilities such as range calculation tools. With long-distance connections, you may also need to use GPS devices and consider issues such as antenna height, power output levels, gain of antennas, and possible object interference in the path of the RF signal.

Detachable Antennas

While APs often come with detachable antennas, the purpose of those antennas is usually very different from the antennas that come with bridges (except when running the AP in bridge mode). When you replace antennas on APs, you want to achieve higher gain output and not impact directionality. For a bridge, the antenna you select depends on the mode of use. If you are creating point-to-point connections, you use semidirectional or highly directional antennas. If you are creating point-to-multipoint connections, you use either omni-directional or semidirectional antennas.

Common Applications

When configuring a wireless bridge link, one of the bridges is in root mode and the other bridge or bridges are in non-root mode. The two main wireless link types are point-to-point and point-to-multipoint. Many devices use other names but are actually wireless bridges, for example, wireless gaming adapters. These devices are basically consumer grade bridges; however, some of them use proprietary communications protocols other than 802.11. To reduce the likelihood of interference with your 802.11 network, choose an 802.11-compliant device that you can configure to a different channel.

Point-to-Point

In point-to-point mode, a single wireless bridge forms a link between two wireless bridges. This configuration is a common one for short-distance WAN links and campus links that bridge just two locations.

Point-to-Multipoint

The use of bridges in a point-to-multipoint application allows for multiple bridging links to a central location. For instance, you might have a main network where the majority of services are located (domain servers, file servers, databases, Internet access, and so on) and smaller networks with some localized services and access to the main network for other functions. In this kind of situation, a point-to-multipoint setup works well.

To configure a point-to-multipoint link, install a bridge with a semi- or highly directional antenna at each remote location. Install an omni-directional antenna and bridge at the central location. You then align the antennas at each remote location so they are aimed properly at the central omni antenna. This central antenna may be semidirectional in scenarios where the two remote locations are relatively close to each other and in the same basic direction away from the central network. (See Figure 1.1 in Chapter 1 for a representation of point-to-point and point-to-multipoint connections.)

Configuration Methods

Wireless bridges are configured through the same basic interfaces as APs. Consumer grade bridges, which are really APs, usually have only a browser-based interface. Enterprise bridges are configurable through HTTP, telnet, SSH, console and custom applications, as well as SNMP.

Wireless Bridges Summary

Wireless bridges provide connectivity between disconnected networks without your needing to run any kind of cabling or pay for leased lines. Another kind of wireless bridge to be aware of is the wireless workgroup bridge. A workgroup bridge is used to connect a group of wired (Ethernet or token-ring) devices to a wireless network. These types of bridges are often used in remote classrooms or campus buildings that are rather small. The main difference between the two bridges is that a workgroup bridge can connect to an AP on a wireless network and wireless bridges connect only to other wireless bridges.

Repeaters

Repeaters have been used in wired networks for many years. A repeater receives the signal at one interface and amplifies it internally and then sends it back out the other interface. This allows data to travel greater distances down the cable. In a wireless network, repeaters perform the same function except they receive and repeat RF signals, and they function with more complexity.

The concept of the repeater goes all the way back to the telegraph system. In order to get electrical signals to travel many miles, you had to repeat or replay the signal periodically. To understand this idea, imagine a person in your backyard telling some information to your neighbor in a loud voice. The person in your neighbor's neighbor's (that is a complicated one, isn't it?) backyard can't hear the comment very well. Your neighbor repeats the comment loudly, and your neighbor's neighbor does the same thing. Eventually, the message reaches the backyard of some individual 20 miles away. This is precisely what a repeater does for electromagnetic signals in a wireless network.

Common Features

A SOHO, or even medium-sized business, is likely to use a standard AP as a repeater; however, dedicated repeaters are available. These consumer-grade repeaters are often called *range extenders*. Because this is exactly what a repeater does, the name makes sense. A wireless repeater is basically a bridge; in effect, the repeater is a client to another AP, and it acts as an AP for wireless clients that cannot reach the distant AP. In other words, the first AP is the root AP and the "repeater" AP is the non-root AP. Figure 4.15 shows a Linksys consumer-grade repeater.

FIGURE 4.15   WRE54G Range Extender

When looking at the features of consumer-grade repeaters, you find that they support many of the basic features of an AP. Remember, an AP can actually function as a repeater or range extender. Other features include

- No Ethernet connection
- Lower cost

No Ethernet Connection

Most wireless repeaters provide an RJ-45 Ethernet port for initial configuration, but when acting as a repeater the device does not need to be plugged into an Ethernet port because the repeater receives RF signals and retransmits RF signals (or at least this is how it appears). In reality, the repeater acts as an AP to the clients that are farther away.

Lower Cost

Because a repeater needs less functionality than an AP and acts as a bridge, you don't need features such as VPN pass-through and firewalls. And the fewer the capabilities, the lower the price point, usually.

Common Applications

Wireless repeaters give you the ability to extend the wireless network into areas the APs connected to your wired infrastructure cannot reach. Repeaters provide a simple solution to coverage in new buildings and previously unused areas of your facility.

Because of the behavior of RF signals, wireless repeaters can be used to "get around corners." In other words, the structure of your facility and the objects it contains may block RF signals from traversing the environment completely. A wireless repeater, well placed, can give you coverage in those hard-to-reach places.

Configuration Methods

Repeaters are generally configured through an Ethernet port initially and then through a browser-based interface on an ongoing basis. Some repeaters do not provide an Ethernet interface, so you configure them through the wireless interface only. Some repeaters have custom client applications to perform the initial configuration as well.

Switches

Wireless switches provide wired and wireless networking solutions with most implementations. They usually come with multiple Ethernet ports, and they can include many different feature sets such as VLANs (virtual LANs) and integrated SPI firewalls. A wireless switch is usually far more powerful and functional than a standard Ethernet switch.

Common Features

The common wireless switch offers the following features:

- Multiple access ports
- Virtual LANs
- SPI firewalls
- Remote manageability
- Power over Ethernet support
- Per-user rules
- Support for RADIUS servers

Multiple Access Ports

Wireless switches generally come with fewer than 12 Ethernet ports in consumer and SOHO models while enterprise models can expand to 20 or more by default. These ports are for connecting APs to the network. This distinction is an important one to make between SOHO wireless switch devices and enterprise wireless switches. The SOHO device is usually a simple switch (just like a standard Ethernet switch) that might support basic VLANs, but seldom enterprise functionality such as QoS. This device is an AP and switch all-in-one. The enterprise wireless switch does not usually contain a radio and is, therefore, not an AP in and of itself. Instead, you plug APs into the Ethernet ports and the switch manages them centrally.

Virtual LANs

Wireless switches provide a logical network infrastructure rather than a physical infrastructure. Because of this distinction, you can use them to implement a virtual LAN (VLAN) easily. A VLAN is a configuration set that dictates a particular Ethernet port will be on "one specified LAN" even though it may not connect directly to that LAN physically. Said another way, a VLAN is a group of devices that may actually be on separate physical network segments bordered by routers that act as if they were on the same network segment. The nodes on the VLAN are generally unaware that the other devices are not literally on the same physical segment.

VLANs help to provide better roaming and also allow for great flexibility in configuration management. For example, you can configure multiple VLANs in the switch and then require different security specifications for the various VLANs. This way you can put stronger security mechanisms in place, which can also slow communications, but only where they are needed, instead of on the entire network.

SPI Firewalls

SPI, or stateful packet inspection, firewall functionality is often built in to wireless switches. The most powerful switches allow you to create different firewall rule sets for different VLANs. You can then create protected network segments that exist only in software configurations rather than requiring many different hardware elements.

Remote Manageability

Remote management features allow you to configure not only the switch but also the APs connected to the switch. This mechanism is very useful in large enterprise installations, but loses its benefit quickly in a smaller environment with just one or two APs. This is due to the fact that one or two access points can be configured, maintained, and secured quickly without remote management on the same level as needed by large enterprises.

Power over Ethernet Support

Many switches allow the pass through of PoE power to APs via switched Ethernet ports. Then you can power PoE-compliant APs through the switch instead of down the line from the switch.

Per-User Rules

Per-user rule sets allow you to treat users in different ways on the network. For example, you can restrain certain users from routing through to the Internet while allowing others unrestrained access. You can also identify the time of day when particular users are allowed on the network to reduce the possibility of nighttime attackers.

Support for RADIUS Servers

If you are using AAA (Authentication, Authorization, and Accounting), most wireless switches can pass off this authentication to a central Remote Access Dial-In User Service (RADIUS) server such as Microsoft's Internet Authentication Service (IAS) or other software-based and hardware-based RADIUS devices. This gives you centralized control and management of authentication, authorization, and accounting (logging) parameters.

Common Applications

Most environments utilizing full wireless LAN switches are large enterprise installations. The cost of the switches (often in excess of $3,000) is a tremendous barrier to entry for SOHOs and even many medium-sized businesses. When working with a small company, standard APs connected to standard wired hubs usually provide sufficient functionality and are much more cost effective.

In larger enterprises, installing a wireless switch at each location and using that switch to manage the APs is a great solution. You can manage the switches across the LAN or WAN easily and this gives you centralized administration of a very decentralized concept—wireless networking.

Configuration Methods

Because you are configuring many different APs at once, configuring a wireless switch is much more complex than configuring a single AP. However, the fact that you can configure all of these devices from one interface is usually a timesaver overall.

Configuration interfaces usually include HTTP and HTTPS as well as Telnet or SSH. Because each vendor provides different applications and interfaces, the configuration of every switch will vary a little. For this reason, you should consider standardizing on a single switch provider for many, if not all, of your networking needs.

Wireless VoIP Gateways

A wireless VoIP gateway device provides VoIP services to wireless client devices such as wireless IP phones. Wireless VoIP gateways are also called *VoIP routers*. In many cases, VoIP routers are also standard 802.11 wireless routers providing both networking and VoIP support. VoIP routers may also provide interfaces for conversion allowing the use of analog phones with the VoIP network.

VoWLAN Fundamentals

To fully understand the features and applications of wireless VoIP gateways, you need to understand the fundamentals of VoWLAN. These fundamentals include its basic functionality, benefits or advantages, and the devices used to form a VoWLAN network.

Functionality

First, a VoWLAN requires a wireless LAN infrastructure with the needed throughput capabilities for VoIP traffic in addition to the traditional networking traffic that will still be traversing the network.

The second item you need is a wireless VoIP phone. These phones come in many forms and types, but they all have wireless radios in them for communications with the wireless network. Select a phone supporting the wireless standard of your wireless VoIP router or gateway, which is usually 802.11b/g.

The third component in your VoWLAN implementation is the wireless VoIP router—generally a standard wireless AP with telephone ports for connecting to your VoIP service such as Vonage or another service provider.

The final element required to build a VoWLAN network, if you want to communicate outside of your organization using VoIP, is a VoIP service provider. This provider provides the link between VoIP and PSTN so you can actually place calls outside of your IP-based network.

Advantages

The advantages of VoWLAN are potentially huge. First, you have the benefit of mobility. This benefit leads to greater productivity, as you can have that important phone conversation while you are walking down the hall to that important meeting. Having those phone conversations on the go might call for new "corporate etiquette" programs, however. Overhearing the conversation of coworkers is already annoying and disruptive. Imagine the problems caused by employees not ending phone conversations abruptly at the beginning of meetings. Setting these possible problems aside, productivity improvements will likely outweigh the drawbacks.

A second advantage of wireless VoIP is the reduced cost of phone service. Small businesses can subscribe to Internet-based phone services for a fraction of the cost of older public switched telephone networks (PSTN). It's predicted that the cost of Internet telephony will continue to drop as competition increases and bandwidth becomes more of a low-cost commodity.

Devices

The two major devices used in a VoWLAN are the wireless VoIP gateway and the wireless VoIP phones. I'll cover the features, applications, and configuration interfaces of the VoIP gateways in a moment. First, I discuss the basic types of wireless phones that you can use with a wireless VoIP gateway. These include

- Wireless IP phones
- PDAs
- Computers

Wireless IP phones are hardware devices created to communicate with wireless VoIP networks. These devices are sold by Cisco, Zyxel, and other vendors. Features often include call waiting, call forwarding, and often speed dialing and memory options for contacts. LCD displays show messages related to caller ID and waiting voice mails.

PDAs, with the appropriate software installed, can be used as wireless VoIP phones. Software, such as EN-PDA Softphone and NetZeroVoice, allows you to configure your PDA to use VoIP services and make and receive phone calls on your portable device as long as you have Internet access. You can often configure these packages to work with your own VoIP gateways as well.

Because software can perform the operations of a VoIP phone, a laptop or desktop computer can also be converted into such a device. In these scenarios, you would need a microphone, but microphone/headphone combos are readily available to serve this purpose.

Common Features

There are features common to all or most VoIP systems. These features provide the basic functionality needed by most IP-based telephone systems.

- **PSTN backup**   This feature allows you to connect a standard PSTN line for telephone operations in the event of a power failure.
- **Analog phone support**   This feature lets you connect analog phones and operate them across the wireless VoIP network.

- **SIP support** The Session Initiation Protocol (SIP) provides for roaming capabilities and commonly replaces Mobile IP.
- **QoS management** This feature lets you limit the bandwidth consumed by non-VoIP traffic when VoIP traffic is present.

Common Applications

VoIP telephone systems provide advantages over traditional analog phones in that they often provide services that are not offered by PSTN phone service providers. These services include receiving your voicemail as email attachments, creating virtual presences in remote cities, providing various phone numbers for your company in different area codes, and even connecting to the Internet to make phone calls from any location. Because of these benefits, you can use wireless VoIP solutions to provide

- "Anywhere" access to telephone service for traveling employees
- Centralized voicemail services accessible from home or the office
- Internal-only communications with VoIP technology
- The ability to share a limited number of lines to the outside world through automatic switching on the internal VoIP network

Configuration Methods

Because wireless VoIP gateways are often standard APs as well, you configure them in the same ways as an AP, which means HTTP, custom configuration software, and SNMP are generally supported.

Media Gateways

Wireless media gateways fall into two main categories: *centralized media sharing devices* and *wireless display connections*. A centralized media sharing device, the main focus of this section, is used to share videos, graphics, and audio files across the wireless network with multiple device types including computers and televisions. As shown in Figure 4.16, a wireless display connection is usually called a wireless presentation gateway.

These kinds of presentation gateways are often used to create a connection to a projection device without the need for cables. You can use them to run PowerPoint presentations or play digital videos for presentations and events.

FIGURE 4.16   D-Link DPG-2000W wireless presentation gateway

The device shown in Figure 4.16 actually allows multiple presenters to install the client software and then switch between presenters on-the-fly to dictate which client device controls the presentation at any given time. With customizable banner pages, you can even determine what the "null" screen will look like. This screen is the one shown when there is no active connection, which is great for in-between conference sessions. Although these devices are not generally referred to as wireless media gateways, some vendors do reference them as such. For our purposes, we'll refer to them as wireless presentation gateways.

The rest of this section focuses on the centralized media sharing devices truly known as wireless media gateways. Remember, wireless presentation gateway devices usually have HTTP (browser-based) configuration interfaces. Since they do not actually provide access to any sensitive data, the security concerns usually demanding a console interface are irrelevant.

Common Features

Common features of wireless media gateways include

- Remote control interfaces
- Support for graphics, videos, and audio

- Support for Internet streaming services
- Extra capabilities such as internal storage and print servers

Remote Control Interfaces

Most wireless media gateways make it simple to access data by providing a remote control interface. Simple navigation and basic functionality keep the learning curve to a minimum. The downside to this is that most of these media gateways are very basic in what they allow you to do and have limited expandability (for example, you generally cannot add newer video codecs or audio codecs). For this reason, some installations require a custom solution, such as an actual PC functioning as a client to a wireless presentation gateway connected to a video screen or television. In this instance, you are basically building your own wireless media gateway device with full expandability, and in some cases (some wireless media gateways are more than $700–$1,000), this is a less expensive solution.

Support for Graphics, Videos, and Audio

Most media gateways support standard image formats such as JPG and TIFF, but check the specifications closely to ensure support for your media type. Videos support almost always includes MPEG1 and MPEG2. Some devices support other video codecs including XVID, though that support is less common than the MPEG format. Audio formats supported generally include MP3, WAV, and various other formats.

When it comes to compatibility, if the wireless media gateway does not support the codecs (coding/decoding algorithms) in which your videos are stored, you have to re-encode hundreds of videos. If you've done this before, you know that it takes many, many hours. The same reality applies to any graphic files you wish to access.

Support for Internet Streaming Services

Services such as Rhapsody and Napster are often supported by wireless media gateways, allowing you to access massive libraries of music and spoken word audio. These extra services require monthly subscription fees, but can be less expensive than buying individual CDs and are extremely popular.

Extra Capabilities

Capabilities above and beyond the basics include print servers, internal hard drives for storage of data, and connectivity with Windows XP Media

Center Edition for access to TV and other Media Center features, such as DVD playback and TV schedule guides.

Common Applications

While the most common application of a wireless media gateway is to provide access to all forms of digital entertainment and information for home use, small and large businesses are using them to create central points of access for multiple kiosks in various entrances to their facilities and for streaming of CEO presentations to employee break rooms. This kind of creative use provides centralized control over decentralized distribution of media of all kinds.

Configuration Methods

The standard configuration interface for a wireless media gateway is web based and very few support any other options. Connector types include Ethernet, USB, VGA, RCA, S-Video, and other video connections. USB ports are used to connect USB printers, when they are supported, or external USB hard drives for extra storage space.

Firmware upgrades are important for wireless media gateways as they provide extra functionality, such as support for new streaming services, audio codecs, and video codecs. As with APs, apply firmware updates through the Ethernet port when possible to reduce the likelihood of corruption.

Power over Ethernet Devices

Power over Ethernet (PoE) provides the delivery of DC voltage to an AP or a wireless bridge over standard CAT5 or CAT6 Ethernet cables, powering the unit with the same cable that carries the data to the unit. Basically, PoE lets you use an AP or bridge that cannot be located near a power outlet.

Functionality

PoE is used when AC power outlets are not available in the location of the AP or bridge and it is more cost effective and time efficient to use PoE instead of installing a power outlet. Administrative advantages include the ability to cycle devices (power off and on) from a remote location such as through a PoE compatible switch interface.

Let's say you want to provide wireless coverage in a city park. While there may be power outlets in the park, they may not be located where you need them. Using a traditional setup, you would have to trench and lay pipe and wiring just to get power to the AP. With PoE, you could run an Ethernet cable through the air or bury it just a few inches deep and provide power through this cable. Figure 4.17 demonstrates this scenario and the placement of PoE devices and wireless devices.

Sometimes PoE can be useful even when power outlets are available. PoE requires one cable and it provides centralized power administration. Don't, however, confuse this with centralized device configuration. You cannot configure the WPA settings on an AP just because it is powered with PoE, but you can cycle the device to reset when software errors occur or during security emergencies.

To use PoE you will need at least two devices. The first is the PoE compatible wireless device and the second is the PoE injector. A possible third device is a PoE or active Ethernet switch that performs the role of the injector. A generic term used to refer to power injectors, switches, or any device that can provide Power over Ethernet is *power sourcing equipment* or *PSE*.

PoE Devices

Many APs and bridges contain built-in support for PoE. This support is usually noted on the vendor's website and in the documentation. Because having

FIGURE 4.17   PoE installation in a park

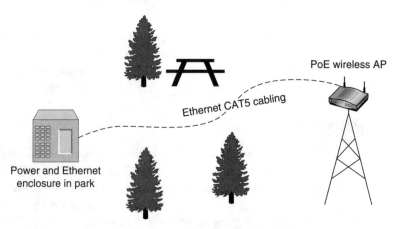

an alternate power source is an advantage, PoE-compatible devices may be slightly more expensive.

Do not confuse *PoE* with *PPPoE*. Though not usually made in daily operations, this is a common mistake when taking a test. PoE is, of course, Power over Ethernet. PPPoE is PPP over Ethernet and is a protocol for connecting remote hosts to the Internet over a DSL connection by simulating a dial-up connection. It is not used as frequently any more, but in times past, it was essential and supported by many DSL gateway wireless routers.

There are usually no configuration settings to manage in PoE-compatible devices. These devices detect the use of PoE for power and utilize it automatically. In effect, sending power down the Ethernet cable from the PSE "turnson" the wireless device.

If you lack PoE support in your chosen APs or bridges, you might be able to use PoE through a *DC picker* or *DC tap*. These devices are sometimes called *active Ethernet splitters*. They pull (or pick/tap) the DC power off the CAT5 cable and then make it available to the equipment through the standard DC power jack.

To use PoE, you need either an injector plus a PoE device or an injector, plus a DC picker, and a standard device to provide extra flexibility in your power configuration. DC pickers come as either passive or regulated. A passive picker/tap takes whatever DC power is injected and routes it to the DC port unchanged. A regulated DC tap converts the power to another voltage when necessary.

PoE Injectors

PoE injectors come in many forms and with various capabilities. For example, a multiport injector provides DC power through multiple CAT5 cables and a single port injector provides power to only one cable. PoE injectors can be large and rack mountable or small footprint devices that are mounted individually to a wall or shelving system.

One important feature to look for in PoE injectors is 802.3af compliance—the IEEE standard for PoE devices. If your APs and bridges, as well as injectors, are 802.3af compliant, they should work together without any problem. It's still important to verify pin usage and power levels. Injectors may run power on different wires and can damage your equipment if

FIGURE 4.18 Single and multipPort injectors

not installed properly. Figure 4.18 shows both single port and multiport power injectors.

PoE Switches

If you need to power many APs using PoE, you might want to use a PoE-capable Ethernet switch. These devices act as both switches and PoE injectors in one unit. The D-Link DES-1316 switch, shown in Figure 4.19, is such a device. This device is also a great example of a common reality with these switches: only 8 of the 16 switch ports on this device are 802.3af or PoE ready. This is an important characteristic to watch for when selecting a PoE switch.

With a beginning cost of less than $500, PoE switches are viable candidates for small and medium-sized businesses as well as the large enterprise. These devices usually support standard switch features such

FIGURE 4.19 D-Link DES-1316 PoE/802.3af switch

as VLANs and QoS management. They generally include either consol or HTTP configuration interfaces or both.

PoE Ethernet switches carry the PoE benefits even further than stand-alone PoE injectors. One of the great benefits of PoE is the fact that you have to run only one cable to the wireless device. With a switch, you have only one device to install in the closet or switch location. When you use a PoE injector, you need both a switch (or sometimes a hub) and the PoE injector in the closet, but when you use a PoE switch, you need only the switch.

Cycling an AP that is in the ceiling or some other hard-to-reach location, such as the top of a tower, is not as simple as opening your web browser and clicking a few buttons. PoE switches allow you to stop and start the power to any given port through the management interface, which is a huge benefit.

Finally, 802.3af-compliant PoE switches perform PoE device sensing, which means the switch detects if the device connected to the port is an 802.3af device and if it's not, it cancels power to that port. Some non-802.3af vendors also provide this functionality. Remember that non-PoE devices should not be damaged by the flow of power anyway, as the power flows on unutilized wires.

Enterprise Class Devices

As mentioned at the beginning of this chapter, there are more powerful devices that are not used in SOHO, consumer, or smaller business environments. Though not the main focus of this book and the Wireless# certification, it is important to know what these devices are and the functionality they provide.

A great source of information on these enterprise class devices is the *CWNA Certified Wireless Network Administrator Official Study Guide (Exam PW0-100), Third Edition* by Planet3 Wireless and published by McGraw-Hill (2005). This book prepares you for the CWNA exam and provides valuable information about more advanced wireless equipment than what is covered here.

Among the many enterprise class devices, the most common ones include

- Enterprise Wireless Gateways
- Enterprise Encryption Gateways

Enterprise Wireless Gateways

Enterprise Wireless Gateways (EWGs) are specialized devices that provide authentication and connectivity for wireless clients. These devices offer role-based access control, QoS management, VPN tunnels, and more.

Role-based access control (RBAC) allows you to configure different levels of wireless access based on particular job descriptions or functions in the organization. RBAC can provide an extra level of security in your environment because users cannot even access the network on which the secure data resides, much less access the data once they get there. Not only is RBAC capable of limiting access to resources but also it controls the bandwidth consumed by a role on the wireless network. This helps reduce bandwidth consumption by users who do not really "need" bandwidth-intensive applications—such as those Internet newscasts they might want to watch at work. Finally, RBAC can also restrict access to particular time windows so that specific roles cannot access the network except at assigned times.

An EWG can authenticate users with a variety of mechanisms, including RADIUS, LDAP, 802.1x, and internal proprietary databases. Because of this flexibility, many client types are supported by the EWG.

Some EWGs are so complex that in order to master their capabilities and configuration options it's necessary to attend the vendor's training class. For smaller businesses with tighter budgets, many modern wireless routers are beginning to incorporate some of the features of an EWG, though they perform at lower levels. The Buffalo Technology WZR-RS-G54, seen in Figure 4.20, is just such a device.

This device is a perfect example of an entry-point device that provides some features of an EWG without the cost (this particular device is under $200). Of course, you lose many features; for example, the Buffalo Technology WZR-RS-G54 supports only PPTP VPN end points and offers no support for L2TP/IPSec VPN client connections, though it does allow for all types of VPN pass through. The PPTP end point also uses a built-in user database. There are two internal antennas (one vertically polarized and one horizontally polorized) for better support of laptops and desktops, and there is also an external antenna port. The main difference between a device such as this and an EWG is that an EWG is not an access point in and of itself; instead it connects to and manages access to access points. The Buffalo Technology WZR-RS-G54 is an all-in-one device that gives you some features of an EWG.

FIGURE 4.20   Buffalo Technology WZR-RS-G54

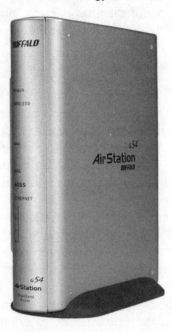

Enterprise Encryption Gateways

An Enterprise Encryption Gateway (EEG) handles the encryption processes for your wireless LAN. The EEG has both an encrypted and an unencrypted side. The unencrypted side is generally your wired LAN, and the encrypted side is the wireless LAN. The major benefit of an EEG is that it can offset the overhead created by encryption from your APs to the more powerful EEG device.

Antennas

Antennas are possibly the most important devices in wireless networks. You can have the best APs, routers, switches, and even power them with standard 802.3af PoE devices and still accomplish nothing if there are no antennas to propagate the wireless signals into the air. Antennas come in all shapes and sizes with different purposes and capabilities. Selecting the right antenna, however, is a science and not an art. With the right knowledge and testing equipment, you can choose the best antenna for any situation.

When evaluating antennas, the technician must understand the basics of antenna functionality, the types of antennas available, and how to choose the best location for the different antenna types. This section covers all three of these important elements.

Antenna Functionality

An excellent way to think of antennas is to consider the analogy of a water hose and a nozzle. The hose is the coaxial cable carrying the RF energy from a transmitter to the antenna. Just as the hose contains the water, the coaxial cable contains the RF energy until it reaches its destination. The nozzle is the antenna; it sprays the RF energy into the air much like the water hose nozzle sprays the water into the air.

Just as different nozzles create different spray patterns, different antennas have different RF propagation patterns. This way, you can use a standard transmitter (for example, an access point) and propagate the RF energy differently in a range of places by using various types of antennas. Some antennas propagate the energy relatively the same in all directions and others propagate most of the energy in a narrow path in one direction. Select the antenna that creates the appropriate propagation pattern depending on your needs.

The Isotropic Radiator

Most antennas are compared to a mythical antenna known as an *isotropic radiator*. I call it a mythical antenna because humans cannot create one. The isotropic radiator is an antenna that propagates RF energy in all directions in a completely equal spherical pattern. With this type of antenna, the RF energy is propagated up, down, side-to-side, and in all other directions with the exact same energy. As you recall from Chapter 2, dBi measures the gain of an antenna. The *i* stands for isotropic and is used to compare the actual gain in the advertised direction of the antenna. If an antenna is an omni-directional antenna with a high gain (12–15 dBi), then the doughnut shaped propagation pattern is flatter. In other words, less of the RF energy travels in an upward direction and more of the RF energy travels in an outward direction.

The longer an omni-directional antenna, the flatter the RF propagation pattern. This means, in the inverse, that the shorter the antenna, the more spherical the propagation pattern, so to create a perfect sphere, the antenna would have a length of zero, which means, of course, that the antenna does not exist.

Am I the only one who fears saying that something cannot be done? After all, people once said that objects heavier than air could not fly, and that if you floated too far in a boat, you would fall off the end of the Earth. I feel safe in saying that with the current technology and information available, it is impossible to create an isotropic antenna. So when someone reads this book in 1,000 years (over a wireless network using a true isotropic radiator at 100 exabits per second, or more), I won't look too foolish.

Polarization

You do not have to be a physics expert to implement and support wireless LANs. That is the good news. However, you should know enough about the concept of polarization to determine proper antenna placement. *Polarization* references the physical orientation of the antenna in relation to the earth. Understanding the impact of horizontal versus vertical polarization is important.

Simply put, when omni-directional antennas are in a vertical position, the RF waves are propagated horizontally. When the antennas are placed in a horizontal position, the RF waves are propagated vertically. Here is the catch: vertically polarized antennas are in a vertical position and horizontally polarized antennas are in a horizontal position. In other words, the polarization of an antenna is not referred to by the propagation of the wave, but by the position of the electric field, in the wave, to the ground.

The electric portion of an electromagnetic wave is propagated parallel to the propagation device. If the antenna is vertical, the electric wave is vertical. Now you know where the term *vertically polarized* comes from; it references the polarization of the electric field in relation to the earth. Even though the waves propagate horizontally when an omni-directional antenna is vertical, the antenna is said to be vertically polarized. The easiest way to remember this is that polarization refers to the position of the antenna.

I don't want to leave the impression that absolute vertical and horizontal polarization are the only options. If you have worked with any AP attached antennas, you know they can be positioned at many angles. The vertical and horizontal planes simply provide an easy way to think of antenna propagation behavior. In fact, it is not uncommon to position an antenna in a way that might be called *angled-polarization*. This positioning allows the RF waves to propagate to multiple floors in a building and is often seen in hotel hotspot installations.

The most important thing to remember about polarization is that the sending and receiving antennas should be positioned using the same polarization. Configuring the antennas with different polarizations causes a reduction in signal strength at the receiver and can impact throughput greatly. For example, if you place one antenna close to the ground and another 100 feet away and 30 feet higher, you have to angle the antennas so they are parallel to each other to achieve the best signal reception.

Antenna Gain and Loss

An antenna is a passive device, which means it does not create actual gains and losses. You cannot use an antenna to increase the amount of RF energy radiated from the antenna. As a passive device, the antenna produces gain by propagating more of the energy in a limited scope of directionality, meaning the antenna sends the energy only in certain directions and, therefore, the energy can travel farther.

Returning to a water analogy, if you have exactly one gallon of water and throw it in all directions at the same time with the same velocity, it will go a certain distance. The distance it travels should be the same in all directions, in a spherical pattern, assuming gravity has no impact on it. However, the water dissipates over distance because it evaporates in the air. Now, take that same amount of water and throw it in one direction with the same lack of gravity. The water travels a greater distance, in that direction, before it evaporates.

You can think of RF energy in a similar way. The energy is absorbed and the wave front broadened as it travels until, eventually, the energy dissipates. If you propagate more of the energy in one direction, you logically propagate that energy over a greater distance. For this reason and to address security concerns, you should use directional antennas for long-distance links. More of the energy travels in the desired direction and for a greater distance. Why is all this so important? The answer is simple: wireless devices have a receiving sensitivity rating. This rating indicates the RF signal strength that must exist for the wireless device to communicate. Because the RF signal weakens over distance, you eventually reach a point where RF energy exists but is so weak that the wireless device can no longer detect it.

There is a simple formula you can use to determine the received signal strength at the wireless receiver. This formula is

Received signal = RF transmitter output power – losses in the path to the transmitting antenna + transmitting antenna gain – free space path loss + receiving antenna gain – losses in the path to the receiver

Using this formula, you can decide which antenna type to select. In many cases, the most important thing to consider is the gain of the antenna. With indoor networks, you frequently use omni-directional antennas placed in centralized locations in the facility. These antennas ship with APs but can be replaced with more powerful models to increase the signal strength. Realize, however, that increased strength usually means a flatter horizontal distribution, so the signal will not travel as far vertically.

While many of the figures needed to calculate the preceding formula are available from the hardware vendors (antenna vendors, AP vendors, cabling vendors, and so on), the missing element is the estimate for free space path loss. Use Table 4.1 for this purpose.

For example, assume you have gathered the estimates listed in Table 4.2 for a particular connection between an AP and a client. Using the RF math rules covered in Chapter 2, you determine that the receiver has a signal strength of roughly –74 dB from the original 50 mW. This ends up being approximately 2 nanowatts (0.0000002 milliwatts). Because most receivers have a receive sensitivity of –70 dBm or better (better being lower than –70), this connection will likely work just fine though the data rate will be lower.

Let me explain this further. The math to determine the –74 db is as follows (from Table 4.2):

–3 dB + 6 dBi = 3 db

3 dB + –80 dB = –77 dB

–77 db + 6 dBi = –71 db

–71 db + –3 dB = –74 db

TABLE 4.1   Free Space Path Loss Estimates

Distance	Loss (in dB)
100 meters	80.23
200 meters	86.25
500 meters	94.21
1,000 meters	100.23

TABLE 4.2   Power Levels at Measurement Points

Measurement Point	Power Level
AP output	50 mW
Connectors	−3 dB
Antenna	6 dBi
100 meters	−80 dB
Antenna	6 dBi
Connectors	−3 dB

You could also state it like this:

$$(-3) + 6 + (-80) + 6 + (-3) = (-74)$$

Once you have determined the loss in dB, you can use the rules of 3s and 10s to determine the signal strength at the receiver.

Antenna Types

Antennas come in dozens of form factors, but these many form factors can usually be categorized into three basic types of antennas. While the most common type of antenna installed in small networks is the basic omni-directional or dipole antenna, you need to understand all three types so you can select the best one for any situation. These three types are

- Omni-directional/dipole
- Semidirectional
- Highly directional

Omni-directional/Dipole

Omni-directional antennas propagate RF waves out from the antenna horizontally in all directions, assuming the antenna is vertically polarized. Another way to say this is the omni-directional antenna sends out the RF waves in a perpendicular direction to the antenna itself. Imagine an ever-growing circle around the antenna and you have the right concept. Omni-directional antennas do not emit a perfectly circular radiation patter, but this concept is the best way to generalize the omni-directional antenna's functionality. This circle is often referred to as a doughnut because the RF wave does not propagate in an outward direction only; some of the wave propagates upward, but this upward propagation increases for a distance and then lessens forming the shape of a doughnut.

The applications of omni-directional antennas vary. First of all, nearly all APs come with an omni-directional antenna—specifically a dipole antenna. These antennas are sometimes called *rubber ducky antennas* because of the rubber shielding covering the actual antenna element. Because these antennas are omni-directional, if you use an AP with the default antenna configuration, place the AP in the center of the desired coverage area.

Other omni-directional antennas are intended to send waves a greater distance, and they do this by flattening the wave. In other words, the wave looks more like a circle and less like a doughnut when you look at the propagating pattern. An example of such an omni-directional antenna is shown in Figure 4.21.

FIGURE 4.21   Omni indoor wireless antenna (D-Link ANT24-0400)

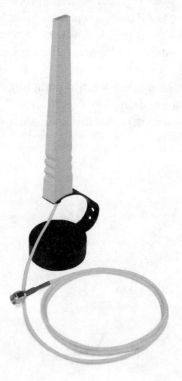

Outdoor omni antennas are available in high gain versions which can be very useful for creating hotspots or covering large outdoor areas such as parks and corporate campuses. These antennas range in dBi from 4 to better than 15.

Semidirectional

Semidirectional antennas come in a wide range of styles with a large variance in RF propagation patterns. Common form factors are the patch, panel, and yagi antennas. The patch and panel antennas are generally flat form factors and the yagi (pronounced *YAH-gee*) antennas look like long rods with tines sticking out (though these tines are often covered by tubing). Figure 4.22 shows the three types of semidirectional antennas.

These antenna types are useful for providing coverage down hallways and corridors inside buildings. For example, if you need to provide coverage to a group of offices along a long narrow hallway, mount a patch or panel antenna at one end of the hallway facing inward. This placement usually provides coverage in the offices—as long as the hallway is not too long. If the hallway is of greater length, place a patch or panel antenna at each end of the hall and connect each one to a different AP using a separate channel. Sometimes using a yagi antenna solves this type of problem as it has a narrower beam-width than the patch and panel antennas. However, the yagi may not provide coverage in the offices nearest the antenna.

Yagi antennas can also be used in point-to-point links spanning distances of more than 3 kilometers (approximately 2–2.5 miles). Vendors often cite distances of more than 5 kilometers, but this estimate is often unrealistic

FIGURE 4.22   Patch, panel, and yagi antennas

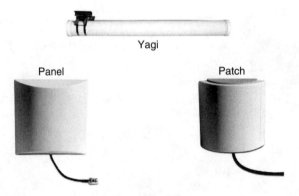

in real-world implementations because of interference by weather, trees, and buildings. In other words, a portion of the RF energy is lost due to absorption, reflection, and refraction.

Highly Directional

Highly directional antennas are generally used for WAN links such as point-to-point or point-to-multipoint. The parabolic dish and grid antenna are common examples of these antenna types. Using these antennas, you can create a link that spans up to 35 miles. With prices under $500 in many cases, creating a single link (two antennas, two wireless bridges, connectors, and mounting kits) can cost less than $1,500. Assuming the air is uncongested with RF traffic, this link can be less expensive than the cost of leasing a line for two months. If the wireless link provides the needed bandwidth, it is a great cost/benefit solution.

Figure 4.23 shows an example of a parabolic dish antenna, and Figure 4.24 shows the grid antenna. Notice the similarities between the parabolic dish and a satellite dish. This form factor allows for less of the signal to propagate behind the antenna and therefore provides more strength in the desired direction of propagation. The grid antenna, with the holes in the back panels, withstands heavy winds well and is useful to maintain alignment in high wind areas.

FIGURE 4.23   A parabolic dish

FIGURE 4.24   A grid antenna

Antenna Accessories

You will need more than just an antenna and a wireless device to get your wireless connections working. In many cases, connectors, amplifiers, and mounting kits are all needed.

Connectors

Antennas come with different types of connectors. Common connector types include

- N-type
- F-type
- SMA
- BNC
- TNC

In addition to the different types, there are also variations on each type. For example, the N-type connector comes in standard, reverse polarity, and reverse threaded models. When selecting antennas, connectors should match your equipment. When selecting an RF connector, make sure it matches your equipment in type and impedance. Look closely at the packaging for the antenna and the device to ensure they both use the same connector type.

In some cases, adapters are available to convert from one connector type to another, but you must verify that the use of a pigtail adapter does not breach FCC regulations. The FCC states that an adapter can be used only if it is part of a certified system. While it is not illegal to sell the pigtail adapters, it may be illegal to use them with your equipment.

This is reminiscent of the old days when crackers would phone phreak the telecom network with tone generators. It was legal to buy all the items to build the tone generator at your local electronics store, but if you used them to break into the phone network, you were, of course, committing a crime. If you've heard of blue boxing, you've heard of phone phreaking. Blue boxing, a kind of phone phreaking, was a method used to access the long-distance mode of the telephone network without paying for it. You might think of it as using licensed wireless bands today without paying for them—only then someone really paid for the implementation of the infrastructure.

Amplifiers

Amplifiers are used down line from the antenna to increase the strength of the RF signal. Amplifiers are useful when creating a wireless WAN link with a 15 dBi antenna that supports up to 100 mW of input power if your bridge outputs only up to 50 mW. You can double the RF signal before it reaches the antenna and then get the full benefit of the antenna's gain (while remaining within FCC regulations).

Mounting Kits

Mounting kits come in all shapes, types, and sizes. For simple situations, you can generally use the default kit that comes with the antenna. If you need to mount the antenna outdoors, you might need to purchase extra mounting kits and even build custom kits in many situations. With point-to-point and point-to-multipoint links, it is very important that you mount the antennas firmly so they do not lose alignment.

Placement

The placement of your wireless antennas depends entirely on the antenna type, link type, and power output. In most small networks (SOHO and small businesses), you install omni- or semidirectional antennas to create indoor coverage. Place omni-directional antennas in locations that are central to the desired coverage areas and the semidirectional antennas on the outer edge of the coverage area with the antenna aimed so the RF energy is propagated inward.

When creating wireless WAN links, use semidirectional or highly directional antennas in most cases. Aim these antennas at each other to establish a link. When creating a point-to-multipoint connection, however, use either an omni- or semidirectional antenna at the central hub of the network.

A final important note about antennas is that multiple antennas do not automatically mean MIMO technology. In fact, multiple antennas have been used in single wireless APs for a long time. These dual antennas allow for *antenna diversity*. Basically, the antenna with the best reception is used for wireless communications.

Summary

Wireless repeaters are basically access points configured as repeaters, or they are permanently configured to act as a repeater. Either way, they are used to increase the range of the wireless network.

Switches are often used in wireless implementations to centralize the management and control of infrastructure devices such as wireless access points and routers. The term wireless switch is sometimes used to refer to a wireless router with a built-in switch. In enterprise terms, a wireless switch is a "wireless aware" switch. This means that it is a special switch capable of controlling thick or thin access points. Thin access points have no localized configurations and are managed through the centralized controller, the wireless switch.

Media gateways allow you to watch streaming video or listen to streaming audio of wireless connections. They allow you to share your digital media library throughout your home with your televisions and media players. A wireless presentation gateway allows you to display the output from your computer on a projector using a wireless connection.

Power over Ethernet gives you an alternate way to power wireless devices. These can be enterprise devices or SOHO devices. The power is carried over the standard CAT5 or CAT6 cabling to the device.

There are many types of antennas for many different purposes. Select omni-directional antennas for indoor use and coverage of small to medium outdoor areas. Semidirectional antennas are used indoors for narrow and long coverage patterns and outdoors for short-distance wireless links. When you need to create a long-distance link, you need to upgrade to parabolic dish and grid antennas.

When selecting antennas, it is important to consider the gain of the antenna and the advertised coverage pattern. The proper gain and coverage pattern allows you to "fill" the coverage area with RF signals and create a functional wireless LAN. To ensure consistent coverage and connections, mount your antennas firmly and install them properly.

Key Terms

- ☐ access point
- ☐ antennas
- ☐ highly directional antennas
- ☐ omni-directional antennas
- ☐ Power over Ethernet
- ☐ semidirectional antennas
- ☐ VoIP gateways
- ☐ wireless bridge
- ☐ wireless media gateway
- ☐ wireless presentation gateway
- ☐ wireless repeaters
- ☐ wireless routers
- ☐ wireless switch

Review Questions

1. Access points can operate in different modes depending on the need of the network. Select the two modes from the following list that are available on most access points.

   A. Console mode

   B. Root mode

   C. Repeater mode

   D. Switch mode

2. What are the benefits of adjustable power output levels on access points? Select two.

   A. Reducing the size of the coverage area

   B. Increasing data throughput

   C. Decreasing security

   D. Preventing interference with other nearby networks

3. You are a network administrator in a small company, and you want to use WPA on your network instead of WEP. However, when you access the HTTP interface for your AP, it does not seem to provide WPA support. Other than buying a new AP, what could you try to get WPA support on your existing AP?

   A. Upgrade the client software to convert dynamically between WEP and WPA so at least the clients are more secure.

   B. Implement WPA over WEP using a RADIUS server.

   C. Check with the vendor of the AP to see if they offer a firmware upgrade that provides WPA functionality.

   D. Connect a WPA adapter in-line between the AP and the antenna.

4. What is the reason for configuring an access point, or any infrastructure device, before connecting it to the network infrastructure?

    A. Because the default settings are often insecure and the moment it is connected to the infrastructure it makes the infrastructure insecure

    B. Because you cannot configure the device while it is connected to the infrastructure

    C. In order to prevent the device from corrupting the encryption settings on the network

    D. Because the device allows users to become administrators in the network realm

5. Which of these are common configuration and management options for access points?

    A. Custom configuration client tools

    B. HTTP

    C. SNMP

    D. Telnet

6. What is the main difference between a wireless access point and a wireless router?

    A. The wireless router can perform MAC filtering.

    B. The wireless access point can perform MAC filtering.

    C. The wireless access point provides routing based on IP addresses and the router does not.

    D. The wireless router provides routing based on IP addresses and the access point does not.

7. As a network manager, you need to allow IP packets from outside your wireless network to pass through to a specific device inside your network when they are destined for a certain port. Which feature should you configure in your wireless router?

   A. Port routing

   B. Port redirection

   C. Port forwarding

   D. Port blocking

8. You have installed a wireless router on your network. The wireless clients complain that they cannot get to devices that are not on the wireless segment. You are sure that your wired routers are configured to use the RIP routing protocol. What feature should you enable in the wireless router to allow it to self-configure?

   A. Enable the RIP protocol

   B. Configure a static route to the RIP server

   C. Configure a static route to another RIP router

   D. Enable the IP routing engagement feature

9. You have a remote site that is not connected to your network. The organization has decided to create a wireless link with the site that is located approximately one mile from the headquarters. You have the antennas, mounting equipment, cabling, and connecters. What other device will you need to create this link?

   A. Wireless switch

   B. Wireless bridge

   C. Wireless repeater

   D. Wireless media gateway

10. The network you manage has been attacked by a scanning-type worm. This kind of worm appears to seek out open networks that allow unrequested traffic into the network and then attacks them. Because your organization will not budget for a full firewall, what feature can you enable in your wireless router to provide some level of protection?

    A. Firewall

    B. VPN pass through

    C. VPN end point

    D. MAC filtering

11. What is the most common difference between a device sold as a bridge and a device sold as an AP?

    A. The intended use

    B. Bridges cannot be access points

    C. Access points cannot be bridges

    D. The antenna size

12. You have a wireless network that has been providing adequate coverage. However, the organization is adding a new wing that will be beyond the reach of the current wireless network by just a few dozen feet. What one device could you install to extend the wireless network into this area?

    A. Wireless workgroup bridge

    B. Wireless bridge

    C. Wireless repeater

    D. Wireless media gateway

13. A wireless workgroup bridge is used to connect a group of wired devices to a wireless network.

    A. True

    B. False

14. RBAC, which is implemented in some wireless switches, stands for
what feature?

    A. Rule-based access control

    B. Role-based access control

    C. Rights-based access control

    D. Remote binary access control

15. Microsoft's IAS (Internet Authentication Service) is an example of
what kind of server?

    A. Active Directory

    B. Firewall

    C. RADIUS

    D. RRAS

16. What feature of wireless switches allows wireless clients from all over
the network to appear as if they were on the same IP segment?

    A. VWAN

    B. VPAN

    C. VLAN

    D. VMAN

17. If you want your users to be able to communicate over the Internet
with VoIP phones, what three items do you need at a minimum?

    A. VoIP service provider

    B. VoIP router or gateway

    C. Telephone

    D. VoIP phone

18. What type of devices can act as a wireless VoIP phone? Select two.

   A. PDAs

   B. Laptops with 802.11 NICs

   C. Desktop computers with Ethernet NICs

   D. Analog phones

19. What is the difference between a wireless media gateway and a wireless presentation gateway?

   A. A wireless presentation gateway provides only the display of a computer's video on a remote device.

   B. A wireless media gateway provides only the display of a computer's video on a remote device.

   C. A wireless media gateway cannot display video on a television.

   D. A wireless presentation gateway can provide centralized management of storage media.

20. What does PoE stand for?

   A. Power on Ethernet

   B. Power over Ethernet

   C. Power on Extension

   D. Portable Omni-Extension

21. You have purchased an AP that uses PoE and plan to place it in the ceiling of your facility where there is no power outlet. You have run the Ethernet cable from the PoE compatible switch to the AP and it is still not powering up. What should you check?

   A. Make sure you have not used all PoE capable ports in the switch

   B. Make sure you have selected a PoE-compatible CAT5 cable

   C. Make sure the toggle switch on the AP is set to PoE instead of DC

   D. Make sure the DC port cover is closed on the AP

22. You are creating a wireless link between two remote locations (approximately .3 kilometers from the central offices) and the central offices. This connection will be a point-to-multipoint link set with the remote locations and the central office. What antennas should you use?

    A. Semidirectional antennas at the remote locations and a highly directional antenna at the central location.

    B. Omni-directional antennas at the remote locations and a semidirectional at the central location.

    C. Semidirectional or highly directional antennas at the remote locations and an omni-directional antenna at the central location.

    D. Highly directional antennas at the remote locations and a highly directional antenna at the central location

Review Answers

1. **B, C.** Access points support at least four modes of operation. These modes include root mode, bridge mode, repeater mode, and client mode. In root mode, an access point is acting as the "center of the network." Bridge mode is used to create wireless links between two disconnected LANs. Repeater mode is used to extend the wireless network into uncovered areas. In client mode, the AP acts as a client to the wireless network and routes information back through its internal Ethernet port.

2. **A, D.** Adjusting the output power levels can reduce the size of the coverage area and therefore help prevent interference with other nearby wireless networks.

3. **C.** Vendors can provide upgraded firmware to give support for WPA; however, they may not be able to support WPA2 (802.1x) with a firmware upgrade because the processor may not be powerful enough to support the encryption demands.

4. **A.** While the timeframe between connection and secure configuration is small, it provides unnecessary window of opportunity for hackers. Many wireless devices have built-in DHCP servers that are enabled by default. This can cause problems as clients might receive improper configuration settings.

5. **A, B, C, D.** All four of these are common configuration interfaces. Other common configuration interfaces are the console, HTTPS, and SSH.

6. **D.** The main difference in functionality between an access point and a wireless router is that a wireless router inspects and directs IP packets. A wireless access point basically acts as a bridge since the wireless clients have the same IP network configuration and wired clients on that segment. With a router, the wireless clients are on one segment while the wired network is on another. Both the wireless access point and router can usually perform MAC filtering.

7. **C.** Port forwarding allows you to redirect incoming traffic that is destined for a particular port to a specific internal machine on your network. Also called *port redirection* in some documents, but the more common phrase is *port forwarding.*

8. **A.** Enabling the RIP protocol for inbound announcements should allow the wireless router to self-configure and provide routes for the wireless clients so they can access the wired network.

9. **B.** A wireless bridge is needed at each end of the connection. This can be a dedicated bridge device or an AP in bridge mode.

10. **A.** Enable the firewall. The firewall will usually be an SPI firewall, which means it disallows any incoming data that was not originally requested by an internal device. Enabling MAC filters does not help because they protect only the wireless side of the wireless router and not the wired side. MAC addresses can be easily spoofed as well, so they are not a perfect solution for protecting the wireless side.

11. **A.** The only major difference between a wireless AP and a bridge is the intended use. This is because most bridges can be configured as APs and most APs can be configured as bridges. They usually come preconfigured for their intended use.

12. **C.** A wireless repeater allows you to extend the network into this new area. Wireless repeaters are often called *wireless range extenders.*

13. **A.** Wireless workgroup bridges allow you to connect multiple wired devices to a wireless network. These devices can be useful for connecting remote classrooms to central networks.

14. **B.** RBAC stands for Role-based access control and is used to limit client capabilities based on the role of the user on the network.

15. C. IAS is a RADIUS (Remote Access Dial-In User Service) server providing authentication, accounting, and authorization for wired, wireless, VPN, and dial-up clients.

16. C. A virtual LAN (VLAN) allows client devices from many areas to appear as if they were on the same IP segment for management and administration purposes.

17. A, B, C. You will not need a VoIP phone if you have a VoIP gateway that allows the connection of a standard analog telephone. Therefore, the minimum required is a wireless gateway, VoIP service provider, and telephone.

18. A, B. PDAs, tablet PCs, desktops, and laptop computers with Wi-Fi cards can act as wireless VoIP phones with the right software installed. While a computer using only Ethernet could act as a VoIP phone, it could not act as a wireless VoIP phone as the question asked. Analog phones cannot act as wireless VoIP phones, though they can be used with VoIP technology.

19. A. A wireless presentation gateway provides only the display of a computer's video on a remote device, whereas a wireless media gateway provides display of a computer's video and access to the computer's data storage as well as the internal data storage of the wireless media gateway. Many wireless media gateways also provide extra features such as print servers. In the end, the wireless media gateway is much more powerful than a wireless presentation gateway and is intended for different use.

20. B. Power over Ethernet. PoE is a standard that provides DC power to wireless devices over standard CAT5 or CAT6 cables.

21. A. In many PoE switches, only some of the ports are PoE capable or only a limited number can be configured to use PoE. Make sure you have not used all the PoE ports in the switch. If you have not, enter the configuration interface to check that PoE is enabled for the port to which you have connected the AP.

22. C. The most common point-to-multipoint configuration uses highly or semidirectional antennas at the remote locations and omni- or semidirectional antennas at the central location.

Wireless Client Devices

Wireless# Exam Objectives Covered:

❖ Summarize the characteristics, basic attributes, and advantages of VoWLAN

- Wireless VoIP phones characteristics

❖ Identify the purpose, features, and functions of the following client devices. Choose the appropriate installation of configuration steps in a given scenario.

- CardBus PC cards

- USB/USB2 devices

- Compact Flash devices

- SDIO devices

- PCI devices

- Mini-PCI devices

- Client utility software and drivers

- Bluetooth connectivity devices

- Wireless IP phone

- Wireless gaming adapter

- Wireless print server

- Wireless IP camera

- Wireless hotspot gateway

- Wireless presentation gateway

Once your wireless infrastructure is in place, you need to connect the client devices to the network. There are many different client devices available for all the various scenarios you may encounter. If you need to connect an older PC to the wireless network, wireless client devices are available for that. If you need to connect a laptop to the wireless network, you can connect—even without a built-in wireless or PCMCIA port—by using a wireless USB adapter. Whatever the situation, there is likely a way to connect without great difficulty.

This chapter covers the many wireless client devices that you can connect to desktop PCs, laptops, PDAs, and tablet PCs. You'll also discover client devices such as gaming adapters, wireless presentation gateways, and IP cameras. Finally, you'll learn about print servers—their functionality and benefits—and hotspot gateways as well.

Client devices come in many forms and styles. I'll cover devices categorized as

- PCI
- MiniPCI
- SDIO
- Compact Flash
- CadBus PC cards
- USB devices

PCI and MiniPCI

PCI wireless adapters are generally installed in desktop computers. Older cards might actually be PCMCIA placeholders that support various PCMCIA radio cards. This can be a benefit. You can slide a PCMCIA card into the PCI card's slot and turn on the computer to have wireless access from your desktop. Later, you can remove the card from the desktop and insert it into your laptop for portable wireless access.

Most modern PCI wireless adapters have radios built in and, therefore, no longer need the PCMCIA cards to communicate. There are benefits to this scenario as well. The wireless PCI card with a built-in radio has a larger antenna that provides better reception. However, if you can connect it to the back of the computer only, the antenna can also be a disadvantage; the back of the computer is a bad location because it's more difficult for the antenna

FIGURE 5.1   PCI client device with cabled antenna

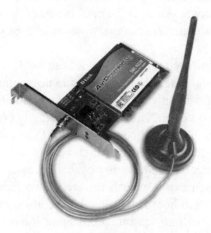

to pick up and send radio signals. Some PCI devices support cabled antennas that you can place some distance from the computer, like the one shown in Figure 5.1. This setup helps overcome the issue with common PCI cards.

When installing a PCI card, take the usual precautions. Ensure that the PC is powered off and that you discharge any static electricity that might have builtup in your body. This static discharge can be done by using specifically designed ESD (Electrostatic Discharge) wrist straps connected to a grounding point or by touching the internal metal frame of the computer while it is connected to a power source. Find an open PCI slot and slip the device, like the one shown in Figure 5.2, into the open slot. You then replace the cover and turn on the computer. If device drivers are available for the card,

FIGURE 5.2   Standard PCI client device

your system detects that card and installs the drivers (assuming you have a modern plug-and-play system). If the card is newer than the OS, you might have to install the drivers manually because the OS might not recognize the device.

Another form factor used with PCI devices is the *Mini-PCI* device. These small devices are generally installed in laptop computers and tablet PCs. They provide built-in antennas, and their reception is generally at least as good as a USB device with a built-in antenna (such as a USB thumb wireless client). One great benefit to Mini PCIs is the fact that they can usually be upgraded to support newer standards and specifications. Of course, this upgrade means you have to physically replace the hardware and not just upgrade some drivers or firmware. Many laptops have built-in (soldered onto the system board) wireless so the ability to purchase new Mini PCI hardware is still an advantageous benefit over the standard soldered or integrated wireless, which often cannot be replaced without changing the entire system board.

SDIO

The Secure Digital Input Output (SDIO) wireless network adapter is used in PDAs and looks like a long Secure Digital (SD) memory stick, as shown in Figure 5.3. You might encounter the rare laptop that supports SD slots for more than memory sticks, but it's not common.

FIGURE 5.3   SDIO wireless client device (Socket WL6200-480)

Before using a client device, it's important to understand what it requires. For example, the vendor of the device shown in Figure 5.3 says that "all you need is a Pocket PC 2002 or Pocket PC 2003 (running Windows Mobile™ 2003) with an SDIO slot running SDIO *Now!,* and you can use the SDIO WLAN Card to access the Internet, email, and corporate servers." To use this device, you have to be running Windows Mobile 2003, have an SDIO slot supporting SDIO *Now!,* and your PDA has to be a Pocket PC 2002 or 2003. Remember, not all SDIO cards work with all devices. Check the specifications closely.

Compact Flash

Like SDIO cards, Compact Flash (CF) cards are used in handheld devices. As Figure 5.4 shows, CF cards have a different form factor than SDIO in that they are much larger and often support only 802.11b. They are intended for use with handheld devices with lower battery levels and processing power, so do not let vendor literature fool you when it says they can roam from 802.11b to 802.11g access points. Many have taken this to mean that the CF card supports both 802.11b and 802.11g, when in reality if the card is listed as an 802.11b card, it can't communicate with any AP that doesn't allow 802.11b mode.

CardBus PC Cards

CardBus is a high-performance version of PCMCIA. PCMCIA cards usually work in CardBus slots, but CardBus cards do not work in PCMCIA slots (except for *rare* instances where a CardBus card is backwardly compatible

FIGURE 5.4   Netgear MA701 CF wireless card

FIGURE 5.5   Belkin Cardbus wireless NIC

with PCMCIA). Think of CardBus as PCI and PCMCIA as ISA. If you're familiar with standard PC hardware of the past, this makes a lot of sense. If not, just know that CardBus devices are faster and more capable than PCMCIA. A CardBus wireless device looks like a PCMCIA device, as Figure 5.5 shows. Thankfully, the cards usually have CardBus printed on them clearly.

USB Devices

As the name implies, USB devices are beneficial in that they are universal (USB stands for Universal Serial Bus). By this, I mean that any USB device can be used in a laptop, tablet PC, or desktop computer as long as the computer has a USB port and the port is capable of the device's USB version requirements.

There are two versions of USB at this time: USB and USB 2. USB 2 supports faster throughput (up to 480 Mbit/s) than USB (12 Mbit/s) and is the preferred device type for wireless networking. However, older laptops support only USB 1.0 or 1.1 and thus limit your options.

The form factor of USB devices varies. Figure 5.6 shows a thumb-type USB adapter, and Figure 5.7 shows an external USB adapter with a built-in

FIGURE 5.6   USB thumb-type wireless adapter

FIGURE 5.7   USB external wireless adapter

positional antenna. The benefit of this device is that it allows more precise positioning of the device and antenna and therefore greater reception. The benefit of the thumb-type USB adapter is obvious—it's extremely portable and can be carried easily for when you need wireless access most.

Client Drivers

Once you've selected the right wireless client device type, you need to install and configure the device. Installation can be as complex as updating firmware to support the wireless standards you are using and as simple as connecting the device and watching it magically work.

To help you understand the process of installing and configuring a client device, I'm going to walk you through the installation and configuration of a ZyXEL ZyAIR G-220 USB thumb-type wireless NIC. This is a standard USB wireless client having a small form factor for easy portability. These devices, although not as capable as a USB device with an external antenna, provide greater mobility and flexibility. This device is shown in Figure 5.8.

The steps to install a wireless client are as follows:

1. Verify system requirements.
2. Connect the device.
3. Install the drivers.
4. Test connectivity.

FIGURE 5.8   ZyAIR G-220

Verify System Requirements

The first step is to ensure that the wireless hardware is compatible with your system. You can usually do this by reading the included vendor documentation or by visiting the vendor's website.

The ZyAIR G-220 lists the following requirements:

- Pentium II 300 MHz or above
- 6MB available hard drive space
- 32MB RAM
- CD-ROM drive
- An open USB port
- Windows 98 SE, Windows ME, Windows 2000, or Windows XP

There are two important things to note about these requirements. First, the device is compatible with newer Windows operating systems only. Sometimes you can find drivers on the Internet for operating systems other than those listed, but it's a difficult and time-consuming process and, with USB devices, often fails. For this reason, you must be certain that the device you select supports the operating system you wish to run.

Second, note the CD-ROM requirement. While listed as a requirement, you can often ignore it. If you download the drivers from the Internet and copy them to the computer's hard drive, you do not need a CD-ROM drive. The reason it's listed as a requirement is for driver and software installation.

I'll be installing the client device on a P4 3.4 GHz processor with 2GB of memory and a 120GB hard drive. I have four open USB ports and a CD-ROM drive, and my operating system is Windows XP Professional.

Based on the requirements and these PC specifications, installation should not be a problem.

Connect the Device

The second step in the installation process is to connect the device. If this were a PCI device, I'd turn off the computer and then remove the cover and install the PCI card. Because I'm installing a USB device, I simply plug it into an available USB port or hub.

Install the Drivers

When I've placed the device in the USB port, since I'm running Windows XP Professional on my laptop, the dialog shown in Figure 5.9 appears. This dialog alerts me that a new device has been detected and provides options for installing the device. I click No, Not At This Time to indicate that I do not want to search Windows Update for drivers, and then I click Next.

On the next screen, I select to install the drivers from a list or specific location and then route the installation to my CD-ROM drive where the

FIGURE 5.9   Hardware detection screen

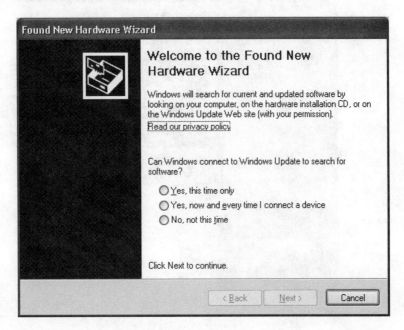

ZyXEL CD is waiting. My system quickly notifies me that the driver has not passed Windows logo certification, but this is not uncommon so I choose to continue anyway. After the system copies a few files, I click Finish to complete the driver installation.

Test Connectivity

Now that the drivers have been installed, I can test connectivity. In my case, I used the Windows XP Wireless Zero Configuration (WZC) and its built-in wireless management interface, shown in Figure 5.10. Here you see two available wireless networks. I select the one labeled Netgear and click the Connect button. In moments, I'm connected and my wireless client has been configured.

Because this is an open network, there is no need for WEP or WPA configuration (WEP and WPA are security options). This is common for hotspots and, sadly, for many small networks. If you are implementing

FIGURE 5.10   WZC configuration interface for Windows XP

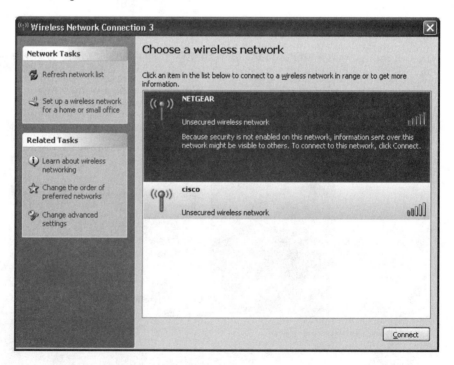

a business or home network, you should implement wireless security to protect your data and privacy. I'll talk more about wireless security in Chapter 11.

Client Software

If you choose not to use Windows' wireless connectivity features (WZC), you need to install the client software that comes with your wireless client. To install the software, you insert the CD into CD-ROM drive, and the installation process begins automatically. If it does not start automatically, open the CD and look for a SETUP or INSTALL executable and double-click that file to begin the process.

The ZyXEL device I just installed comes with its own client software. When I insert the CD into my CD-ROM drive, I see the screen shown in Figure 5.11, where I can choose from several options. I select Install Utility.

Once you've installed the vendor utilities, they often take precedence over the WZC feature, and you will no longer be able to configure the wireless connection using this tool. While not always the case, you should be aware that it is a possibility. The client software that comes with the ZyXEL USB wireless device is similar to client software that comes with other USB, PCI, or any other form-factor client devices.

FIGURE 5.11   ZyXEL autorun installation routing

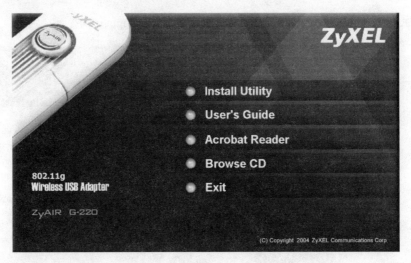

FIGURE 5.12   ZyXEL Site Survey software (6 feet from the AP)

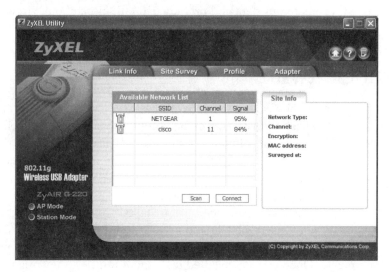

One interesting feature offered by most client software programs is a site survey feature. The capabilities of this feature vary, but it's useful for discovering where you have RF coverage in your facility. Figure 5.12 shows the site survey mode of the client software when I've positioned my laptop close to the AP (approximately 6 feet away). Figure 5.13 shows the same site survey mode when my laptop is more than 100 feet away from the AP. Notice the difference in signal strength.

FIGURE 5.13   ZyXEL Site Survey software (100 feet from the AP)

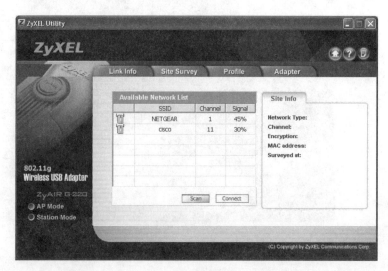

You can see how you could use this software to perform a site survey. More complex tools are available, and I discuss those in Chapter 12, but in many cases, this simple tool is all you need for a small network for home users or small businesses.

Wireless IP Phones

Wireless IP phones, discussed briefly in Chapter 4, are client devices used to access VoIP networks through wireless networks. These devices can be dedicated wireless VoIP phones, or they can be computing devices configured to operate as wireless VoIP phones.

Dedicated wireless VoIP phones come in different shapes, sizes, and feature sets. For example, the Cisco wireless IP phone 7920, shown in Figure 5.14, includes the following features:

- Six multiline appearance-extensions or speed dials
- Calling name and number display
- Call waiting
- Call forwarding
- Call transfer

FIGURE 5.14   Cisco 7920 wireless IP phone

- Three-way calling (Conference)
- Predialing before sending
- Redial
- Call hold/resume
- Call mute
- Call park
- Call pick-up/group pick-up
- "You Have Voice Mail" message on display
- Hotkey for keypad lock
- Hotkey for voice-mail access
- Nine speed dials configurable in the set
- Programmable speed-dial hotkeys 2–9
- Time/date display
- Idle/call state-based soft keys
- Keypad lock/vibration icon indicators
- RF and battery level indication
- Comfort noise generation (CNG), voice activity detection (VAD), adaptive jitter buffer, and echo cancellation
- Language support: English, French, and German in the first release
- Local phone book

Most of these devices support standard security features such as WEP and WPA as well as phone locking capabilities. When the phone is locked, only someone who knows the unlock code can make a call. WEP or WPA ensures that the VoIP communications are encrypted to prevent eavesdropping.

When using a PC or laptop as a wireless VoIP client, the software usually provides features similar to those listed for the Cisco 7920 phone, and, of course, the device provides standard wireless client connectivity at the same time.

Gaming Adapters and IP Cameras

Wireless gaming adapters and IP cameras—while they seem to have nothing in common, other than being wireless—actually have another important feature in common. They are both noninfrastructure devices used on wireless networks.

The gaming adapter connects a gaming machine, such as the XBOX, to a wireless network, and the IP camera provides video surveillance or other video purposes across the wireless infrastructure.

Gaming Adapters

Gaming adapters come in 802.11a, b, and g versions and support most gaming consoles without the need for drivers. Figure 5.15 shows a Linksys WGA54G wireless gaming adapter. Wireless gaming adapters usually work in one of two modes: *console-to-console connections* or *console-to-Internet connections*.

Console-to-Console Connections

A console-to-console connection is created when you use two wireless gaming adapters together. One connects to each gaming console through the console's Ethernet port and then they connect to each other wirelessly. This allows for head-to-head gaming in one area.

FIGURE 5.15   Linksys WGA54G

Console-Internet Connections

When creating a console-to-Internet connection, you use just one wireless gaming adapter connected to your existing wireless network, which provides an IP configuration to the wireless gaming adapter that allows routing out to the Internet and to DNS servers. In this way, the gaming console can connect to gaming services on the Internet to allow for online game play.

IP Cameras

Wireless IP cameras, also commonly called *wireless Internet cameras,* allow you to implement video surveillance, video conferencing, or low-quality video recording. Figure 5.16 shows a wireless IP camera that could be used for video surveillance or environment monitoring.

In Figure 5.16, you can see the antennas that are used to form the wireless connection. This particular camera supports 802.11g and allows for connectivity to your standard wireless network. It also supports 2-way audio and 4x zoom functions as well as built-in motion detection and email notification. With this device installed, a small business owner can be notified by email if someone (or something) is in their building.

These cameras are often referred to as *Internet cameras* because you can view the video feed through an Internet browser that supports the software. Many cameras use ActiveX controls for viewing and, therefore, require you to use Internet Explorer on the clients unless your alternate browser supports ActiveX controls.

FIGURE 5.16   Wireless IP camera from D-Link

While wired IP cameras are certainly available, not having to run cabling is a huge benefit of using a wireless camera. You can install the camera in any area where power is available, as you need to provide DC power to the camera for functionality.

Most of these devices also support recording of the video feed to a network-attached storage (NAS) device. This device can be configured to record video based on a schedule, by motion detection, or all the time. With this camera in place, you have automatic NAS archival of video feeds for security purposes, should they ever be needed.

Wireless Presentation Gateway

Wireless presentation gateways were briefly mentioned in the last chapter in the section on "Wireless Media Gateways." As stated there, wireless presentation gateways (WPGs) are often referred to as wireless media gateways, though they should really be differentiated. A WPG, as its name implies, is intended for delivery of presentations. Figure 5.17 shows an example of a wireless presentation gateway.

FIGURE 5.17   D-Link DPG-2000W

A WPG may have any, or all, of the following features:

- Ability to display PowerPoint presentations
- Ability to display anything on the computer screen
- Ability to display JPEG, TIFF, or BMP images
- Functions with MAC or PC
- Supports multiple presenters, though not simultaneously
- Configured through web-based interfaces and custom client drivers

Of these many features, the one that I've found most useful is the ability to support multiple presenters. I've been in many situations in which several people needed to present the information on their computer to the group. With a wireless presentation gateway, and a quick client install on each laptop, we were able to share a single projector without connecting and reconnecting VGA cables.

Another great benefit of a wireless presentation gateway is the available range. You would have to purchase 25 feet of VGA extension cable to position the projector far enough away to fill the screen in a large room. With a wireless presentation gateway, you just position the wireless gateway beside the projector, and you're off and running.

Wireless Print Servers

Print servers are devices that allow you to connect a printer to the network for client use. These are sometimes called *netprint devices* or *printer sharing devices.* A wireless print server is a device that can share the printer, or printers, on the network and connects to the network using either a wireless connection or both wired and wireless connections.

Wireless print servers come with two connection types: parallel (LPT) or USB. Figure 5.18 shows a device with a parallel connection, and Figure 5.19 shows a device with a USB connection.

Other devices may support multiple ports. These devices usually contain one LPT port and one or more USB ports. However, you can acquire devices that support multiple ports of each kind to meet your needs regardless of the number of printers you have.

Wireless print servers will usually provide configuration interfaces that are browser-based and may provide telnet support as well. Features may include support for multiple protocols, built-in memory buffers, and remote power cycling for maintenance and support.

FIGURE 5.18   Parallel wireless print server

Hotspot Gateways

A wireless hotspot gateway allows you to share Internet access publicly while maintaining the integrity of your private network. Figure 5.20 shows the D-Link DSA-3200, which is a wireless hotspot gateway with built-in 802.11g support. You can also get hotspot gateway devices that do not include wireless APs and that you connect to external APs to actually provide wireless access.

FIGURE 5.19   USB wireless print server

FIGURE 5.20   D-Link DSA-3200 802.11g hotspot gateway

A hotspot gateway provides a WAN port and two interfaces: one public interface and one private interface. You can connect one or more APs to the public interface (to connect more than one AP, you usually have to connect a switch to the public port so you can support more than one device) to provide wireless Internet access. You can then connect multiple devices, again through switches, to the private side and be certain that devices on the public side cannot access devices on the private side.

Many devices, such as the one shown in Figure 5.20, support either external authentication or authentication through the internal user database. The D-Link DSA-3200 can support up to 250 users when using the internal database. Because support is provided for external LDAP or RADIUS authentication, you can create and support an unlimited number of users. However, it's important to distinguish between how many users can be supported and how many users can be connected. According to the documentation, only 50 users can connect to the Internet simultaneously.

Using standard browser-based interfaces, you can configure the public interface, private interface, and wireless settings to your liking. Think of these devices as server-based firewalls with multiple network interfaces configured for access to, and control of, multiple networks.

Summary

Choosing the right wireless client device is essential to building an operational wireless network. These devices include PCI, Mini-PCI, SDIO, CardBus, CF, and USB devices. You should also understand how print servers, wireless presentation gateways, and hotspot gateways function in order to choose and manage these devices when you need them.

You also learned about IP cameras and gaming adapters and their proper use. You can use a gaming adapter to connect to the Internet or to another gaming console. You can use an IP camera for video conferencing and environment surveillance.

To learn more about any of the devices covered in this brief chapter, visit the various vendors' websites and read the product specifications and product manuals for these products. This will help you in two ways: you will know the devices better for the Wireless# exam, and you will be better prepared to select and implement these devices in your environment.

Key Terms

- ☐ **CardBus**
- ☐ **Compact Flash**
- ☐ **Mini-PCI**
- ☐ **PCI**
- ☐ **PCMCIA**
- ☐ **SDIO**
- ☐ **USB**
- ☐ **wireless hotspot gateway**
- ☐ **wireless presentation gateway**
- ☐ **wireless print server**

Review Questions

1. You need to purchase a wireless client device for a laptop computer. Which of the following device types would be viable options? Select two.

   A. PCI

   B. PCMCIA

   C. SDIO

   D. USB

2. What is one of the major benefits of Mini-PCI built-in wireless networking in laptop computers?

   A. The Mini-PCI wireless devices support 802.11i.

   B. The built-in wireless networking does not support speed doubling.

   C. The Mini-PCI card can usually be upgraded through hardware replacements.

   D. The built-in wireless networking does not support new driver updates.

3. USB wireless devices come in two major form factors. One is a cabled wireless device that sits on the desk and has a positional antenna that can be moved and angled in different ways. What is the other form factor?

   A. Converter dongle to connect to Mini-PCI

   B. Pigtail converter to connect to Compact Flash

   C. Thumb-type connector

   D. Battery pack–sized connector

4. You are preparing a room for a large-scale presentation by your company president and three VPs. They have informed you that they want to run different presentations, and they will need to switch back and forth

among their screens randomly throughout the event. What device would help you accomplish this?

A. Wireless hotspot gateway

B. Wireless presentation gateway

C. Wireless media gateway

D. Wireless gaming device

5. You are a networking and systems consultant located in a small town. A client in this town has requested that you install security cameras in their place of business that they can monitor from home. They inform you that it is very important to them that they can present video footage to law enforcement in case of a break-in. What feature will the IP camera you choose need to support?

A. Remote control

B. 802.11g

C. NAS archival

D. MPEG compression

6. How many interfaces does a wireless hotspot gateway usually have?

A. 1

B. 2

C. 3

D. 4

7. A multiport wireless print server is a wireless print server that can connect to Ethernet or Wi-Fi, whereas a single-port wireless print server can only connect to Wi-Fi.

A. False

B. True

8. Wireless gaming adapters can be configured to provide console-to-console connections or console-to-Internet connections. How many gaming adapters do you need to implement a console-to-console connection?

A. 1

B. 4

C. 3

D. 2

Review Answers

1. **A, D.** While some laptops support more than SD flash memory cards, this is extremely rare. Most likely, you will have the options of a PCMCIA card or a USB device. PCI slots are not available in laptop computers and would be available only if the client were a desktop-class machine.

2. **C.** Mini-PCI wireless cards can usually be replaced with models supporting newer wireless standards and capabilities, and this is a great advantage.

3. **C.** Thumb-type connectors look like thumb drives and usually have LEDs that inform you of the wireless connectivity of the device. They often include full wireless client feature sets, including the ability to act as an AP and the inclusion of site survey software.

4. **B.** A wireless presentation gateway allows you to do just what the president and VPs are requesting. Once you've installed the client software on each of their computers, assuming they have wireless cards in them, they can switch among their machines and share the presentation screen through the wireless presentation gateway.

5. **C.** NAS (network-attached storage) archival allows you to dump the video feed to a network storage device for later presentation to law enforcement if the need arises.

6. **C.** While the features of hotspot gateways vary, they usually have three interfaces: one for the WAN (Internet), one for the private network, and one for the public network.

7. **A.** False. A multiport wireless print server usually has an Ethernet port and a Wi-Fi radio just as a single-port wireless print server does. The difference is that a multiport wireless print server supports more than one printer and can support both USB and parallel or LPT ports.

8. **D.** You need two wireless gaming devices to connect two gaming consoles console-to-console. You connect one to the Ethernet port on each gaming console, and they create a wireless link between them.

WiMAX

Wireless# Exam Objectives Covered:

❖ Summarize the characteristics, basic attributes, and advantages of WiMAX

- Fixed vs. mobile and frequencies used

- Data rates, throughput, range, and line-of-sight parameters

- Quality of Service (QoS) and security features

- Different wireless MAN standards—802.16-2004, 802.16e, ETSI HiperMAN, Wi-Bro

❖ Identify and describe common WiMAX applications

- Campus and wireless ISP broadband wireless access (point-to-multipoint)

- Wireless voice and data backhaul (point-to-point)

- Security/surveillance

- Enterprise private networks

WiMAX (Worldwide Interoperability for Microwave Access) is an often misunderstood technology. This confusion is born out of a misconception of its intended use. WiMAX is *not* intended to be a replacement for Wi-Fi, but rather a complement to the features and capabilities of the 802.11 family of networking technologies. Phrases such as "WiMAX is the next version of Wi-Fi" and "When will WiMAX replace Wi-Fi?" have led many to believe that WiMAX is indeed an upgrade to Wi-Fi. It is not.

Some people refer to WiMAX as WiFiMax, but WiFiMax is not a current standard or certification. While bridging devices that connect Wi-Fi networks with WiMAX networks will likely come onto the market, no current standard uses this terminology.

In this chapter, I provide you with a clear understanding of what WiMAX is and its intended purposes according to the WiMAX Forum. You will learn about the features and capabilities of WiMAX, so you can plan where and how to fit it into your organization's networking plans. Finally, you'll learn about the different WiMAX standards around the world and the various real-world applications of this technology.

WiMAX Overview

According to the WiMAX Forum, an organization dedicated to furthering WiMAX technologies and specifications,

> "WiMAX is a standards-based technology enabling the delivery of last mile wireless broadband access as an alternative to cable and DSL. WiMAX will provide fixed, nomadic, portable, and, eventually, mobile wireless broadband connectivity without the need for direct line-of-sight to a base station. In a typical cell radius deployment of 3 to 10 kilometers, WiMAX Forum Certified™ systems can be expected to deliver capacity of up to 40 Mbps per channel, for fixed and portable access applications."

This sounds exciting and has for a few years now. In the winter of 2005/2006, we're just beginning to see the reality of WiMAX hardware and networking potential. Vendors predict 2007 and 2008 timeframes for actual implementations and widespread use of WiMAX technologies.

So what is this technology and why has it taken so long to appear in the marketplace? The answers follow, but first I want to give you a clear and concise definition of WiMAX that you can use as a starting point when you talk and learn about WiMAX technologies.

WiMAX is a radio frequency technology that uses licensed and unlicensed bands to provide wireless connections for non-line-of-sight real implementations with speeds up to 40 Mbps per channel and a cell radius up to 10 kilometers for fixed and portable access situations, and speeds up to 15 Mbps and a cell radius of 3 kilometers for mobile situations. In line-of-sight implementations, WiMAX can provide link distances up to 50 kilometers.

In the WiMAX terminology, portable access means you can access WiMAX networks from different locations, but not necessarily while moving. Mobile WiMAX is accessible while on the move.

From this definition, you can see why WiMAX has been such a popular topic in the wireless industry. The ability to provide multiple channels at 40 Mbps for cell sizes from 3 to 10 kilometers is well above what can be accomplished with standard 801.11g or 802.11a wireless point-to-point links (at least as far as distance goes—remember, these cell sizes support point-to-point or point-to-multipoint client connections). In addition, non-line-of-sight (NLOS) features of some WiMAX technologies provide the potential for better coverage in wooded or congested areas.

A WiMAX network consists of two major components: a *base station* and a *subscriber station*. Base stations provide connectivity to one or more subscriber stations and are implemented by service providers to provide Internet, voice, or WAN link access. Figure 6.1 illustrates how a base station communicates with multiple subscriber stations in a WiMAX implementation.

These base stations are similar to Wi-Fi APs as they provide centralized access to backend connected networks. They use different standards than Wi-Fi, however, so the comparison ends there. While subscriber stations are uniquely designed for 802.16 networks, the reality is that they provide a connection to the network and you can still route internal 802.11 devices through the 802.16 subscriber station for network access.

History

The 802.16 standard was first published on April 8, 2002 (after two years in development). The WiMAX Forum was formed in April of 2001 and established in June of 2001. This order might seem odd, but it's common

FIGURE 6.1   WiMAX base stations and subscriber units or stations

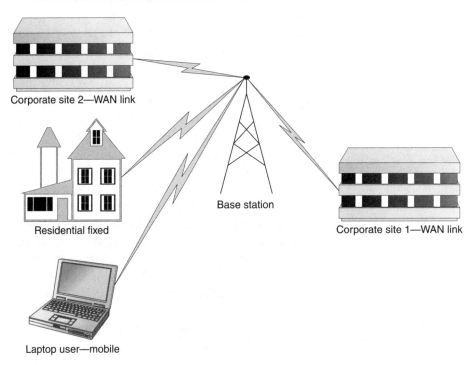

to form certification bodies before completing or ratifying a standard. The WiMAX certification will certify that a technology is compliant with WiMAX specifications—not 802.16. This is because the WiMAX Forum created a certification that is compatible with a portion of the 802.16 standard. WiMAX certified hardware should be compatible with other WiMAX certified hardware, but not necessarily with 802.16-compliant hardware. This is important to remember.

The founding organizations of the WiMAX Forum included Wi-LAN, Ensemble, CossSpan, Harris, and Nokia. The OFDM Forum and Fujitsu joined in 2002. In 2003, Aperto, Alvarion, Airspan, Intel, Proxim, and others joined the group. At this time, the forum has over 200 members with representatives from service providers, system manufacturers, chip vendors, and ecosystem organizations. The major focus of this organization is to provide interoperability between vendors' WiMAX hardware.

In January 2005, at a WiMAX conference called "WiMAX: Beyond the Hype," Gordon Antonello clearly stated that

- There are no WiMAX networks today.
- There are no WiMAX Forum Certified products available today.
- WiMAX Forum Certified testing will begin later this year (2005).
- Vendors are shipping pre-WiMAX products today.

These statements are important because you must understand that WiMAX is brand new and any existing 802.16-compliant hardware might, or might not, work with future WiMAX Forum Certified hardware. However, some vendors are promising to provide upgrades through firmware or chip replacements to meet the WiMAX specifications.

The WiMAX Forum began lab trials in the third quarter of 2005 and field trials in the fourth quarter of 2005. General production deployments are expected in 2006 as true WiMAX Forum Certified equipment enters the marketplace.

The final standard being implemented in hardware systems today will support the 802.16-2004 specification of the IEEE. Vendors are building their hardware to this specification and then sending that same hardware to the WiMAX Forum for certification.

Capabilities

WiMAX is expected to do for metropolitan area networks (MANs) what Wi-Fi has done for local area networks (LANs). WiMAX is not intended to replace Wi-Fi, but to complement it by connecting Wi-Fi networks to each other or the Internet through high-speed wireless links. You can thus use WiMAX technology to extend the reach of Wi-Fi (providing backhaul between WLANs) and cellular networks. However, in developing countries, WiMAX may become the only wireless technology because Wi-Fi and cellular have not penetrated areas that can be reached with WiMAX technology.

Data Rates and Throughput

Real-world performance of a WiMAX implementation will vary just as a Wi-Fi implementation varies and for the same reasons: environmental factors

TABLE 6.1 WiMAX Standards Throughput and Data Rates

WiMAX Standard	Expected Throughput	Advertised Data Rates
Fixed LOS (802.16-2004)	40 Mbps	70–75 Mbps
Mobile NLOS (802.16e)	15 Mbps	30 Mbps

and radio performance. Table 6.1 lists the different WiMAX standards and expected throughput as well as advertised data rates.

Range and Line-of-Sight

With line-of-sight (LoS) links, WiMAX can support from 30 to 50 kilometer distances (31 miles). This is a great improvement over 802.11b/g or 802.11a. When implementing NLOS cells, WiMAX supports ranges from 3 to 10 kilometers and using advanced modulation algorithms can overcome many interfering objects that Wi-Fi systems cannot pass through.

Quality of Service Features

A variety of WiMAX features contribute to excellent Quality of Service (QoS) management. Just as on a Wi-Fi network, WiMAX users share a data pipe and QoS can degrade as more users are added to the network. Using the QoS features of WiMAX, service providers can guarantee certain users specific bandwidth amounts by limiting the bandwidth consumption of other users.

The first aspect of QoS in WiMAX networks is a grant-request mechanism for access to the network. The WiMAX implementation of contention allocates only a fixed amount of time be given to these grant-requests. *Contention* refers to the act of vying for access to the network. Because of the limited amount of time available, bandwidth cannot be consumed by contention requests. When a contention request comes into the network, the system compares the request with a service level agreement for the consumer making the request, and they are granted, or denied, access accordingly.

Another benefit of WiMAX QoS is link-by-link modulation schemes. In other words, the base station can use different modulation schemes for different links. The modulation scheme used is related directly to the distance of the link. Rather than all users' links being downgraded by the user farthest away, link-by-link modulation allows closer users to use higher data-rate modulation schemes.

By optimizing the use of bandwidth through contention time limitations and link-by-link modulation schemes, an excellent foundation is provided for QoS. Add to this the support for differentiation between voice, video, and data, and you have an environment that provides for good QoS management.

Fixed and Mobile

You need to understand the differences between fixed and mobile WiMAX. Remember, *portable* does not equal *mobile*. *Portable WiMAX* is WiMAX that you can access from multiple locations, but it's not intended to support high-speed movement during connections and communications. *Mobile WiMAX* is intended to support connections while moving. To help you remember the difference, you could say that portable means portable-fixed. An example of portable WiMAX is using your laptop in a coffee shop. You are actually stationary, but are connected to the WiMAX subscriber service. An example of mobile WiMAX is walking down the street while browsing the Internet on your PDA or a police officer accessing the network from their cruiser.

Fixed WiMAX provides last-mile delivery of access to the Internet and other networks, which means locations that have not been reached by DSL and cable broadband providers will receive access. Fixed WiMAX is also used for backhaul connections and WAN links in place of T1 and other leased lines. Fixed WiMAX uses the 3.5 and 5.8 GHz frequency bands.

Mobile WiMAX provides network access while mobile. City employees such as fire, police, and emergency response teams need network access while driving in a vehicle. Salespeople working in a metro area or individuals who need network access while on the go could also take advantage of mobile WiMAX. Mobile WiMAX uses the 2.3 and 2.5 GHz frequency bands.

Organizations

Just as the Wi-Fi Alliance certifies and supports 802.11 standards, the WiMAX Forum certifies and supports 802.16-based technologies. To be WiMAX Forum Certified, a piece of equipment must pass conformance and interoperability tests. *Conformance testing* means that the equipment is tested as a stand-alone unit. The system is run through a series of tests to be sure the device works according to the WiMAX system profile. To pass *interoperability testing,* the equipment must communicate with at least two other vendors' devices. Once passing both of these tests, the equipment is certified as WiMAX Forum Certified.

Treat any pre-WiMAX equipment as proprietary in your network management and implementation plans because the equipment has never been tested independently to verify interoperability. However, if you have the resources and time to test the equipment, it might function well and can be used as long as it meets your demands.

WiMAX Standards

As with Wi-Fi, many standards are often referred to as WiMAX or broadband access standards. Technically, WiMAX supports 802.16 specifications and will continue to evolve as the specifications evolve, but other standards have also been created based on the 802.16 specification. Some of them are extensive enough to demand attention by the WiMAX Forum, including HiperMAN and WiBro. WiMAX effectively embraces all of these standards.

802.16-2004

This standard is the formal one being used for current fixed and nomadic (meaning that the connection cannot be maintained while moving, but it can be created in more than one stationary – fixed – location) LOS and NLOS WiMAX implementations and is based on and backwardly compatible with 802.16 and 802.16a. The WiMAX Forum profiles supporting 802.16-2004 are in the 3.5 GHz and 5.8 GHz frequency bands. Vendors are currently creating indoor and outdoor customer premise equipment (subscriber stations) and laptop PCMCIA cards to support this specification. This standard will be used for cell creation in nonmobile scenarios and LOS distance links. Table 6.2 is provided as a reference for 802.16-2004 specs matched with WiMAX Forum certification profiles.

The concept of duplexing refers to the management of upstream and downstream traffic flows (transfer of information). Frequency division duplexing (FDD) uses two channels (frequency ranges separated by what is sometimes called a *guard band* to avoid interference). One channel is used for upstream traffic and the other is used for downstream traffic. Time division duplexing (TDD) uses a single channel, and the devices at each end must alternate between sending (transmitting) and receiving.

TABLE 6.2   802.16-2004 Frequencies, Duplexing Schemes, and Channel Widths

Frequency (GHz)	Duplexing Scheme	Channel Width (MHz)
3.5	TDD	3.5
3.5	FDD	3.5
3.5	TDD	7
3.5	FDD	7
5.8	TDD	10

802.16e

This standard is an extension to the 802.16-2004 specification and supports mobile communications. This mobility is provided through handoffs and roaming support built in to the standard. While intended to provide mobility, this technology is used by service providers to provide fixed access as well. This specification operates in the 2.3 and 2.5 GHz frequency bands.

ETSI HiperMAN

The European Telecommunications Standards Institute created the HiperMAN standard for broadband wireless MAN implementations. The HiperMAN standard operates in the frequency ranges between 2 GHz and 11 GHz. Created in close collaboration with the IEEE, it is based on 802.16 and is compatible with the 802.16a-2003 specification. HiperMAN, like WiMAX, supports both point-to-multipoint and mesh network implementations.

Wi-Bro

WiBro, an acronym for *Wireless Broadband,* is a Korean standard similar to 802.16e. The WiMAX Forum has decided to support this standard, which means 802.16e-compliant hardware should interoperate with WiBro-compliant hardware. Much as HiperMAN is compatible with 802.16-2003, 802.16e is expected to interoperate with WiBro.

WiMAX Applications and Uses

There are many different uses and types of WiMAX access. Table 6.3 summarizes the various access types, according to the WiMAX Forum, and their features related to location, speed, handoff (transfer during mobility), and standards. In the handoffs column, *hard* means the connection might not be consistent during handoff and *soft* means the handoff is seamless to the user.

Campus and WISP Broadband Access

Providing wireless broadband access is a major objective of WISPs (wireless Internet service providers). Having a centralized base station communicate with remote towers and then with remote customers offers the possibility of Internet access for rural or under-serviced areas.

These WISP connections can be configured to use WiMAX only for the backhaul (from the localized communication towers to the centralized base stations), or they can use WiMAX all the way to the customer. If WiMAX is used only for the backhaul, Wi-Fi or some proprietary technology can be utilized from the localized towers to the customers.

TABLE 6.3   Types of WiMAX Access

Type of Access	Devices Used	Location/Speed	Handoff	802.16-2004	802.16e
Fixed	Outdoor/Indoor CPEs	Single/Stationary	No	Yes	Yes
Nomadic	Indoor CPEs, PCMCIA cards	Multiple/Stationary	No	Yes	Yes
Portability	Laptop PCMCIA or mini cards	Multiple/Walking speed	Hard	No	Yes
Simple mobility	Laptop PCMCIA or mini cards, PDAs, smartphones	Multiple/Low vehicle speeds	Hard	No	Yes
Full mobility	Laptop PCMCIA or mini cards, PDAs, smartphones	Multiple/High vehicle speeds	Soft	No	Yes

Seeing how many campuses cover large areas, both in the educational and the business sector, WiMAX technology could be utilized to create a single cell of coverage for a campus. Picture a scenario where 10–12 APs are used to provide Wi-Fi coverage for a college campus. Now imagine replacing all those APs with a single base station for communications with mobile or fixed WiMAX clients. Of course, you'll have to wait until the WiMAX clients become more readily available, but the good news is you could leave your Wi-Fi network in place and move to WiMAX for the future or continue to use both technologies on an ongoing basis.

Voice and Data Backhaul

Another possible use of WiMAX technology is VoWiMAX (don't worry—you won't be tested on that odd acronym), or VoIP using WiMAX to transfer voice data. Some estimates range as high as 4800 business or 7200 residential subscribers per WiMAX cell. While allowing the mix of voice and data traffic, this technology competes directly with local telephone service providers, possibly lowering the cost for consumers in that area as well.

Security and Surveillance

Using devices such as IP cameras, you can configure large-scale security and surveillance systems much more easily with WiMAX. Cameras can monitor all your locations with video feeds going to a centralized location across WiMAX networks. By installing IP cameras at each of your facilities and implementing WiMAX links between these facilities, you can centralize security management across an enterprise.

A municipality could carry this concept even further. A city could install IP cameras at bridges, intersections, and other areas for real-time monitoring and control. This same functionality could be provided to public school systems, water management plants, military installations, and any other environment needing centralized monitoring of localized activities. Considering the motion detection capabilities of many modern IP cameras, you can understand the improvement in surveillance capabilities when combined with WiMAX.

Enterprise Private Networks

As with Wi-Fi links, private networks can be either point-to-point or point-to-multipoint. You can deploy them quickly, and while the equipment costs more than Wi-Fi equipment, the available communication distances and bandwidths will be greater. These links can provide reliable transport of voice, data, and video information.

Summary

In the end, the major benefits of a WiMAX network are

- Lower costs
- Wider coverage
- Higher capacity
- Standards-based

Lower costs are expected because of commonalities among devices. For example, we expect the same chips will be used in customer premise equipment (CPE) devices as are used in PDAs and personal computers. As the volume of deployments increases, greater integration of radios will likely increase, eventually driving the prices downward as well.

Where Wi-Fi networks measure the distance of coverage in feet or meters, WiMAX networks measure coverage in miles or kilometers, resulting in wider coverage areas and lower costs because single units provide greater coverage. WiMAX also provides for higher capacities in the areas of data rates and actual throughput.

Finally, standards-based technology means greater interoperability. You won't have to worry about a subscriber station from one vendor being able to connect to a base station from another, as you do with proprietary equipment based on 802.16.

Key Terms

- ☐ **802.16-204**
- ☐ **802.16e**
- ☐ **base station**
- ☐ **fixed**
- ☐ **HiperMAN**
- ☐ **mobile**
- ☐ **nomadic**
- ☐ **subscriber station**
- ☐ **WiBro**
- ☐ **WiMAX**

Review Questions

1. What is the Korean equivalent of 802.16e?

   A. WiBro

   B. WiMaxE

   C. HiperMAN

   D. FHSS

2. What standard is similar to the ETSI HiperMAN standard?

   A. 802.11g

   B. 802.11a

   C. 802.16b

   D. 802.16-2004

3. WiMAX fixed networks use what two frequency bands?

   A. 3.5 GHz

   B. 2.4 GHz

   C. 5.8 GHz

   D. 5.4 GHz

4. To implement security and surveillance systems that use WiMAX for video feed delivery to a centralized location, what other remote devices do you need?

   A. Wi-Fi access points

   B. Wi-Fi client cards

   C. IP cameras

   D. Digital conversion units

5. When a user moves while connected to a WiMAX network, the handoff from one base station to another can be either soft or hard. What is the difference?

    A. A hard handoff maintains the connection, but a soft handoff is not guaranteed to do so.

    B. A soft handoff maintains the connection, but a hard handoff is not guaranteed to do so.

    C. A soft handoff does not support IP transfer across VLANs.

    D. A hard handoff does not support IP transfer across VLANs.

6. You are responsible for creating a network connection to a remote and rural area. There are no leased-line providers in the area, but the area is close enough to use Wi-Fi or WiMAX technology. What is one thing that might move you to use WiMAX instead of Wi-Fi?

    A. Wi-Fi provides greater bandwidth.

    B. WiMAX is more widely implemented.

    C. WiMAX uses licensed frequencies that you can guarantee for your use, but at a cost.

    D. Wi-Fi uses licensed frequencies, but they may not be available.

Review Answers

1. **A.** WiBro. The Korean WiBro standard was created and implemented to begin rollouts of 802.16e-type solutions while the 802.16e standard was still being completed. WiMAX and 802.16e have been and continue to be developed with consideration for support for WiBro through interoperability between standard 802.16e equipment and WiBro.

2. **D.** 802.16-2004 is both similar to and interoperable with HiperMAN. The WiMAX Forum is measures to ensure that certified equipment interoperates with HiperMAN equipment as well.

3. **A, C.** WiMAX fixed networks use the 3.5 GHz and 5.8 GHz frequency bands. The 5.8 GHz frequency band provides 10 MHz–wide channels for the greatest throughput.

4. **C.** You would need to install IP cameras in the remotely monitored locations. You can connect these cameras to a Wi-Fi router that connects to a WiMAX subscriber station or, in the future, to directly compatible WiMAX network connections.

5. **B.** A soft handoff, which is only truly supported by 802.16e-based WiMAX, guarantees a consistent connection whereas a hard handoff does not.

6. **C.** WiMAX can use licensed or unlicensed frequencies, and if you choose to pay a license fee, you can guarantee that the frequency is uncontested in your area. There are no licensed Wi-Fi frequencies available.

Bluetooth

CHAPTER 7

Bluetooth

Wireless# Exam Objectives Covered:

❖ Summarize the characteristics, basic attributes, and advantages of Bluetooth

- Frequencies used

- FHSS hop rates and adaptive frequency hopping support

- Data rates, throughput, and range

- Power classification

- Different wireless PAN standards—802.15.1, 802.15.2, 802.15.3, Bluetooth 1.2, Bluetooth 2.0+EDR

❖ Identify and describe common Bluetooth applications

- Computer peripherals (GPS receivers, printers, keyboards, mice, digital cameras)

- Mobile audio (Cell Phones, MP3 Players, Headsets)

- Mobile data devices (PDAs)

- Unique devices (automotive diagnostics, wireless sensor links, gaming devices)

In This Chapter

Bluetooth Overview

Bluetooth Technical Details

802.15 Standards

Wireless PAN Applications

Chapters 3–5 covered the functionality and basic components of a Wi-Fi network and how to build a wireless LAN. Then in Chapter 6, you learned about the newer WiMAX technology and using it to create a wireless MAN. In this chapter, you learn about another RF-based technology used for much "smaller" networks—wireless PANs (Personal Area Networks).

A wireless PAN connects peripheral and data devices in a small area, usually no larger than 20–30 feet in diameter because the signals cannot reach out farther than this. These peripheral and data devices include PDAs, headphones, speakers, and PC-to-PC connections, among others.

One of the most popular technologies used in the creation of a wireless PAN is Bluetooth. Bluetooth was originally developed by one company, but they later opened it for standardized, multiorganizational development.

In this chapter, you'll learn about the development of the Bluetooth specification and its purpose. You'll review the available Bluetooth hardware along with specific applications of that hardware, and you'll also learn about the versions of Bluetooth and the important feature differences among those versions, as well as other PAN standards such as 802.15.1, 802.15.2, and 802.15.3.

Bluetooth Technology

Bluetooth is a short-range communications technology used to create a wireless PAN. With Bluetooth, you connect peripheral devices, such as headphones or hands-free cell phones, to a computer or other host device without using cables. According to the Bluetooth Special Interest Group (SIG), the key features of Bluetooth include

- Robustness
- Low power
- Low cost

Development of the Standard

Bluetooth was an idea born internally at Ericsson in 1994. The company started looking into the feasibility of low-power, low-cost radio interfaces between mobile phones and their accessories. The primary goal was to do away with the need for cables.

As the idea grew into the potential for real hardware solutions, the *Bluetooth SIG* was formed in 1998 and consisted of five different companies: Ericsson, IBM, Intel, Nokia, and Toshiba. Eventually, four additional companies joined (Motorola, Microsoft, Lucent, and 3COM) to form what is called the *Bluetooth Promoter Group*. Since that time membership has grown quickly, and the original intention of Bluetooth has expanded over time to produce a modern specification that serves a number of applications.

You may be wondering why this technology is known as Bluetooth. The answer lies in a bit of history. Harald Blatand is known in Danish history as the king who united separated countries (Denmark and Norway). His nickname, Bluetooth, comes from unknown origin, but the technology was named for him. As King Harald united countries, Bluetooth unites technologies in that it allows technologies from different vendors to communicate with each other using a standardized methodology.

Bluetooth Applications

Bluetooth technology has been used in many types of equipment and applications. Some of these include

- Computer peripherals
- Mobile data
- Audio
- Industry-specific (unique) devices

Computer Peripherals

There are many Bluetooth computer peripheral devices. Some of these devices act as gateways or connectors to non-Bluetooth devices and others are direct connect Bluetooth devices in that they connect directly to each other using only Bluetooth standards with no intermediary gateway. In order to use any Bluetooth device, however, your computer must have Bluetooth support. You can install support with a USB Bluetooth device like the one shown in Figure 7.1. This particular device works with either PC or Mac computers to provide Bluetooth connectivity.

FIGURE 7.1   D-Link DBT-120 Bluetooth connector

Figure 7.2 shows a PCMCIA and Compact Flash combo unit from Belkin that allows you to use the device with a laptop computer or a PDA. Simply remove the Compact Flash card from the PCMCIA adapter and plug it into your compatible PDA to install Bluetooth capabilities in your PDA. Leave the Compact Flash card in the PCMCIA adapter and plug the card into your laptop to provide Bluetooth support to the laptop.

Many newer laptop computers, and a few desktop systems as well, come with Bluetooth capabilities built in. For systems without built-in support, a USB or PCMCIA Bluetooth adapter can provide the needed support. If you have an older desktop without USB support, you may need to purchase a PCI Bluetooth card such as the G & W PICO PCI adapter in Figure 7.3. You then connect an appropriate antenna to the antenna connector shown.

FIGURE 7.2   Belkin F8T006 Bluetooth CF/PC combo adapter

FIGURE 7.3   G & W PICO PCI Bluetooth adapter

Once you've installed a centralized Bluetooth device to act as the master to your Bluetooth network, you can begin using the many Bluetooth devices on the market, such as

- Printer connectors
- Speakers
- Headphones
- Keyboards and mice
- GPS devices
- Digital cameras

Printer Connectors

Printer cables are just one more item to fit behind or under your desk. With a Bluetooth printer connector, you can connect to a printer without USB or parallel cables. The DBT-320 print adapter, shown in Figure 7.4, is an example of a Bluetooth printer connector.

FIGURE 7.4   D-Link DBT-320 printer adapter

To use an adapter such as this, you need a Bluetooth-capable PC that supports the Hard Copy Replacement Profile (HCRP), used for printing, and the Serial Port Profile (SPP) Bluetooth profiles. A *Bluetooth profile* is a set of specifications for communicating with certain device or application types. You plug the adapter into the USB port on your printer and then create a Bluetooth connection with the device from your PC. As with most Bluetooth devices, the operating range is up to 10 meters, but depending on the environment it may be less.

Speakers and Headphones

Bluetooth speakers connect wirelessly to your laptop or PDA, giving you better quality audio than you might get with the internal speakers in your device. Bluetooth headphones come in two categories: standard headphones and cell-phone headsets. Standard headphones provide the same benefits of cabled headphones without the need to run cables. With cell-phone headsets, you can talk on your cell phone in hands-free mode. These devices are combo units with both a headphone and a microphone.

Keyboards and Mice

Bluetooth keyboards and mice are available from many different vendors. You can select single keyboards or mice, and you can purchase complete desktop systems that include both the keyboard and mouse.

GPS Devices

You can purchase a global positioning system (GPS) device to communicate with your laptop, desktop, or PDA computer. These devices can also interoperate with mapping software to provide directions to service locations such as restaurants, gas stations, and department stores. They can also show your exact location on a map and provide audible turn-by-turn directions while you are driving. Figure 7.5 shows a GPS device that connected to a laptop can provide GPS data and coordinates to mapping software.

Digital Cameras

Digital cameras usually come with a USB cable for connectivity to your computer; however, some cameras allow for Bluetooth connections as well. This way, you can transfer data from the camera to your laptop or desktop computer quickly and easily without cables.

FIGURE 7.5   Bluetooth GPS device

Mobile Data and Audio

PDAs are becoming more popular every year. The devices are slowly replacing the old binder-based time-management and planning portfolios. Many PDAs provide Bluetooth connectivity for synchronizing data. If you're a road-warrior, wireless connectivity is much more convenient than having to travel around with your PDA cradle to synchronize information with your laptop computer each night. (At least, I hope I'm not the only one who travels with both a laptop and a PDA.)

Finally, MP3 players often support Bluetooth for connectivity with headphones and portable speaker sets.

Industry-specific Devices

Bluetooth can be used in wireless sensor networks, though ZigBee-type devices seem to be more popular because of their greater communication distances and feature sets. (ZigBee and wireless sensor networks are covered in Chapter 9.) In addition, Bluetooth devices are used in the automotive repair industry for automobile diagnostics. Finally, gaming devices have been created using the Bluetooth specification, such as the controller/headset combo for XBOX Live play shown in Figure 7.6.

FIGURE 7.6   XBOX Bluetooth controller with headset

Bluetooth Concepts

To grasp the true functionality of Bluetooth devices, there are some basic concepts you need to understand. These concepts include the Bluetooth stack, links, channels, and protocols. Before covering these topics, we'll address the more high-level concept of how Bluetooth networks are formed. You can create two kinds of Bluetooth networks: piconets and scatternets.

Piconets

When up to eight Bluetooth devices are communicating with a shared hopping sequence (such as FHSS discussed in the "Frequency Hopping" section later in this chapter) in a local area, you are using what is called a *piconet*. In a piconet, one device acts as the master and up to seven other devices can connect to the master. Because of the way piconet channels are utilized, there is a probability of interference from other piconets of approximately 1.5 percent—which means you can operate multiple piconets in an area without any likely interference. When using Bluetooth keyboards and mice in a corporate work area, you can see how important this would be. When five or more devices are within range of each other, they need some way to communicate without overriding each other. They do this through FHSS hopping sequences.

Collisions are nonissues in a piconet because the master assigns a communications time slot to each of the seven slave devices. The slave devices can communicate only during their assigned time slot. As you add more slave devices to the piconet, you reduce the throughput of each individual device; however, most of these devices are not bandwidth intensive, so this is not likely to cause problems.

Scatternets

When you have more than one piconet interoperating in some way, you've created what is called a *scatternet*. In a scatternet, the master in one piconet acts as a slave in another piconet. The master then acts as a bridge between the two piconets. While allowable according to the Bluetooth standards, in reality this setup reduces throughput to an unacceptable level.

The Bluetooth Stack

Think of the Bluetooth stack as the communication layers in a Bluetooth network. This model is similar to the OSI model and, in fact, you could refer to the baseband portion of the Bluetooth stack as the Physical layer. Figure 7.7 illustrates the basic components of the Bluetooth stack.

FIGURE 7.7   Bluetooth stack

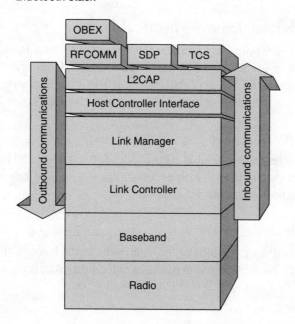

Radio and Baseband

In a Bluetooth device, the radio receives RF signals through the antenna, and these signals are processed by the baseband. Think of the baseband as the translator converting data to be sent into RF signals and RF signals into data to be received. The baseband compresses and encodes the data for transmission on the RF medium.

Link Controller

The Link Controller (LC) supervises baseband operations and acts in a support role to the link manager. The LC performs the following functions:

- Sends and receives data
- Identifies the device sending data
- Performs any needed authentication and encryption functions
- Determines the type of frame needed for each time slot

Link Manager

The Link Manager layer is responsible for discovering other link managers (active Bluetooth devices) and communicating with them. For the Link Manager layer to do its job, it depends on the lower layers or the Link Controller and baseband.

Host Controller Interface (HCI)

The Host Controller Interface (HCI) communicates the information from the lower-level protocols (baseband and Link Controller/Link Manager) to the host device whether that device is a PDA, cell phone, or computer. The main component that communicates with the HCI is the L2CAP processor.

L2CAP

This layer is responsible for packet segmentation and reassembly. It is also responsible for QoS information communications and relies on the baseband to transmit information.

Protocols

The remaining portions of the stack include the basic protocols for Bluetooth operations. RFCOMM provides serial communications emulation as if the device had a serial port. SDP is the service discovery protocol and is used to determine the services available on another linked device. When you need voice and data call control, the telephony control protocol specification (TCS) is used. This protocol provides for group call-management capabilities as well. Finally, OBEX is borrowed from the IrDA Object Exchange Protocol and allows for synchronization, file transfer, and object push such as virtual business cards.

Links

A Bluetooth link references the actual data transmission method used in a piconet or among devices. Bluetooth devices support both synchronous and asynchronous links. *Synchronous links,* called Synchronous Connection-Oriented (SCO) links, are used for voice communications and *asynchronous links,* called Asynchronous Connectionless (ACL) links, for data.

Frequency Hopping

As you learned in Chapter 2, frequency hopping spread spectrum systems actually hop from one frequency to another during communications, reducing narrowband interference. Bluetooth uses FHSS technology.

Frequencies (Channels) Used

Bluetooth uses the same 2.4 GHz frequency range used by 802.11b and 802.11g. Although interference could be a major issue, it is usually resolved because of the characteristics of Bluetooth wireless communications.

The use of FHSS reduces the likelihood of interference to some degree. There are 79 channels available for the creation of hop sequences in the U.S. and Europe. Other countries provide for only 23 channels, so interference may be a greater issue in those places.

FHSS Hop Rates

Bluetooth devices use FHSS in an advanced mode with 1600 frequency changes (hops) per second. Because of this, the availability of any one frequency within the range is increased and the number of devices that can be used in the 2.4 GHz spectrum rises as well.

Adaptive Frequency Hopping

Version 1.2 of the Bluetooth standards introduced a new interference resistance technology known as *adaptive frequency hopping* (AFH). In previous Bluetooth implementations, information was sent to the slave from the master on one channel and then the response was returned on a different channel, so you couldn't tell if the bad channel was the sending channel or receiving channel. All you knew was that the data needed to be retransmitted as it had not been received properly.

As of Bluetooth 1.2, data is sent and received on the same channel during a hop, and if communication fails, the channel is marked as "bad." The hop sequence can then be modified to avoid this channel dynamically in future communications, which results in adaptive frequency hopping.

Interference can come from Wi-Fi networks in the same location or from other Bluetooth networks. Either way, you experience fewer interference problems with Bluetooth 1.2 and achieve greater throughput.

Bluetooth devices do not actually know what causes the interference. This is a benefit because the devices account for any interference and do not look for specific patterns or signatures from particular technologies. In addition, coexisting Wi-Fi networks do not have to be modified to accommodate the Bluetooth devices.

Bandwidth and Range of Coverage

The high-end data rate for standard Bluetooth data communications is 1 Mbps. This data rate is also the most commonly available in devices on the market today.

You can expect throughput to be less than the actual data rate with any wireless technology because of administrative overhead. However, in Bluetooth networks, administrative overhead is not as great as in Wi-Fi networks. While an 802.11b network usually provides only about half the data rate in actual throughput, a Bluetooth network provides 723 Kbps throughput, or approximately 75 percent.

Version 1.2 of the Bluetooth standard supports 1 Mbps data rates and version 2.0 with EDR supports up to 3 Mbps.

The general distance of Bluetooth devices is limited to 10 meters. However, this distance varies with the class of device being utilized. Some devices can communicate over greater distances and others over shorter distances. The deciding factor, just as in Wi-Fi LANs, is determined by the power output levels.

TABLE 7.1   Bluetooth Power Classes and Ranges

Power Class	Range
1	100 meters (300 feet)
2	10 meters (30 feet)
3	1–3 meter (3 feet)

Power Classifications

Bluetooth devices come in three power classifications known as class 1, class 2, and class 3. Table 7.1 outlines the different power classifications and the range of communications they provide.

According to the Bluetooth SIG, the most common radio is a class 2 device. This radio usually uses 2.5 mW of output power.

Bluetooth and Related Standards

There are many standards related to wireless PANs, so it's beneficial to understand what these standards represent and their purposes.

802.15.1

The standard for wireless PANs is 802.15.1. It is not Bluetooth, and Bluetooth is not it, but this standard is almost identical to the Bluetooth stack covered in "The Bluetooth Stack" earlier in this chapter. Referring back to the brief discussion of the OSI model in Chapter 1, you can think of the relationship between 802.15.1 and Bluetooth much like the relationship between the OSI model and most networking technologies. You can usually map the networking technology to the OSI model, but as with TCP/IP, it seldom matches directly. The same is true for Bluetooth and 802.15.1. Bluetooth came first and then 802.15.1, and they are not identical.

802.15.2

The 802.15.2 specification details methods for the coexistence of 802.15.1 (Bluetooth) networks and 802.11 (Wi-Fi) networks. The 2.4 GHz spectrum, which is used by both Bluetooth and Wi-Fi, can become congested very quickly in any area. For this reason, a specification was needed to allow for the coexistence of these networks.

Bluetooth and Wi-Fi technologies are complementary rather than competitive, which means users want to access both devices in the same space. Because Bluetooth uses FHSS, it can recover from interference errors, but at the cost of reduced throughput. The same is true for Wi-Fi in an environment where Bluetooth is being utilized. Wi-Fi most likely functions but often suffers from reduced throughput.

802.15.3

The 802.15.3 standard is a specification for high bandwidth communications. Data rates specified include 11, 22, 33, 44, and 55 Mbps. Actual data throughput can exceed 45 Mbps with this newer technology. As with Wi-Fi technology, the farther you get from the wireless PAN center, the lower the data rate. The 802.15.3 specification requires that devices be backwardly compatible with Bluetooth and other 802.15.1-type technologies.

Bluetooth 1.2

Adopted in November of 2003, this newer standard implemented the following new features:

- Adaptive frequency hopping
- Anonymity mode
- Faster connections
- QoS improvements

Bluetooth 2.0+EDR

Bluetooth 2.0+EDR was adopted in November 2004, just one year after 1.2. This standard provides for faster data transfers and longer battery life in battery powered devices. The main reason for this longer battery life is that with faster data transfers, you can burst data in shorter windows of time and allow the devices to sleep longer. Of course, 2.0 is backwardly compatible with 1.2 and 1.1.

Summary

Bluetooth is an excellent alternative to using cables and provides a less cluttered environment. Bluetooth, however, uses the same 2.4 GHz frequency range as that used by Wi-Fi. For this reason, interference issues may arise. While Bluetooth is great for peripheral device communications, it's not the best choice for "true" networking because of its limited 1–3 Mbps data rate and even lower throughput levels. However, being able to synchronize data between portable devices and desktop computers is a big plus.

Key Terms

- ☐ **802.15.1**
- ☐ **802.15.2**
- ☐ **802.15.4**
- ☐ **adaptive frequency hopping**
- ☐ **Bluetooth**
- ☐ **Bluetooth stack**
- ☐ **piconet**
- ☐ **scatternet**

Review Questions

1. A network of Bluetooth devices consisting of eight or fewer total devices sharing the same hopping sequence is known as a

   A. Scatternet

   B. Wireless LAN

   C. Piconet

   D. Wireless MAN

2. The term used to describe the way Bluetooth devices function in the creation of and management of links is

   A. Bluetooth stack

   B. Bluetooth 2.0+EDR

   C. 802.15.1

   D. 802.15.3

3. What is the data rate of a standard Bluetooth 1.2 device?

   A. 1 Mbps

   B. 723 Kbps

   C. 128 Kbps

   D. 3 Mbps

4. What is the range of a class 1 Bluetooth radio?

   A. 10 meters

   B. 1 meter

   C. 100 meters

   D. 30 feet

5. What is the name of the technology introduced in Bluetooth 1.2 that helps to prevent interference?

   A. Adaptive interference management

   B. Adaptive frequency hopping

    C. Adaptive channel hopping

    D. Adaptive channel management

6. A Bluetooth device performs how many hops (frequency changes) per second?

    A. 79

    B. 23

    C. 2.4

    D. 1600

7. Which of these items are examples of common Bluetooth devices? Choose three.

    A. Headphones

    B. Printer adapters

    C. Gaming units

    D. Home cordless phones

Review Answers

1. **C.** A network of multiple Bluetooth devices communicating with each other using the same hopping sequence is a piconet. A piconet can have a maximum of eight devices, with one device acting as the master. The remaining seven devices act as slaves in the network.

2. **A.** The Bluetooth stack is the layered structure of communications between Bluetooth devices. This stack includes the radio and baseband layers and all layers above this that allow for communications.

3. **A.** The data rate of a 1.2 device is maxed out at 1 Mbps. The actual throughput is less—usually around 723 Kbps.

4. **C.** The range of class 1 Bluetooth radio is 100 meters. These devices are usually seen in industrial situations.

5. **B.** Adaptive frequency hopping was introduced in Bluetooth 1.2 and allows for the designation of "bad" channels so they can be removed from the hopping sequence.

6. **D.** A Bluetooth device performs 1600 hops per second to allow more Bluetooth devices (because of more possible hopping sequences) in an area to communicate in different piconets.

7. **A, B, C.** Home cordless phones do not generally use Bluetooth technology.

Infrared

Wireless# Exam Objectives Covered:

❖ Summarize the characteristics, basic attributes, and advantages of infrared technology.

- Frequencies used

- Data rates, range, and line-of-sight parameters

- Protocol types

- Interfering sources

- Different wireless PAN specifications—Serial Infrared (SIR), Medium Infrared (MIR), Fast Infrared (FIR), Ultra Fast Infrared (UFIR), Infrared Simple (IrSMP), Infrared Financial Messaging (IrFM), Infrared Transfer Protocol (IrTran-P)

❖ Identify and describe common infrared applications

- PDA data communication and synchronization

- Point-of-sale systems

- Laptop computer data communication

- Financial Messaging (IrFM)

Up to this point, I've mostly covered wireless technologies that use some form of radio frequency communication. These types of wireless technologies are often NLOS and have the ability to communicate over long distances (WiMAX and Wi-Fi) and short distances (Bluetooth, WiMAX, and Wi-Fi). There is another type of wireless technology, which has been around for a long time, and is generally used for short-distance communications with LOS; that technology is Infrared Data Association (IrDA). IrDA is a term used for both the technology itself and the consortium of organizations that provide standards for the technology.

IrDA is a communication system that uses infrared light. It is used in mobile devices for inexpensive and quick point-to-point communications. A few examples of these devices include laptops, mobile phones, PDAs, and digital cameras. In this chapter, you'll learn about this technology, including

- History and development of IrDA
- IrDA applications
- IrDA functionality (range and LOS, bandwidth, and protocols)
- Interference issues
- Infrared standards

History and Development of IrDA

The development of IrDA goes back as far as Sir William Herschel's discovery of the infrared light spectrum in the year 1800. His discovery of *infrared* light, light that is beyond the visible spectrum seen by human eyes, led to the development of all kinds of infrared technologies, including IrDA and infrared imaging, which has changed our understanding of our own planet. Military forces around the world use infrared goggles that detect heat signatures, giving them "eyes in the dark." Recent developments related to infrared data communications include the development of remote controls, calculators, the formation of the Infrared Data Association, and this association's creation of standards.

While the focus of this chapter is on using infrared for data transfer, it is useful to compare remote controls with modern IrDA. The first remote control, called the Flash-Matic, was produced by Zenith in 1956. Today, you rarely find a TV, CD player, VCR, or DVD player that does not come with remote control features built in.

Remote controls are related to IrDA in that data is exchanged between the remote control and the receiver (VCR, DVD player, and so on); however, the concept is much simpler in a remote control. A remote control system is comprised of a *receiver* (the device you communicate with using the remote control) and a *transmitter* (the remote control itself). Communications are unidirectional, or one way. The remote control communicates with the receiver using predefined patterns of high and low energy levels. These high and low energy levels are representative of 1s and 0s. Each button on the remote control sends different variations of 0s and 1s that have been partially standardized by the remote control industry, which is why you can often purchase universal remote controls.

This is where the similarities between remote controls and modern IrDA devices begin to disappear. Remote controls are one-way communication devices (the receiver has no way to communicate with the remote control); IrDA devices are two way (bidirectional) because each device is a transceiver and acts as both a transmitter and a receiver. Remote controls send very little data to the receiver, and IrDA devices can send and receive potentially large data objects. Remote controls do not have error checking. The remote control sends the data, and if the receiver does not receive it, the user has to retransmit the data—push the button again. IrDA devices implement protocols for communication that perform error checking and automatically retransmit data. The wavelengths of remote controls vary between 880 nm to 950 nm, but an IrDA wavelength is fixed at 880 nm in most implementations. Finally, remote controls are intended to travel across rooms and even bounce off objects, but IrDA devices are designed to communicate with other devices within a boundary of about one meter. Table 8.1 lists the comparison data for remote controls and IrDA devices.

TABLE 8.1   Remote Controls and IrDA Comparison

Feature	Remote Controls	IrDA Devices
Communications	Unidirectional	Bidirectional
Data transfer	Small amount	Larger amounts
Distance	3–7 Meters	1 Meter
Wavelength	880 nm to 950 nm	850 nm to 900 nm
Protocols	No error checking; human monitoring required	Error checking protocols; automatic retransmission

TABLE 8.2   IrDA Standards

Standard	Date
Serial Infrared (SIR)	September 1993
Link Access Protocol (IrLAP)	June 1994
Link Management Protocol (IrLMP)	June 1994
Fast Infrared (FIR)	October 1995
Infrared Mobile Communications (IrMC)	January 1997
Infrared Object Exchange (IrOBEX)	January 1997
Infrared Wristwatch (IrWW)	October 1998
Infrared Financial Messaging (IrFM)	October 1999

The first use of infrared for actual data exchange was the HP48 calculator. This device, based on research performed by Hewlett-Packard in 1987, was able to beam data objects back and forth with other HP48 calculators. While the research was performed in 1987, the product was released in 1990.

After the release of the HP48 calculator, interest in infrared communication began to grow, and in June of 1993, 50 companies joined to form the Infrared Data Association (IrDA), which has become synonymous with the technology itself. The IrDA was formed to provide a platform for discussion and standardization of infrared devices and communication specifications. The first specification for IrDA communications was already available by September of 1993 and was the Serial Infrared (SIR) physical layer standard. The initial release date of this and other IrDA standards is provided in Table 8.2.

Today, more than 200 years after Sir William Herschel's discovery of infrared light, there are literally thousands of products on the market that contain infrared ports. These include laptop computers, PDAs, mobile phones, and more. You'll learn about them in the next section of this chapter.

Infrared Applications

The possible uses of a short-range communication technology with moderate bandwidth capabilities are many. In this section, I cover the three most common applications:

- PDA synchronization
- Point-of-sale systems and Financial Messaging
- Laptop data communications

PDA Synchronization

Much like Bluetooth, IrDA PDA synchronization eliminates the need for PDA cradles. Since these cradles can be somewhat large, they defeat the portability purposes of a PDA in many scenarios. With an IrDA port on the PDA and an IrDA port in a laptop or desktop computer, you can often synchronize the PDA with the PC without using the cradle that shipped with the PDA. Not all PDAs support synchronization using IrDA, however. If you plan to use it in this way, be sure to verify support for this feature first.

Another benefit of having IrDA ports in PDAs is the ability to transfer objects between PDAs. For example, let's say you're in a meeting with some of your peers and you discover during the course of the conversation that two of your colleagues need contact information for an individual that you have stored in your PDA. With IrDA ports, you can take out your PDAs and transfer the contact file from your PDA to theirs without connecting cables or wires. This is obviously a big timesaver.

Point-of-Sale Systems and Financial Messaging

A *point-of-sale system* is a system used to process purchases at the "point-of-sale." These systems usually include a keyboard and monitor for data input and often include infrared technology as well. One common application of infrared technology in point-of-sale systems is the use of an infrared connected printer.

The standard developed to allow for financial transactions across IrDA is *Infrared Financial Messaging* (IrFM). IrFM introduces the concepts known as *point-and-pay, point-and-shoot,* or *position-and-pay.* Imagine replacing all the credit cards and cash in your wallet with a single device that also organizes your life. This concept is what IrFM offers you through point-and-pay. You simply take out your PDA and point it at the vending machine, cash register, gas pump, or any other transaction point, and your purchasing information is transferred automatically to the payment transaction device and the amount is deducted from your checking account or charged to your credit card account.

This sounds wonderful until you realize that when you lose your PDA, you lose your life. A friend of mine was having a fun afternoon, sitting on the edge of a massive culvert with a flood of water flowing out of it to form a waterfall that dropped many feet into a deep pool. In one brief moment, his PDA fell from his "securely mounted" hip cradle into the watery abyss below. Needless to say, it was never seen again.

In my friend's case, he lost some contacts and schedule information. That's not necessarily the end of the world. What if he had left a PDA with all his financial information on it sitting on a picnic table in a park? That would be a different story. If IrFM is to really grow in this area of point-and-pay, security is critical. At the same time, you don't want IrFM to implement the same security that credit cards use because they are notoriously prone to theft and unauthorized use. Security mechanisms should be put in place that actually make IrFM *more* secure than traditional payment methods.

Because IrFM deals with financial information, security is extremely important. IrFM handles security concerns using digital signatures, session encryption, and PIN (personal identification number) codes. Not all IrFM implementations use these security mechanisms, but they are available to vendors who choose to implement them. Ultimately, you're responsible for ensuring that proper security precautions have been taken.

Laptop Data Communications

For a long time, IrDA ports were standard in laptop computers. Nowadays, it's not uncommon for a laptop computer to have Bluetooth instead of an IrDA port, which is the case with the laptop I am using to write this book. It is a new laptop with integrated Wi-Fi and Bluetooth, but no IrDA, and it falls in the $2,800–3,000 price range. Clearly, not all laptops support IrDA at this time because more Bluetooth and Wi-Fi peripherals are being sold than IrDA. Still, many vendors are creating laptops with IrDA ports built in. For those laptops without IrDA ports, you can acquire a USB-to-IrDA adapter such as the one shown in Figure 8.1.

FIGURE 8.1   USB to IrDA adapter

Using an IrDA port, you can create quick ad hoc connections between two laptop computers. You can also synchronize your PDA data with your laptop, and you can connect some mobile phones to the laptop or desktop to back up and restore your contact information and other mobile phone data.

With Wi-Fi capabilities included in most laptops today, building a network using Wi-Fi technology is more common. This can be a benefit since IrDA requires physical LOS and Wi-Fi does not because of indoor reflection, refraction, and scattering (the bouncing around of the RF signal). By the same token, physical LOS offers a certain level of security because a hacker has to be in the same area to access your data or devices.

Infrared Functionality

IrDA uses the electromagnetic spectrum known as *infrared*. Wi-Fi, WiMAX, and Bluetooth also use portions of the electromagnetic spectrum; however, they use a completely different frequency set and therefore do not interfere with IrDA, and IrDA does not interfere with them in most situations.

You might remember from Chapters 2 and 3 that wireless networks usually provide for coexistence through the use of different frequencies. IrDA is not quite the same. While you can operate several IrDA connections using different wavelengths, or frequencies, the cost is prohibitive. Most IrDA devices use one standard frequency. Because this is the case, you may wonder how IrDA devices can coexist with other active devices. The answer is *spatial separation*. Most IrDA implementations work at 1 meter or less.

To understand the functionality of IrDA, you must learn about the frequencies used, the bandwidth and data rates available, the range and LOS parameters related to infrared communications, and the standard protocols available according to the IrDA specifications.

Frequencies

The frequencies used by IrDA are sometimes called *optical frequencies* because they are dealing with light—something that is of the nature of light and visible, though not to the human eye. Do not confuse IrDA with Free Space Optics (FSO). FSO is used as an alternative to fiber-optic cabling and allows for speeds up to 1.25 Gbps and distances up to 10 kilometers (6.2 miles).

Frequencies used by IrDA are referenced in wavelengths, such as 850 nm or 880 nm. This spectrum is license free, so you do not need approval from the FCC or other regulating bodies. Remember, while IrDA devices communicate in the 880 nm range, their communication range may vary from 850 nm to 900 nm.

Bandwidth and Data Rates

The data rates of infrared links depend on the link type. There are four basic link types: *serial infrared (SIR), medium infrared (MIR), fast infrared (FIR),* or *very fast infrared (VFIR).* Table 8.3 provides a breakdown of these different link types and the data rates provided.

While the data rate for FIR link types is advertised at 4 Mbps, in reality the throughput is between 2 and 3 Mbps because of link parameters and management overhead. The same holds true for the other link types; they do not achieve a throughput equivalent to their data rate. This bandwidth can also be shared in a multipoint configuration with up to 16 devices, limiting the effective throughput for any given device participating in the configuration.

All discovery and link negotiations take place at 9600 Kbps, so all link types support this speed. You should also know that IrDA devices are really half-duplex devices. This makes a lot of sense: if one device sends light, the other device is blinded by that light as it receives it. This is why part of the IrDA standards specifies something called *minimum turn around time* and *maximum turn around time.* These are the time intervals allowed before the receiving device becomes the sending device. Think of it as the "unspoken etiquette" in human communications. When you're trying to listen well to others, you wait for a "minimum turn around time"— also called a pause—in their speaking before you begin to speak. IrDA communications work in much the same way; only this pause is clearly defined, usually through time-division multiplexing (TDM).

TABLE 8.3   IrDA Physical Layer Link Types and Data Rates

Link Type	Data Rate
SIR	2.4 Kbps–115.2 Kbps
MIR	0.576–1.152 Mbps
FIR	4 Mbps
VFIR	16 Mbps

TDM is a way to put multiple data streams into a single signal by separating the signal into multiple fixed segments, each with a short duration. Individual data streams are then reassembled at the receiver based on predefined timings, or segment lengths.

Range and LOS

IrDA devices require physical LOS. In other words, though invisible light is used to implement the communications, you must be able to see visibly the device you are communicating with. Of course, there are scenarios where you cannot see the device, but the link is established with a mirror or some other reflecting device. In normal operations, however, physical LOS is required.

The fact that infrared requires physical LOS is one of the main reasons that security is not a chief concern of infrared communications in most implementations. Of course, IrFM is an exception to this, but with PDA synchronization and laptop-to-laptop links, security is not usually as big of a worry. As long as you can control who connects, you are not usually worried about the data in a connection being secured because it would be difficult for a hacker to intercept the data without your knowledge. Therefore, session encryption is usually implemented only for financial transactions through IrFM.

When considering LOS, you must consider possible sources of interference in the IrDA link. Sunlight is the most common interference source; however, any bright light, flurescent or otherwise, has the potential to cause interference. Remember, although you cannot see it, infrared communications are light based.

To understand the potential for interference from other bright lights, imagine you are standing outside on a bright sunny day and your neighbor is standing a few hundred feet away from you holding a flashlight. From your position, you may not even be able to see if the flashlight is on or off. This is because the visible light is being made invisible by the interference from another brighter visible light—the sun. Turn off that brighter visible light (or just wait until dark—it's a little easier than turning off the sun), and you can clearly see the flashlight's beam.

Remember Sir William Herschel? He discovered infrared light by passing the sun's light through a prism to separate the colors, which means that sunlight has the potential for infrared and, therefore, can cause interference in infrared communications.

Protocols and Standards

Central to the IrDA group is something called a *Special Interest Group* (SIG). SIGs work toward the creation of standardized protocols to allow for infrared communications in various usage scenarios. This section covers the most important SIGs and the standards they have created so you will be comfortable with this information both for the Wireless# exam and when selecting IrDA devices and software. The protocols covered include

- IrPHY
- IrLAP
- IrLMP
- Tiny TP
- IrTran-P
- IrOBEX
- IrLAN
- IrCOMM
- IrMC
- IrFM
- IrSMP/IrSimple
- IrTM

IrPHY

The *infrared physical layer* (IrPHY) is the foundation for the other layers and protocols used in IrDA communications. The IrPHY defines the range, angle, speed, and modulation type for the IrDA link. The possible IrPHY standards common today include SIR, FIR, and VFIR with UFIR in development. UFIR is the *ultra-fast infrared* specification and is intended to provide up to 100 Mbps communications.

The data rates of these physical layer standards were covered in Table 8.3. Refer to this table to ensure the selected devices meet your data transmission needs. Figure 8.2 illustrates where these various protocols and standards fit into the IrDA specifications.

As you can see in Figure 8.2, there is a layer known as the *framer* or *framer driver* between the IrPHY and the IrLAP layer. This framer is responsible for two major tasks: performing packet framing based on the physical specification and acting as the device driver for the transceiver controller. While this layer exists in reality, it's not actually mentioned

FIGURE 8.2   IrDA protocols and standards

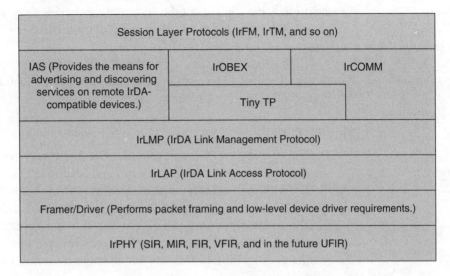

in the IrDA specifications, though they reference its functionality in the sections on the IrPHY and the IrLAP and developers have come to call it the framer.

IrLAP

As is implied by the name, the *IrDA Link Access Protocol* (IrLAP) is responsible for constructing and maintaining the link between two remote devices for the transmission of data packets. This process involves device discovery and negotiation. An IrDA device can be in one of two basic states: normal disconnect mode (NDM) and normal response mode (NRM). The link is established while in NDM and the link is maintained and data transmitted while in NRM.

When an IrLAP link is created, one device functions as the primary and the other as the secondary. The primary device is responsible for discovery, negotiation, and link maintenance. The secondary device is responsible for responding and acting in accordance with the rules put forth by the primary device. This process is similar to what occurs in a Bluetooth connection.

IrLMP

The *IrDA Link Management Protocol* (IrLMP) is responsible for multiplexing, service discovery, and general link control.

The multiplexing service allows you to connect multiple IrDA devices to the primary device without the client devices having to coordinate access. To provide this service, the IrLMP actually uses the discovery, link control, and data transfer services of the IrLAP.

To provide service discovery, the IrLMP coordinates with the Information Access Service (IAS) seen in the upper left of the illustration shown in Figure 8.2. Think of IAS as a yellow pages service for the IrDA devices.

Tiny TP (TTP)

The *Tiny Transport Protocol* provides two basic services to the IrDA communications process: *flow control* and *segmentation and reassembly* (SAR). Although usually implemented as part of the IrLMP module, Tiny TP is generally referenced as a separate protocol. The flow control algorithms allow for multiple IrLMP connections to operate over a single IrLAP link. The SAR provides for the breakdown of large packets into smaller packets for transmission and then the reassembly of those packets upon delivery.

IrTran-P

IrDA Transfer Pictures/Photos (IrTran-P) is a standard for the transference of digital photos from a digital camera to a PC.

IrOBEX

IrDA Object Exchange (IrOBEX) is the standard for object transfer or exchange and is used by many of the point-and-shoot applications of the session layer protocols, such as IrFM.

IrOBEX provides for the transfer of objects such as digital pictures from digital cameras, electronic business cards, database records, monitoring instrumentation data, or diagnostics and programming information. The concept is to provide for data exchange without the applications having to worry about the technical details of how the exchange takes place.

IrLAN

IrLAN is an optional protocol that serves as a convenient connection between portable PCs and office LANs. When this protocol is implemented, there would be three models of operation: computers attaching to LANs through IrDA access points, two computers communicating with each other as if on a LAN, or a computer attaching to a LAN through an already connected computer with an IrDA port in a bridged or routed fashion.

IrCOMM

Do you want to use QModem-Pro, Procomm Plus, or RipTerm across your IrDA link? If so, you want to take advantage of *IrCOMM*. This standard provides COM port emulation for use with legacy applications along with LPT port emulation for some printing scenarios.

IrMC

IrDA Mobile Communications (IrMC) is a standard for communications between mobile devices or between mobile devices such as PDAs and desktop or laptop computers. IrMC is often used in data synchronization processes and in both IrDA and Bluetooth devices.

IrFM

IrDA Financial Messaging (IrFM) allows for the communication of financial data between IrDA-compliant devices. Security is a chief concern of IrFM implementations. The LOS requirement is often considered a problem for IrDA, but in this scenario LOS actually works as a benefit. The link is inherently more secure than a Wi-Fi link because of the LOS requirement.

In addition to the LOS security, you can implement digital signatures, password authentication, and session encryption to provide even greater security. One potential drawback in the security area is with the IrFM standard for express payment. By its nature, this standard does not require authentication, and this could be a problem if the portable device is stolen. Some argue that people notice quickly when a portable device is stolen, but this certainly depends on how you use the device. In every situation, users should be well educated if IrFM is implemented in your systems.

IrSMP/IrSimple

IrDA Simple (also referred to as IrSimple, IrSMP, and IrSimple Connect) is a standard for quick connection to and transfer of data to home digital devices and appliances. The scenario offered by the IrDA is one of near-instant transferal of a digital picture from a mobile phone to a digital TV for display.

IrTM

IrTM, which stands for *IrDA Traffic Mobility,* is a SIG focused on developing and implementing standards for automatic toll payments. This technology has been implemented in places throughout Asia, South America, and Europe.

Summary

IrDA has been used for many years and has many different applications. Because of its LOS requirements, you wouldn't use it to build a wireless LAN, but for ad hoc connections and short-range fast data transfer, it's exceptional.

Key Terms

- ☐ **FIR**
- ☐ **infrared**
- ☐ **IrCOMM**
- ☐ **IrDA**
- ☐ **IrFM**
- ☐ **IrLAP**
- ☐ **IrLMP**
- ☐ **IrOBEX**
- ☐ **IrPHY**
- ☐ **IrSimple, IrSMP**
- ☐ **SIR**
- ☐ **Tiny TP**
- ☐ **VFIR**

Review Questions

1. If you want to transfer a digital photo taken with your digital camera quickly to a television screen, what IrDA standard might be involved?

   A. IrFM

   B. IrMC

   C. IrSimple

   D. IrSConn

2. You have just walked up to a vending machine and notice that it supports IrDA financial transactions. Your PDA is configured for this, so you point-and-pay. What IrDA standard is involved?

   A. IrFM

   B. IrMC

   C. IrSimple

   D. IrSConn

3. There are multiple types of IrDA transceivers at the IrPHY level. Select the two valid types from this list.

   A. SIR

   B. VSIR

   C. FIR

   D. VMIR

4. If you need to use a legacy terminal application that communicates through a COM or serial port, what IrDA specification is likely involved?

   A. IrTran-P

   B. IrSerial

   C. IrCOM1

   D. IrCOMM

5. You have just purchased a digital camera and notice that it has an infrared port. Assuming this is a standard IrDA port, what protocol would allow you to transfer the images from the camera to your PC?

   A. IrTran-P

   B. IrSerial

   C. IrCOM1

   D. IrCOMM

6. You and a friend who you have not seen since high school just used IrOBEX with your PDAs. What action have you most likely just taken?

   A. You synchronized your PDAs with each other.

   B. You transferred your electronic business cards to each other.

   C. You shared your Internet connection with him.

   D. You looked at pictures on each PDA without transferring anything.

7. A friend tells you that the fastest data rate her IrDA device supports is 4 Mbps. What IrPHY supports this rate as the highest data rate?

   A. SIR

   B. MIR

   C. FIR

   D. VFIR

8. Which three of these options are differences between remote controls that utilize infrared and IrDA devices?

   A. IrDA devices have error checking built in; remote controls usually do not.

   B. Remote controls work at greater distances.

    C. IrDA devices use simple algorithms compared to remote controls.

    D. Remote controls are unidirectional and IrDA devices are bidirectional.

9. You have a laptop computer that supports IrDA and a PDA that supports it as well. What device do you no longer need to carry with you to synchronize the data between these two while you are traveling?

    A. The PDA

    B. The laptop

    C. The PDA cradle

    D. The laptop docking station

Review Answers

1. **C.** IrSimple. Correct answers could also include IrSC, IrSimple Connect, or IrSMP. They all refer to the same standard that allows for very fast link negotiation for data transfer to home appliances.

2. **A.** IrFM is the IrDA Financial Messaging protocol that allows for financial transactions to take place over IrDA links.

3. **A, C.** Serial infrared (SIR) and fast infrared (FIR) are both valid IrPHYs. Others include very fast infrared (VFIR) and ultra-fast infrared (UFIR).

4. **D.** IrCOMM is the serial or LPT port emulator for IrDA communications that allows for the use of legacy serial port applications and printing software.

5. **A.** IrTran-P allows you to transfer digital photos from your camera to your PC.

6. **B.** IrOBEX is used to transfer objects from one IrDA device to another. For this reason, you probably just transferred your electronic business cards to each other or you transferred some other object type. The other options listed do not require the use of the IrDA Object Exchange protocol.

7.   **C.** FIR, or fast infrared, supports data rates up to 4 Mbps and is likely the IrPHY used by your friend's device.

8.   **A, B, D.** Remote controls are unidirectional, and IrDA devices are bidirectional (though they are only half-duplex, they can both send and receive data). Remote controls work over greater distances as IrDA devices are intended to work only within a range of approximately 1 meter. IrDA devices have error checking built in to ensure the data arrives without being corrupted. Remote controls have no such error checking capability, and the user must press the button again if they do not receive the desired results the first time.

9.   **C.** Now that you have IrDA support in both your laptop and PDA, you can synchronize data between them while traveling across the IrDA link (likely using IrMC), and you will no longer need the PDA cradle. The laptop has to be present, of course, if you want to synchronize with it, as does the PDA. You do not need the laptop's docking station, if you have one.

ZigBee

Wireless# Exam Objectives Covered:

❖ Summarize the characteristics, basic attributes, and advantages of ZigBee

- Frequencies

- Power requirements

- Topology models

- Security features

- IEEE 802.15.4 standard

- ZigBee stack

❖ Identify and describe common ZigBee applications

- Building automation and residential/light commercial control

- Industrial control

- Personal healthcare

- PC and peripherals

- Consumer electronics

Wireless technology is very useful for building standard communication networks. However, wireless also gives you networking possibilities you don't have with wired technology. When the wires are removed, new paradigms must be developed and previously unimaginable technologies surface. One of these new technologies is wireless sensor networks. These are networks, not of computing devices as you might think of them, but of sensor devices communicating with some form of centralized control or monitoring service. The two most commonly known standards related to wireless sensor networks are 802.15.4 and ZigBee. Both are covered in this chapter.

The Monitoring and Control Revolution

If you are a student of history, you know that the human race has gone through many great changes. We passed from the hunter-gatherer age to the agrarian age when we began to farm to provide sustenance for ourselves and others instead of hunting and foraging alone. The next step we took was to pass from the agrarian age to the industrial age. The *industrial revolution,* as it was called, brought about massive changes in the way we produce products and, eventually, services. The industrial movement continues to this day and one of its newest elements is the monitoring and control of the machinery that we began to use during the industrial revolution.

Many workers are employed to observe the functioning of machinery and respond to various scenarios. For example, at a water treatment plant, a worker observes the water as it passes through many containers and pipes to verify that the proper changes are being made by testing the chemical makeup of the water at each stage in the process. With monitoring devices, the worker could program them to check this chemical mixture automatically and report the findings to a centralized controller where a decision is made as to whether a human should be notified. These monitoring devices allow for less frequent manual inspections of the process and give the employee more freedom to perform other tasks that bring a cost benefit to the organization.

Consider the scenario in which an assembly line is operated by a standard conveyer belt system. There is a temperature gauge at a particular location where the heat of the conveyor motor is displayed. One of the line workers must check this gauge every 30 minutes and, if the temperature is too high, lower the speed of the conveyer. Then, once the temperature has been reregulated, the line worker increases the speed of the conveyer. What if, instead, there were a control device that monitored the temperature and made adjustments to the speed of the system automatically? In most cases, this would increase line production and decrease the costs to the organization. Such is the potential of monitoring and control devices.

The ZigBee Alliance was created to "enable reliable, cost-effective, low-power, wirelessly networked, monitoring and control products based on an open global standard." The ZigBee specification defines the network, security, and application layers that reside above the PHY and MAC layers of the 802.15.4 standard for monitoring and control devices. This specification is used as an embedded technology in many consumer, healthcare, commercial, and industrial devices.

ZigBee Usage

The benefit of ZigBee-compliant monitoring and control devices is that they are wireless devices based on standard technology. These devices can communicate with central servers without the need for cable runs or Ethernet over power lines. Being standards-based ensures interoperability between devices from different vendors.

ZigBee has many potential uses including

- Building automation
- Control devices
- Personal healthcare
- PC peripherals
- Consumer electronics

Building Automation

Like any infrastructure-type technology, what you do with it depends on the software available to communicate across and with it. In other words, ZigBee has the potential to be and do many things, but whether it reaches that potential depends on the applications that are available or that can be created by an organization. Using the right applications, you can automate nearly any environmental control, including lighting, temperature, purification and oxygenation systems, and more.

You have no doubt experienced motion sensor light switches. These devices detect motion in an area and turn the lights on automatically. Take this a step further and you can see new potential. What if these light switches are smart and attached to ZigBee monitoring devices that reported back to a centralized control system? From one switch, you could provide security monitoring and automatic lighting. You could also learn traffic patterns in your building. You could then use this centralized data to determine if money is being wasted by heating areas that are seldom, or never, used during off hours in your building. You can then adjust the temperature schedule accordingly.

Here is my dream scenario. I walk into my business office and a wireless motion sensor, which can be triggered only from inside the building, detects my presence. This information is sent back to a central server that adjusts the temperature for human comfort automatically and enables the wireless network (Wi-Fi) in my area. These sensors are placed throughout the facility and monitor the presence of movement continually. If an hour passes without any movement, the Wi-Fi network is disabled. Of course, this scenario assumes people are moving around inside the facility throughout the day, but it would be a rare office where someone did not move each hour.

This scenario provides a few advantages. First, the temperature adjusts automatically, and as long as the variance between night temperature and working hours temperature is not too great, the building adjusts to comfort level very quickly. Second, the Wi-Fi network is more secure because it is unavailable anytime after one hour beyond the departure of the last movement reading inside the building. This feature gives you more flexibility than a scheduled shutdown of the network because people can work extra hours without the network administration staff needing to make modifications.

Control Devices

Control devices are used to control environmental and machine-specific configurations based on specifically defined scenarios. Examples of control device markets include

- Home
- Commercial
- Industrial

Home Automation

Like building automation in commercial and government implementations, home automation devices are used to monitor and adjust the temperature, lighting, and even sounds in the home environment. You can also use ZigBee technology in smart home devices ranging from coffee makers to dishwashers. In addition, home security and surveillance systems can use

ZigBee devices, and the future might even include robots and automated lawnmowers based on this technology.

Commercial

Commercial control devices will likely go beyond environmental control more quickly than home automation. While it would be nice if your refrigerator automatically informed the grocery store that you were out of milk, it's not really on anyone's top-ten list of "things we need in our life." However, notifying personnel and modifying configurations on-the-fly would certainly be a big benefit in commercial and industrial situations.

While radio frequency identification (RFID) is used more often for inventory management in a store setting, ZigBee technology can be used to assist an RFID implementation by monitoring other environmental elements and reporting to a centralized controller. For example, ZigBee devices installed in an electronics department can monitor the traffic coming in and out of the area (using motion sensors) and then page for more assistance in that area automatically if too many shoppers arrive in the area. RFID can be used, in this same area, to track inventoried items that are leaving the area. In this way, the two technologies complement each other.

I remember one situation I was in where ZigBee devices could have helped a store make a sale. I was standing at the jewelry counter in a large department store waiting to purchase a ring for my wife. There was no one present behind the counter, and there were no bells to ring, so I waited. After a few minutes, I finally gave up and left. Now, if ZigBee sensors had been installed in the area to detect the presence of a living warm-blooded creature (in this case, a human and maybe the sensors could even use infrared—I'm trying to help you see the potential) and then communicated that information to a centralized controller, the department manager could have been paged, letting them know that a customer was in their area. (You might suggest this possibility to the manager at your local department store after your next long wait at the counter.)

Industrial

The conveyer-belt scenario described earlier in the chapter is a perfect example of industrial use of automatic monitoring devices. We've actually had monitoring devices such as these for a long time. The benefit of ZigBee is that it is a standardized wireless sensor technology. In other words, implementing and maintaining the system is generally easier because you do not have to install any cables.

Other industrial applications include extending your current wired monitoring implementation, discovering equipment performance levels, improving preventative maintenance programs, and enhancing employee safety through the monitoring of environmental and equipment states.

Personal Healthcare

Another excellent use of ZigBee technology is in the arena of personal healthcare. By placing sensor devices in well-planned locations in a hospital, a patient's heart rate and other health indicators could be monitored and reported to a central location. Imagine an assisted living environment where each resident wears a bracelet that communicates with ZigBee sensors installed all over the campus and informs a central monitoring station of a resident's health status at second-to-second intervals. The patient wouldn't have to push a button for help because the staff would be notified the moment a heart beat was missed.

PC Peripherals

When it comes to PC peripherals, the aim is to replace infrared devices or concepts with ZigBee. In other words, instead of aligning the infrared ports on two laptops or a laptop and a PDA, you would just place them in the vicinity of each other and they would connect and synchronize automatically. Think of it as putting the PDA in the cradle and having it synchronize automatically; only now you just place it on the desk near the laptop. The ZigBee devices in each unit detect each other and connect without intervention and synchronize the data. This is a dream, since the technology has not been implemented, but it is a pleasant one.

Consumer Electronics

The potential for use of ZigBee in consumer electronics is large and includes

- Appliance monitoring
- Device access control (consumer NAS, Wi-Fi, and so on)

However, ZigBee consumer electronics are mostly "potential" devices as they are uncommon at this time.

ZigBee Technology

Although ZigBee is used more frequently in commercial and industrial environments, it is considered a PAN technology. As with all 802.15 standards, it uses some form of wireless networking to form these personal area networks; however, you can create ZigBee networks in a mesh-type structure that covers a very large space.

Frequencies

ZigBee technology uses one of three different frequency ranges. In Europe, the frequency range is either 868 MHz or 2.4 GHz, and in the U.S., the range is either 915 MHz or 2.4 GHz. Using the 2.4 GHz band worldwide allows access to the unlicensed ISM frequencies, which makes implementation easy because there aren't any license requirements. These frequencies are summarized in Table 9.1.

Power Requirements

ZigBee devices are wireless and are intended to run on batteries so that wires are unnecessary for networking or for powering the device. For this reason, ZigBee devices require a long battery life (months to years) and therefore have low power consumption. To help with battery life, ZigBee devices come in two basic types: full function devices (FFD) and reduced function devices (RFD). The RFD types require less power as they perform fewer functions. For example, a RFD cannot function as a router or coordinator, but as an end device only. Table 9.2 provides a breakdown of FFD and RFD capabilities.

As you can see from Table 9.2, a ZigBee network generally consists of one coordinator and one or more routers and end devices.

TABLE 9.1   Frequencies Used in the U.S., Europe, and Worldwide

Frequency	U.S.	Europe	Worldwide
868 MHz	No	Yes	No
915 MHz	Yes	No	No
2.4 GHz	Yes	Yes	Yes

TABLE 9.2   FFD and RFD Summarized

	Coordinator	Router	End Device
Function	Network establishment and control	Data routing. Can talk to other routers and the coordinator as well as end devices.	Only talks to routers and/or the coordinator
FFD (full function device)	Yes	Yes	Yes
RFD (reduced function device)	No	No	Yes

ZigBee Stack

The ZigBee stack reveals both the basic functionality of ZigBee and the organizations responsible for managing the components of a ZigBee standard implementation. Figure 9.1 illustrates this stack. The IEEE is

FIGURE 9.1   The ZigBee stack

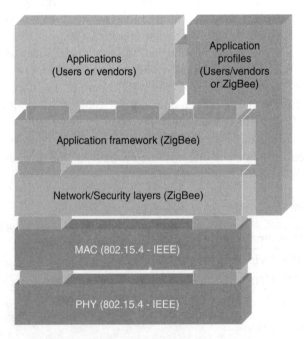

responsible for the 802.15.4 standard, which specified the PHY and MAC layers. The ZigBee Alliance is responsible for defining the Network and Security layers as well as the application framework, while users (generally device vendors) are responsible for the application profiles and applications. In some instances, application profiles are created by the ZigBee Alliance.

Topology Models

There are three basic topology models supported by ZigBee: mesh, star, and cluster tree. The mesh topology is implemented in a way that provides for fault tolerance through multiple communication paths and does not use a coordinator. This topology is similar to a peer-to-peer topology. Most devices in a mesh implementation are FFDs. The star topology does use a coordinator, sometimes called a *PAN coordinator,* which is responsible for managing the communications on the network. At the very least, the coordinator must be a FFD. The noncoordinator devices communicate through the coordinator and may be FFD or RFD devices. With a cluster tree topology, you implement FFD routers that connect multiple networks of ZigBee devices. Each network has a coordinator, or they may be mesh networks in some scenarios. Figure 9.2 illustrates the different topologies.

Security Features

The ZigBee standard implements security through the use of 128-bit AES encryption. By today's standards, this provides adequate encryption

FIGURE 9.2   ZigBee topologies

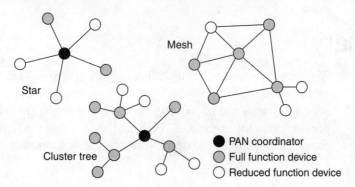

TABLE 9.3 Frequencies, Usage Areas, Channels, Channel Numbers, and Data Rates for IEEE 802.15.4

Frequency	Usage Areas	Channels	Channel Numbers	Data Rates
868 MHz	Europe	1	0	20 Kbps
915 MHz	U.S.	10	1–10	40 Kbps
2.4 GHz	Worldwide	16	11–26	250 Kbps

strength for nearly any type of data. The MAC layer performs the security processing, but the upper layers control and manage this security. Through AES security suites, you can implement confidentiality (encryption), data integrity, and authentication.

Standards

Although the ZigBee Alliance is creating the ZigBee specification, the 802.15.4 standard was created and is managed by the IEEE.

802.15.4

The 802.15.4 standard specifies a MAC and PHY for low power, low bandwidth, and inexpensive wireless communication devices. The standard specifies that DSSS technology be used with the frequencies and data rates specified in Table 9.3.

As you can see from the information in Table 9.3, the maximum data rate for an IEEE 802.15.4, and therefore ZigBee, device is 250 Kbps. These devices are not meant to create high-speed networks, but rather sensor networks that transfer small bursts of data periodically.

Summary

ZigBee is an up-and-coming technology that is likely to change the way we monitor and control our working and living environments. The potential for cost savings and improved performance is huge. The 802.15.4 standard provides stability at the core (PHY and MAC), and the ZigBee specification provides standardization of network communications and operations.

Key Terms

- ☐ **902.15.4**
- ☐ **coordinator**
- ☐ **FFD**
- ☐ **mesh network**
- ☐ **RFD**
- ☐ **ZigBee**
- ☐ **ZigBee router**

Review Questions

1. ZigBee is a complete standard in and of itself and depends on no other standards.

    A. True

    B. False

2. What frequency is available for use worldwide with ZigBee networks?

    A. 868 MHz

    B. 915 MHz

    C. 5.8 GHz

    D. 2.4 GHz

3. Which of these are valid data rates for ZigBee devices according to the standards? Choose all that apply.

    A. 20 Kbps

    B. 250 Kbps

    C. 128 Kbps

    D. 40 Kbps

4. Which ZigBee topology is similar to a peer-to-peer network?

    A. Star

    B. Mesh

    C. Cluster tree

    D. Hybrid

5. To function as a coordinator, what type of ZigBee device should you use?

  A. FFD

  B. RFD

  C. FF-ZigBee

  D. RF-ZigBee

Review Answers

1. **B.** False. ZigBee is a standard for the Network and Security layers, as well as the application framework, that resides above the IEEE 802.15.4 standard. The 802.15.4 and ZigBee standards work together to form a specification for use in wireless sensor networks.

2. **D.** The 2.4 GHz ISM band is available worldwide for license-free implementation of ZigBee wireless sensor networks.

3. **A, C, D.** The supported data rates are 20 Kbps for the 868 MHz frequency, 40 Kbps for the 915 MHz frequency, and 250 Kbps for the 2.4 GHz frequency.

4. **B.** The mesh topology is most like a peer-to-peer network. There is no hybrid topology in ZigBee networks.

5. **A.** You must use a full function device (FFD) if the desired functionality is as a coordinator or router. A FFD can function as an end device as well, but a reduced function device (RFD) can act only as an end device.

RFID

Wireless# Exam Objectives Covered:

❖ Summarize the characteristics, basic attributes, and advantages of RFID

  ▪ RFID system requirements

  ▪ RFID tag types

  ▪ RFID hardware components

❖ Identify proper procedures for installing and configuring common WLAN applications

  ▪ RFID

Radio frequency identification (RFID) systems are being used in many ways today—probably more than you realize. Current implementations include

- Highway toll payments
- Traffic management
- Protected area/garage access
- Theft prevention
- Inventory management and tracking

RFID technology is based on RF communications and has been implemented all over the world. In this chapter, I review the basics of RFID, including what it is, how it works, its common applications, and the basic implementation process for any environment.

RFID Overview

Radio frequency identification (RFID) is a technology that uses radio frequency communications for fairly short-range connections. As a technology, it competes directly with bar-coding systems for inventory tracking, key systems for facilities access, and manual transactions for toll processing.

A basic RFID system is composed of three parts: RFID tags, RFID readers, and processing software. The *RFID readers* read the information from the *RFID tags* and use this information themselves for internal processing, or they send it on to a centralized device for external processing. For example, as a shopper leaves a department store, an RFID reader reads the RFID tag on an item the shopper is carrying. The reader then sends the data from the RFID tag to a centralized server that can determine if the device was purchased at a register. If the device was purchased, the centralized server logs the departure of the item from the building and effectively removes it from inventory. If the device was not purchased, alarms go off and store security personnel can respond accordingly.

This entire process can be wireless. Wireless RFID tags and readers communicate with each other (all RFID tags are RF-based wireless, hence the RF in RFID), and the reader could transmit the data across a Wi-Fi network to the central server. This example demonstrates the technology's potential.

TABLE 10.1   Frequencies by Region

	UHF	HF	LF
North America	902–928 MHz	13.56 MHz	125–134 kHz
Australia	918–926 MHz	N/A	N/A
Europe	865.6–867.6 MHz	13.56 MHz	125–134 kHz
Japan	950–956 MHz	13.56 MHz	12–134 kHz

Frequencies Used by RFID

Like other wireless technologies, RFID uses specified frequencies for communications. Table 10.1 provides a breakdown of these different frequencies and where they are used.

Some applications may use the microwave range (2.4 GHz), but this frequency is not as common as the low (LF), high (HF), and ultra-high (UHF) frequencies. It is also important to note that LF tags differ from UHF tags in power consumption and cost. LF tags cost less and consume less power. The same is true when you compare LF to HF or HF to UHF. The higher the frequency, the greater the cost and power consumption generally.

RFID Components

The most important components of an RFID system are the RFID tags and the RFID readers. As with other wireless technologies, RFID devices (tags and readers) include transceivers (readers) or transponders (tags) and antennas for communicating.

RFID Tags

RFID tags come in three basic types: active, semi-passive, and passive. To select the proper device, you need to know the differences among these types. Table 10.2 outlines those differences.

RFID tags derive their power either from batteries or from the electromagnetic energy generated by the RFID reader. Tags powered by battery are known as *active tags*. Tags powered by the reader's electromagnetic waves are known as *passive tags*. Finally, tags powered by both battery and the reader are known as *semi-passive tags*. These particular tags use the battery to power their local circuitry, but their

TABLE 10.2   Tag Types and Differences

Tag Type	Power Source	Memory	Communication Range
Active	Battery	Most	Greatest
Semi-Passive	Battery and reader	Moderate	Moderate
Passive	Reader	Least	Least

transmission power comes from the electromagnetic waves in the reader. Their range is slightly greater than a fully passive tag's range because they don't have to consume RF energy for circuitry operations. At the same time, their batteries last longer than those in fully active RFID tags.

Active and semi-passive tags are usually larger than passive tags because they require battery enclosures. For this reason and cost factors, passive tags are generally used for inventory tracking at department stores and such, while active and semi-passive tags are used in more permanent scenarios.

A perfect example of a more permanent scenario for active tags is in the area of equipment tracking. Imagine a scenario where a lawn care company wants to track the equipment used by the different teams automatically. Each open-top trailer would have its own active RFID tag as well as each piece of equipment (mowers, weed eaters, and so on). Each morning a trailer is assigned to a crew and they load it with equipment. As they leave the building, the equipment on the trailer is logged as "going out" with that trailer. In the evening, the equipment is logged as "coming in" with that trailer. Any differences between the outbound and inbound equipment would prompt an alert.

RFID Readers

RFID readers come in different form factors, including handheld devices and mounted devices that can be used to communicate with the tags. Figure 10.1 shows a Compact Flash RFID reader that effectively turns a PDA into a handheld RFID reader.

Mounted devices either include antennas or require the purchase of external antennas. The antenna impacts the reading ranges of these devices, but the usual range is from as short as 18 centimeters up to 30–40 feet with some technologies. The latter is very rare in practical implementations, but a range of several yards is not uncommon.

FIGURE 10.1   Compact Flash RFID reader by Socket Communications

RFID Interface Protocols

For the reader and tags to communicate, they must share a protocol. Tag and reader interface protocols define capabilities and frequencies used. Most new RFID implementations use Generation 2.0 interface protocols. Table 10.3 outlines the different protocols and their pros and cons.

TABLE 10.3   RFID Interface Protocols

Protocol	Frequency	Capabilities	Pros	Cons
Generation 1 Class 0	UHF	Preprogrammed tag; end user cannot write new ID to tag	Lower cost	Cannot be customized
Generation 1 Class 1	UHF and HF	Write once, read many (WORM)	Open standard	Can be written to only once
ISO Standard 18000	LF, HF, and UHF	Write once, read many	Managed standard	Can be written to only once
Generation 2.0 Class 1	HF and UHF	Write once, read many	Globally accepted protocol	Can be written to only once

RFID Applications

There are a number of applications of RFID technology, but this section focuses on three common applications:

- Object tracking
- Inventory management
- Payment systems

Object Tracking

Sometimes you just want to track items at your facility. For example, you might want to track the location of computing devices, books, medical equipment, or other items.

A hospital can put RFID tags on mobile medical devices so they can locate the equipment at any time. By placing RFID readers strategically in hospital hallways, they can track the equipment as it moves throughout the facility and then locate when needed.

RFID tracking devices can also be used with animals such as chickens at egg farms and cattle on cattle ranches and dairies. As the cows enter the milking stalls, RFID readers determine which cow is coming in and then track the amount of milk harvested. This data can then be sent to a central server. In advanced implementations, you can track where the cow goes from there and even determine what it eats and how that affects milk output. These are just some possibilities for using RFID in object tracking.

Inventory Management

Inventory management takes object tracking to the next level. Inventory management, although similar to object tracking, is different in that items leave the facility on a permanent or temporary basis. Retail establishments, such as department stores, or service-type organizations, such as libraries, can benefit from inventory management.

Libraries are prime candidates for using RFID to track objects and perform a form of inventory management. For example, imagine each book has a passive RFID tag in it. Library patrons bring the desired books to the checkout counter and place them near an RFID reader. They then scan their library card (with a magnetic strip—or it could even be RFID-based), and the system automatically checks out the books they've placed near the reader. The patron is notified when this process is complete. As the patron leaves the library with the books, the books are scanned again to verify that they have been properly checked out. If they have, nothing more happens. If not, alarms go off notifying the library personnel of the situation.

While this scenario has problems, such as a person placing a book near another patron's books so it will be checked out on that patron's card, these problems can be overcome by having the user verify the books on a touch screen and making sure the checkout booths are separated by enough distance so they do not interfere with each other. This setup would solve a big security problem faced by many libraries today. Many libraries have implemented self-checkout systems, and they are finding that patrons are checking out some of the books in their pile, but not all of them. Sometimes they bring these books back, but sometimes they are never seen again—at least not by the library. This kind of RFID system would make great strides toward securing self-checkout.

Payment Systems

A final common scenario for RFID is in payment systems. The most common implementation of an RFID-based payment system is toll payment processing. Automobiles carry a device with an RFID tag. The toll booths act as RFID readers. As the car passes through, the reader reads the tag and deducts funds from an account associated with that tag's ID.

Amusement parks that charge for each ride could benefit from an RFID-based system. When patrons enter the park at the beginning of the day, they either provide a credit card or pay in advance for a "certain amount of fun." They are then provided with a wristband with an RFID chip installed. As they enter rides throughout the day, the ride gate, outfitted with a reader, identifies them on a screen and asks if they accept the charge and wish to ride. No ride attendants are needed or magnetic strip cards to swipe.

RFID Implementation Process

The RFID implementation process, like many technical projects, can be broken into the following phases:

- Planning
- Testing
- Implementation
- Production

Planning

When planning your RFID implementation, you should consider at least three parts of your business:

- Business processes
- Physical infrastructures
- Technical infrastructures

Analyze your business processes for areas that can be improved through the use of RFID. Consider warehouses where items are received into or taken out of inventory. Look for internal equipment used in the business process that might need to be checked out and checked in. Common items include LCD projectors, laptops, medical equipment, and industry-specific devices.

As you examine the physical infrastructure, think about how the RF waves will propagate throughout the needed coverage areas. With RFID, you seldom need ranges of more than a few feet, so it's not as big an issue as with Wi-Fi, but you must consider it. Look at the areas where you will create *interrogation zones* (similar to RF cells in Wi-Fi and WiMAX implementations, an interrogation zone is the area where tags are read), and ensure that there is ample space provided for mounting the RF equipment.

Your technical infrastructure must handle the backend data transfer from the readers to the processing service. This infrastructure may be a server simply storing the data in databases or it may be a dedicated processing and decision support device. Either way, ensure you have the technology in place to form the communications link. You must also make sure that power and Ethernet, if needed, are available near the interrogation zones.

Testing

You need to test at least two things before you acquire thousands or millions of RFID tags:

- Can the readers effectively read the tags at the distances and speeds you require?
- Will the readers and tags work in the interrogation zones without interference?

You should also test multiple tags. If you're purchasing thousands or hundreds of thousands of tags, you can save a lot of money by ensuring that you purchase only what you need—but not less than you need.

Implementation

As you implement RFID in your organization, continue testing. Though you've performed a preliminary testing phase, things change throughout the implementation. Many implementations take months and years to complete. As you set up each interrogation zone, you want to perform thorough testing to ensure effective operation.

Another important part of implementation, though sometimes performed post-implementation, is end-user education. Two primary groups need training related to the RFID implementation: administrative personnel and users. The administrative personnel need to know how to manage and troubleshoot the RFID technology. The users just need to know how close an item needs to be in order for the readers to pick it up and information such as this.

Production

Once your RFID system reaches the production stage, you are in maintenance, troubleshooting, and upgrade mode. From time-to-time, you might need to update firmware in RFID readers to take advantage of newer tag capabilities (mostly with active tags), and you might need different tags as your needs change.

RFID and ROI

When implementing any new technology, you must consider the financial impact—negative, positive, or both—on the organization. This means discovering the Return on Investment (ROI). Some RFID implementations are based on mandates from customers or suppliers and others are considered for business advantage. If the latter is the case, compare the long-term costs of RFID as opposed to the costs of printed Universal Product Code (UPC) labels for your organization. When using RFID, consider at least the following cost factors:

- Support staff training
- Hardware costs for readers and testing devices

- Ongoing costs of RFID chips (both the devices and inventory and management costs)
- Software costs for data processing both at implementation and over time
- Site survey costs before installation planning
- Ongoing hardware upgrades and maintenance costs including support staff time

When using UPC labels, you have the following costs:

- Printing the labels or ordering them preprinted
- Implementing and maintaining readers
- Employing humans to read the UPC labels (which might cost more than the RFID tags)
- Software costs for data processing both at implementation and over time

These lists are not exhaustive, and you should brainstorm cost factors for comparisons in your specific projects. In the end, the goal is to be sure that, when a mandate is not in place, RFID is used to achieve a return on investment (ROI).

 There has been much debate of late as to whether RFID provides an ROI or not. This debate has yet to be settled, but you can certainly do your part to get the most out of the technology as you possibly can.

Summary

RFID is a technology that has been with us for a long time—dating back to the 1970s and beyond. For inventory management purposes, RFID has taken on new life as the cost of tags has dropped and the availability of the technology has increased. Today, you can use RFID systems for object tracking, inventory management, and payment processing among other things.

Understanding the different hardware components such as tags, readers, and processing systems is the first step; however, to have a successful implementation, you need to plan, test, and probably test some more. Product selection mistakes early on can cause tremendous increases in costs later in the project.

Key Terms

- ☐ **active tags**
- ☐ **interface protocols**
- ☐ **passive tags**
- ☐ **RFID**
- ☐ **RFID readers**
- ☐ **semi-passive tags**

Review Questions

1. RFID uses what type of technology?

   A. Barcodes

   B. Radio frequency

   C. IrDA

   D. Bluetooth

2. What frequency is used by UHF RFID devices in the U.S.?

   A. 902–928 MHz

   B. 121–124 kHz

   C. 2.4 GHz

   D. 915–928 MHz

3. You want a RFID tag that supports longer distance communications and does not rely on the reader to provide power to the tag. What kind of tag do you need?

   A. Passive tag

   B. Semi-passive tag

   C. Active tag

   D. Powered tag

4. In relation to RFID tags, what does the acronym WORM stand for?

   A. Write once, read many

   B. Wireless operating remote monitors

   C. Wireless operating remote management

   D. Wireless operating radio monitors

5. Which of the following are valid applications of RFID technology? Choose all that apply.

    A. Inventory management

    B. Payment systems

    C. Local area networking

    D. Wide area networking

Review Answers

1. **B.** The RF in RFID stands for radio frequency, and it is certainly used in RFID implementations.

2. **A.** The UHF RFID frequency band is 902–928 MHz.

3. **C.** An active tag has its own battery and does not rely on the reader for any function. Its range is greater than passive tags. Passive tags rely on the reader for power to perform all functions, and semi-passive tags rely on the reader for powering transmission but the battery for powering their own circuitry.

4. **A.** WORM stands for write once, read many. This means that you can write your own serialized number to the RFID tag one time and then read from that tag many times.

5. **A, B.** Both payment processing systems and inventory management systems are examples of valid RFID applications. RFID should not be considered for the implementation of wireless LANS or WANS as range and throughput is too low.

Wireless Security

Wireless# Exam Objectives Covered:

❖ Identify and describe the following wireless LAN security techniques. Describe the installation and configuration of each.

- SSID hiding

- WEP

- WPA-Personal

- WPA2-Personal

- RADIUS

- 802.1x/EAP

- Passphrases

- MAC filtering

- Push-button wireless security

- Virtual private networking

In This Chapter

Wireless Security Threats

Wireless Security Solutions

Security Plans and Policies

If you know how to implement a wireless network, but you lack the ability to secure that network, you may find yourself in a very bad situation. Wireless networks are insecure by default because the default settings on most vendors' devices, particularly SOHO and consumer-grade devices, are open and insecure. New technologies, such as push-button security, are attempts at providing greater security, but they do not serve as good replacements for understanding security in a wireless network.

In this chapter, you'll learn about wireless security threats and vulnerabilities, including an overview of the type of attackers who may attempt to gain access to your network. This chapter also includes coverage of a wireless network's vulnerabilities or exposure points.

Following this discussion, you'll learn about the various solutions to these threats and vulnerabilities. You'll discover how to hide your wireless network from unskilled eyes and how to protect it from the skilled attackers as well. You'll also learn to provide authentication, authorization, and accounting for your network and how to do all three with data integrity and confidentiality.

Finally, this chapter concludes with a brief overview of security policies and plans as well as information to include in these documents. These policies tell you what needs to be done and clearly how to get it done.

The Reality of Security

There are many people who believe an environment can be made secure, and there are others who believe that environmental security can never be accomplished. Still, there are those who take a different approach. They will tell you that security is a process and not an end point.

Taking this latter position allows you to have a level of confidence in your network today and at the same time stay on the alert for new vulnerabilities if you are to have that same confidence about your network in the future. Consider the worms that have spread across the Internet in the last few years.

Code Red was a worm that infected certain types of web servers and operating systems. Months before it was launched, the vendor released a patch that, had it been applied, would have prevented any system from being affected by the Code Red worm. Because hundreds of thousands of systems were infected, I think it is safe to say that many people did not apply the patch.

While you can't assume that all the unpatched systems were the result of thinking that once an environment is made secure it will always be secure, you can certainly say that many cases were likely the result of this thinking. From this, you can further say that, if the idea of security as a process had been paramount, many of these machines would have been patched and Code Red would have done little or no damage to them.

This criticism is not meant to minimize the problems created by systems being implemented and supported by nonprofessionals. Many of the systems attacked by Code Red were undoubtedly set up and maintained by people who didn't really understand the security or operations of the system. With wireless technologies, this is also a tremendous problem.

Code Red was just one scenario and there have been many others like it. As long as the idea holds that a system or environment can be made secure and that once secured it will always be secure, security breaches such as Code Red will occur. Support professionals are responsible for staying informed about newer security problems and changing configurations, updating firmware, or patching systems as needed.

You might say that there are no secure systems, if you define *being secure* as *being impenetrable*. However, you can also define a secure system as one having an *acceptable level of risk*. If you hold to this definition, you secure a system based on risk levels. Either way, security is a process, and you must maintain vigilance to reduce the likelihood of attack within your organization and wireless implementations.

It is this security-as-a-process mindset that has given birth to a large new industry—*patch management*. It is sometimes called *update management* as well. An example of patch or update management is the Software Update Services (SUS) from Microsoft. With this technology in place, you can apply patches to all your Windows servers and clients on an automated basis. You should consider this and other similar tools to help maintain the security of your environment. Just like a wired network, wireless network security can be breached if a configured client is breached.

I don't want to cause any confusion, so let me be clear: Microsoft only plans to support SUS until December 1, 2006. After that time, you will have to upgrade to Windows Server Update Services (WSUS sometimes just called WUS) to continue support. Among other things, WSUS now integrates with Microsoft SQL Server for data storage. As of August 4, 2005, SUS cannot be downloaded.

FIGURE 11.1   The Process of security

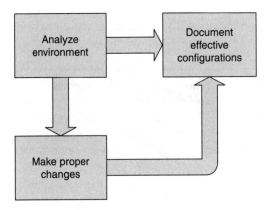

Whether the security process is automated with update and patch management software or performed manually by administrative staff, you must analyze your environment and then make changes, if necessary, and document effective configurations. Figure 11.1 illustrates this process flow. This diagram shows that you will not always need to make changes, but you must continue monitoring the environment and applying changes when needed. Documentation of your security-related configuration is very important; this helps consultants and other employees better understand how your systems are configured.

The Attackers

The term *hacker* has become synonymous with "bad person who wants to get into my computer or network." Among security professionals, a hacker is a "good person who really knows computers," and the term *cracker* is used to reference an attacker with ill intent. However, if you talk about a cracker in front of a nontechnology professional, they might not know what you are referencing. They expect to hear the term *hacker* because it's what they hear and read in the media.

Whether you use the common term *hacker* or the in-the-know term *cracker,* the reality is that understanding the attacker can help you protect against him or her. In this book, I divide attackers into three categories: wannabes, gonnabes, and killerbes.

 For purposes of the Wireless# exam, you do not need to know about these three categories of attackers. However, this categorization helps you analyze the potential threats to your environment and understand how you can protect against them.

Wannabes

The wannabes like to think of themselves as crackers. Usually, they are not extremely technical, but they can use a search engine and follow step-by-step instructions. Believe it or not, these attackers are the most dangerous to you if you do not hold to the notion of security being a process. The reason is the way these attackers decide on their targets. They generally attack anyone who is vulnerable to a known attack. In other words, they are not attacking with directed malicious intent; they just noticed you were vulnerable. If you do not keep your systems up-to-date, they are vulnerable to attack from wannabes.

The process they follow goes something like this:

1. The wannabe finds a script on a website that they can use to discover known vulnerabilities in network systems.
2. He downloads the script and runs it against a block of IP addresses.
3. The report tells him the IP addresses that are vulnerable to the attacks for which he has attack scripts.
4. He runs the proper attack scripts.

As you can see, this attacker does not need to have technical proficiency beyond the ability to run scripts. Frankly, I could teach my mother-in-law to do what they do in about one week (no offense intended, mom). These attackers are also known as *script kiddies* (*skript kiddiez* is also used) or *ankle biters* for this very reason.

The only real protection you have from these kinds of attackers is to implement proper security mechanisms and keep your systems up-to-date with the most recent patches. For those systems that are no longer supported, such as Windows NT 3.5, ensure they are not accessible from the Internet so they cannot be breached.

Gonnabes

The gonnabe has technical proficiency. I like to call them gonnabes because they work for a positive intent and have the true skills of a hacker. They are sometimes called *white hat hackers,* a phrase borrowed from the old westerns where a cowboy wearing a white hat was the good guy and the cowboy wearing the black hat was the bad guy.

These attackers are not a threat because they do not attack networks that don't want them to attempt an attack. They may be "for hire hackers," but they do not attack promiscuously like the wannabes or the next group, the killerbes. This group sometimes attacks vendor hardware and software in their own systems to determine where vulnerabilities might exist, but they do not attack Internet-connected systems or private networks that have not authorized the attack.

Some have coined the term *grey hat hackers* for gonnabes who have possibly crossed the line. These are hackers who discover vulnerabilities and do not just inform the vendor of the security risk but also the media. Some in the field consider this improper behavior and others suggest it is appropriate. For this reason, these gonnabes have become known as *grey hats.*

Today, there are certifications for people who want to be gonnabes. The Certified Ethical Hacker and Certified Penetration Testing certifications are just a couple. Certified gonnabes are often called security auditors, security testers, security assessors, penetration testers, or ethical hackers.

Killerbes

This category is the most skilled and malicious group. Unlike the wannabe, the killerbe knows what they are doing. They are equal in skill to the gonnabe, but they use their skills to attack networks and systems that have not requested a penetration test. They might steal corporate information (a wannabe might do this, too, but they are easier to protect against because of their lower skill level) or prevent access to systems and data needed to operate your business.

The likelihood of an attack on a SOHO or small business network from a killerbe is much less than from a wannabe. This is why you prevent the vast majority of attacks by applying simple security guidelines. These basic security measures prevent a wannabe from getting access to your network, but they do not prevent a killerbe from getting in. To secure your system against attack from a killerbe, you need to implement greater levels of security and train your employees in the basics of social engineering, dumpster-diving, and other human-related attacks.

 You should be aware of the fact that wannabes now have a source that teaches them—step-by-step—how to perform a social engineering attack without having to learn anything about human psychology. This is due, in large part, to the book by cracker Kevin Mitnick, *The Art of Deception*. I generally encourage security professionals to read this book so they can gain a better understanding of this concept. You should also know that this book is in the hands of many wannabes.

I like to think that most skilled hackers are in the gonnabe category (this belief is reflected in Figure 11.2), but this is just a hope that I hold to as there is no actual count. If you implement standard security recommendations for your wireless network, you protect yourself from the vast majority of attackers (wannabes). Then, consider your level of risk for corporate espionage or

FIGURE 11.2   The hacker pyramid

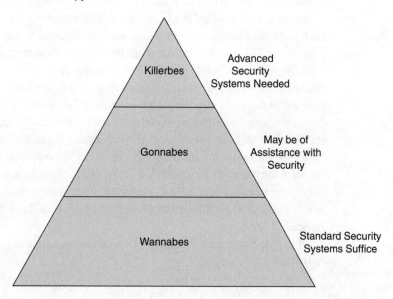

malicious attacks (killerbes) and implement advanced security systems as needed. You might even consider hiring a penetration tester (gonnabes) to verify that you are unlikely to be injured by a malicious attack.

Threats and Vulnerabilities

Threats include the individuals or groups who wish to attack your network and the systems they use to perform the attacks. *Vulnerabilities* are the points where your system is weak and able to be penetrated. You must consider both to implement an effective wireless solution.

Some vulnerabilities are wireless-specific and others are general to all networking types. While most of this chapter focuses on wireless-specific vulnerabilities, I cover other attack points at a high-level as they can provide access to the configuration interfaces of your wireless devices. The first concept you must understand to provide security for your wireless network is the concept of the *attack surface*.

Attack Surface

The attack surface is inclusive of all areas that can potentially be attacked. *Attack surface reduction* is the process of reducing the number of areas where your system can be attacked. This process is in line with the principle of security-as-a-process because attack surface reduction acknowledges that a system cannot have an attack surface reduced to zero and still provide a functional benefit to the organization. Attack surface reduction is about reducing the likelihood of attack by reducing the number of attack points. You can sum it up like this: *If you do not need a particular technology or capability for some beneficial business purpose, do not use it.* John Michael Stewart shared with me an excellent analogy for this concept. Think of it like the booth at the fair where you throw the darts at the balloons. The smaller balloons warrant a bigger prize (the gigantic Elmo for my four year old) because they are harder to hit due to the reduced surface area. In the same way, your network is harder to penetrate when you reduce the attack surface. So go ahead and let the air out of your network's balloon by disabling unneeded services.

There are two general entry points to your wireless devices: wireless entry and wired entry.

Wireless Entry

The wireless attack surface includes all access points, wireless routers, wireless bridges, and other wireless devices. You need to ensure that proper security mechanisms are in place to help prevent unauthorized access through these entry points. One common attack point is a rogue access point. Even well-meaning users can install these points when they want wireless access or a different kind of wireless access in their work area. They don't mean to harm the network, but the default configuration of these devices make them an easy target.

To prevent wireless attacks, you should implement best practices for wireless security. Best practices include hiding the SSID, using encryption, and securing the administration interface. In more advanced implementations, consider the use of 802.1x and EAP for authentication and encryption, which generally involves a centralized authentication, authorization, and accounting server (RADIUS).

Wired Entry

The wired entry point is often overlooked when configuring wireless networks. To understand the impact of this oversight, consider the use of a standard access point. These devices have at least two interfaces: the Ethernet port and the wireless interface. The Ethernet port can be used to access the access point and modify configuration settings, providing an easy attack surface for an attacker.

Imagine an individual slips into a conference room or side office in your small business. This individual pulls out a small footprint tablet PC and connects it to the Ethernet port in the office. Immediately, the attacker notices the LED lights indicating that the port is most likely active. The attacker opens a command prompt and types the command **ipconfig /renew** to see if a DHCP server is available on the network. An IP configuration set comes down to the tablet PC, and the results are displayed on the screen. The attacker now has an IP address on your network.

The next step is to begin looking for devices to access on the network. After a brief scan with a scanning utility, the attacker detects more than 30 active devices. The attacker runs a script that tries to connect to port 80 using HTTP on all the discovered devices (this port is the one used by most web servers). Two of the IP addresses respond positively to the script. The attacker assumes these are infrastructure devices that can be configured through a web interface or that they are actual web servers.

FIGURE 11.3 Access point login screen

One of the two IP addresses that responded positively to the script was 192.168.0.250. The attacker opens the web browser and directs it to the IP address only to see the screen shown in Figure 11.3. Noticing the *Linksys WAP54G* name in the dialog, the attacker remembers that the default logon for this device is no username and the password of *admin*. The attacker attempts this logon and in a moment is looking at the configuration interface for the access point.

This security attack was made worse because the default administrative logon for the access point had not been changed, but if the principles of attack surface reduction had been employed, the attacker wouldn't have been able to reach the access point in the first place. Attack surface reduction, applied to this scenario, demands that the Ethernet port in the spare office be disabled until it is needed. With the port disabled, the attacker could not have used the port to obtain an IP address and then reach the access point to reconfigure it.

Data Flow

Data flow analysis is the analysis of data as it enters, traverses, and is removed from your network. You aren't concerned with the departure point from the network in most wireless implementations, though it is an important concern with security in general and you should consider it as part of your complete security policy and plan.

For wireless networking security, I focus on the flow of data from four perspectives: the data entry point, network traversal, live storage points, and backup storage points.

Entry Point

The data entry point is the beginning of the flow of data. This point is where the user enters the data initially. It might be a laptop computer, desktop computer, or even a web-based interface traveling across the Internet. In any case, you must focus on how the device connects to the network that is responsible for transferring the data from the client to the network. If this is a wireless connection, you must consider how to secure this data.

The level of security needed depends on the type of data. If the only thing you ever use the computer for is Internet access, you might not need advanced security techniques, such as VPN connections and 802.1x/EAP authentication. Access to secure sites should be encrypted with SSL and insecure sites should not need encryption beyond that provided by WPA or WPA2 (I'll cover these later). You might categorize your data into three basic levels of data sensitivity:

- Public
- Private
- Highly private

Public data is data that anyone can see and access. You might want to limit the ability of users to modify the data, but viewing the data is not a concern. If a client uses only public data, you do not need to be as concerned about the security of the connection and standard wireless security practices should suffice.

Private data is data that should be seen only by organizational employees and members, such as human resource information, nonsensitive trade secrets, and other data not needed by the public. The assumption is that any internal individual should be able to view this data at a minimum. You generally use standard wireless security practices and, in some situations, more advanced wireless security mechanisms for this type of data.

Highly private data is described as information that only a select few should see. This data almost always requires advanced security mechanisms such as VPN tunnel requirements for all wireless connections transferring this data and possibly the use of certificates and a PKI (public key infrastructure).

As you can see, the kind of data determines how you protect that data. The underlying issue is the value of the data. Publicly available data is not usually as valuable as data viewed only by limited personnel in your organization. Think of it like this: you wouldn't spend $100 to protect a common modern penny, and you wouldn't spend thousands on security equipment and software to protect data that is worth very little.

This section is not intended as complete coverage of data sensitivity analysis. There are many factors to consider and you should contemplate all the ways in which your data is used in order to provide proper security mechanisms. For more information in this area, check out the book *Network Security: The Complete Reference* by Mark Rhodes-Ousley, Roberta Bragg, and Keith Strassberg (McGraw-Hill/Osborne 2003).

Network Traversal

Once the data leaves the transfer device communicating with the network, it traverses the network and passes through many devices along the way. During this data flow, travel can be interrupted and the data viewed by an attacker if the traversal points are not secured properly. Part of data flow analysis is investigating these connection points and the medium between the connection points.

For our purposes, we are concerned with the wireless medium. Investigate these areas for security vulnerabilities and protect against attacks as much as possible. Consider the network represented in Figure 11.4. Assume that the user enters data in the wireless laptop client and that data is then transferred to the database server on the network.

There are two wireless traversal points. The first is between the wireless laptop client and the access point connected to the wired network. The second is between the two wireless bridges connecting the two wired networks. Both of these wireless connections need to be secured to provide complete security to the data flow. If you enable WPA2-Personal on the access point, but do nothing to secure the wireless bridges, your data, though secure while traveling between the laptop and network, would be at risk while traveling between the bridges. Bridges usually have a narrower RF propagation pattern, but an attacker can still position their device between the two bridges and sniff the traffic from the air.

The concept of *sniffing* the traffic means to pull the packets into your device even though they might not be intended for you. There are many wireless network sniffers (more formally known as network monitors, packet analyzers, or protocol analyzers) available for free. There are also powerful commercial tools available. Do not assume that attackers cannot acquire the powerful commercial tools because of the high cost. Attackers acquire the tools through newsgroups, IRC chat, peer networks, or other sources of *warez,* which is the cracker term often used for pirated software.

FIGURE 11.4   Network traversal diagram

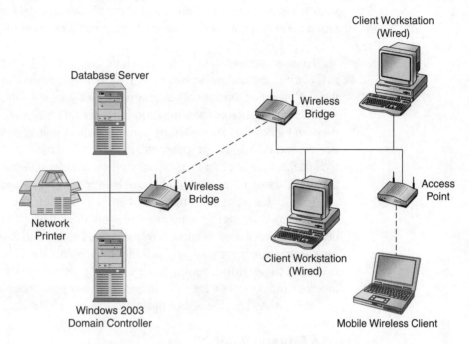

The main purpose of network traversal analysis is to ensure that eavesdroppers cannot gain access to your data easily. You must encrypt the data because you cannot prevent the attacker from pulling the data packets from the air or RF medium. By encrypting the packets, you ensure that, even though attackers can acquire the packets, they cannot view the internal data easily. This precaution helps secure data in transit only, however, and does not protect against data theft during storage, which is discussed next.

Live Storage Point

After the data has traveled the network to its final destination, it is processed in some way. In many cases, the data is stored in *live storage*. Live storage is data stored in a location that can be accessed instantly by authorized users. There are, at minimum, two points of access where this data must be secured: the network and the storage device. When you encrypt the communications between a client device and an access point, you ensure that eavesdroppers can't view the data easily. However, if attackers discover the configuration parameters needed to associate and authenticate with the access point, they can access the network. While discovering these parameters does not give attackers immediate access to the data other wireless clients are transferring with RF technology, it might allow them to view the data as it enters the wired network or, as is the concern here, give them the ability to access the data in live storage.

To protect against the scenario where attackers discover a method for associating and authenticating with your wireless network (in other words, they've breached the network access portion of your security), you should use secure authorization at the point of live storage on the storage device. Create users and groups, as supported by your network operating system or storage device, and then assign proper permissions to those users and groups. Because the attackers are not members of one of these groups and/or are not one of these individuals, they should not be able to access the data.

To truly secure against this kind of attack, you need to understand the security mechanisms of your chosen network operating system or device in depth. You don't need to know how to do this for the Wireless# exam, but you must learn to do it for your production implementations. This understanding is critical to providing complete security to your network because skilled attackers often escalate their privileges once they gain access to the network— this means they become one of those users accessing the data.

Backup Storage Point

The final point of attack is the storage media you use for data backup. Many organizations use physical backup devices that are connected directly to the live storage device. Sometimes organizations transfer the data across the network to an external backup device. In these scenarios, just as when securing the wireless laptop client connections earlier, you must ensure that the traversal path is secure by securing all wireless links in the path.

Wireless Vulnerabilities

There are many vulnerabilities and attack methods unique to wireless networks and some shared with wired configurations. Understanding these attack methods reveals what you are protecting against and how you must go about it. In this section, I cover the most common wireless attack methods, including

- War driving
- Denial of Service
- Eavesdropping

- Hijacking
- Unauthorized use
- Rogue access points
- Humans

War Driving

War driving has become a hobby to some and a devious starting point of attack for others. *War driving* refers to the act of driving slowly through a residential, commercial, or industrial area looking for available wireless networks. Some war drivers even use a GPS unit with their laptop to map precise locations of wireless networks and track whether they are open (no encryption) or closed (encrypted) for future reference.

A common tool used by war drivers, but one that is beneficial to network administrators as well, is the NetStumbler program (see Figure 11.5). This program picks up available wireless networks and shows if they are using encryption, the channel on which they are communicating, and other useful information nuggets for the casual or advanced attacker.

War driving is not just about driving around, however. Sometimes attackers park in your driveway or parking lot to see what they can access. Others walk around (obviously common with teenage attackers who cannot drive)

FIGURE 11.5   NetStumbler

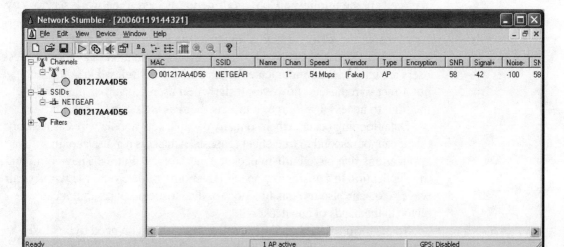

FIGURE 11.6   TrendNet Wi-Fi locator

with PDAs and Wi-Fi detectors to see what they can find. Figure 11.6 shows a Wi-Fi detector that allows you to find wireless networks without drawing much attention to yourself. For this reason, and the fact that they can often plug into USB ports to act as access points or wireless clients, these devices have become very popular in the war-driving community.

Denial of Service

A Denial of Service (DoS) attack can be launched against a wireless network in a number of ways. These include:

- Data flooding
- Standards vulnerabilities
- RF signal senerators

As its name implies, a *DoS attack* denies access to network services by valid client devices. This prevents users from performing productive work on the network. A DoS attack is illustrated in Figure 11.7. In this figure, an attacker has flooded the network with so much information that other wireless users are unable to communicate. In most cases, a wireless DoS attack does not affect wired users; however, if the wired users go across the wireless medium to access a resource, it affects them as well.

Data flooding occurs when so many data packets flood a wireless network that it cannot respond to true client requests. Attackers can use certain software applications that have built-in packet generators to do this. They command the application to transfer any specified amount of data onto the wireless air waves. You can also use this function for diagnostic purposes, but it can wreak havoc in the hands of an attacker.

To perform a data flooding attack such as this, you need to be close to the access point and have a high-powered client device (output power

FIGURE 11.7   Denial of Service attack

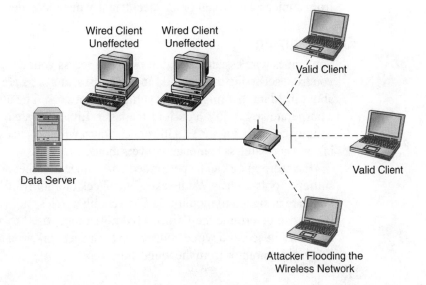

should be great) that allows your client to "drown out" any other clients on the network. This DoS attack is "wireless only" because the wireless client device performing the attack cannot take over the wired network (if the wired network is designed properly anyway) with a simple data flood such as this. Using quality of service features, the switching and routing mechanisms could override such an attack on the wired side. However, this attack method can effectively block acceptable wireless communications for the other wireless clients connected to the same access point.

Another method of creating a DoS attack is by exploiting the standard's vulnerabilities. For example, part of the security mechanism in WPA is to turn off the radio in the access point if more than two specially formed errant packets arrive at the access point within a certain time window. This behavior is normal in order to prevent certain types of attacks; however, it provides the opportunity to perform a DoS attack as well. The attacker can intentionally send these specially formed packets and shoot down the access point.

The third method of executing a DoS attack is to use an RF signal generator. These devices flood the entire frequency spectrum with RF energy in an area, which causes valid RF communications to fail. You should not assume an attack is under way if you detect RF signal generation in your environment, however. The signals could be coming from a microwave oven or an "accidentally installed" device.

Eavesdropping

Sometimes wireless attackers don't want to access your network or prevent you from accessing the network. In these cases, attackers are often just curious about the data that might be traveling the network. The attacker might be a corporate spy or just a curious teenager. Either way, eavesdropping is a security concern. Figure 11.8 illustrates how a wireless attacker might "listen in" on your wireless computer conversations.

Eavesdropping can be performed with either Ethernet or wireless-specific sniffers. Tools such as WildPackets' AiroPeek or Tamo Soft's CommView for WiFi are designed to monitor data traversing wireless networks specifically. If you can determine the IP block (address range) used by wireless clients and you can access a wired connection to the network, you can use a tool like Ethereal to monitor from the wired side.

Hijacking

Hijacking occurs when an attacker takes over a valid user's session on the wireless network. Using a signal generator on the frequency of the valid access

FIGURE 11.8   Eavesdropping

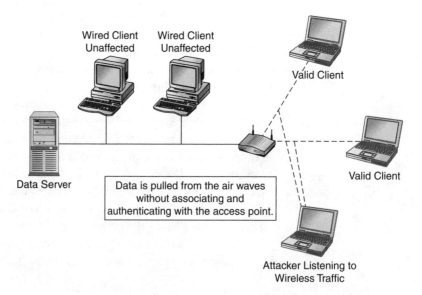

Wired Client
Unaffected

Wired Client
Unaffected

Valid Client

Data Server

Data is pulled from the air waves
without associating and
authenticating with the access point.

Valid Client

Attacker Listening to
Wireless Traffic

point, the attacker causes the client to disconnect from with the access point. The attacker, however, has another access point (or computer with a software-based access point) configured just like the valid access point (same SSID and/or encryption settings) closer to the client and on a different channel. The client finds this access point and connects to it thinking that it is a valid device. The attacker can now begin to launch attacks against or through the client device.

At first, you might not see how an attacker could launch an attack through the hijacked client since it is no longer connected to the proper network, but there is at least one scary possibility. The attacker can push a worm or virus to the hijacked client and then turn off his or her temporary access point. This will cause the client to reconnect to the proper network and, if network-wide anti-virus is not in use, spread the worm or virus across the entire network: wireless and wired.

Unauthorized Use

Unauthorized use can range from basic access to the Internet to more troublesome situations such as accessing sensitive internal data. Unauthorized use begins by first launching another type of attack against the network to discover WEP keys or WPA pass-phrases. In other words, if you provide good security, unauthorized access attacks are harder to achieve and you can worry less about data theft or network misuse.

Rogue Access Points

A rogue access point is a wireless networking device, installed by an unauthorized user, that has been configured to act as an access point. These devices can be installed maliciously or innocently. Either way, they can cause serious security problems.

Users may install an access point because they become impatient waiting for the IT group to implement a wireless network for them. These delays are often caused by security concerns or a lack of understanding of the users' needs among the IT professionals. There are also valid reasons for not installing a wireless network. In any case, the access point installed by the end user is unlikely to be secured properly.

If an attacker installs a rogue access point, it is probably for one of two reasons: to give them access to the Internet through your wired network (this happens a lot in hotels that have Internet in their business office, which is not secured but is not wireless) or to attack the wireless clients on your network. When the attacker gives themselves wireless Internet access, it is a twofold problem. First of all, they might perform illegal acts across this connection and it will appear that you perpetrated the acts. Second, if they do not secure the access point, your users might be able to access the Internet while bypassing your usual Internet filtering rules.

Whatever the reason for the installation of a rogue access point, and regardless of who does it, it can be a potentially large problem. For this reason, use a tool such as NetStumbler periodically to discover any unauthorized access points on your network. More expensive automatic detection tools might not be cost-effective for SOHOs and small businesses and certainly not for home users.

Humans

The final point of vulnerability, whether using wired or wireless networking, is the humans who utilize your network. Through social engineering or dumpster-diving, attackers can gather a lot of information about your organization. Both social engineering and dumpster-diving are caused by human vulnerability.

Social engineering is the act of manipulating users into providing information they should not provide. For example, let's say you sent an email to users who have a desktop computer and a laptop with step-by-step instructions for configuring their laptop for wireless network access. An attacker might guess that the user has such a document and call saying that she (the attacker) is from the support group and needs to verify that they have received the proper instructions. The attacker can proceed to have the user read the WPA pass-phrase from the document, and she now has access to the wireless network. This is just one example of how social engineering might work. Figure 11.9 illustrates this concept.

People often throw papers out without thinking about their contents. Some documents may contain wireless SSIDs, passwords, WEP keys, or other information that can help an attacker gain access to your network. Dumpster-diving often reveals many such documents.

Both of these issues can be addressed only through user education. There is no software program that you can implement, but you can implement enforced policies that discourage users from giving out information. Random audits (fake phone calls to see what users might reveal) can be utilized, but be cautious as privacy rights should not be violated.

FIGURE 11.9   Social engineering

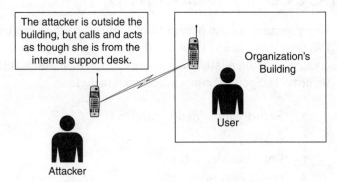

Layered Security
==================

As you can see from the information provided up to this point, a single security mechanism is seldom enough to provide true security to your environment. This is why *layered security,* or *defense-in-depth,* is so important. Layered security gives you the peace of mind that comes from knowing that even if attackers penetrate one layer, they have yet another to get through. If that layer is penetrated, there is still another, and so on. Figure 11.10 illustrates this concept. If the attacker does gain the information needed to configure their machine for WPA or WPA2 authentication, he still has to have a network user account. Even if he accomplishes this, it may not be the right user account for acquiring the data the attacker is after. This layered security approach helps greatly reduce the likelihood of data loss in many situations.

FIGURE 11.10   Layered security

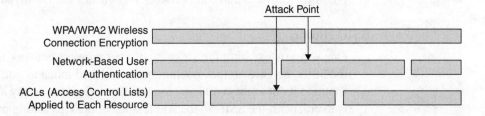

General Security Measures

Every technology can benefit from some of the most basic security concepts. Wireless technology is not any different and in this section, I review these concepts and then talk about specific implementations related to wireless security. The general concepts covered include

- Security through obscurity
- AAA
- Data confidentiality
- Data integrity
- Physical security

Security Through Obscurity

The concept of security through obscurity is a reference to securing the network by making it less visible. I prefer to say "less visible" instead of "hidden" because the network is not really hidden. Think of it as being similar to this statement:

> I was unable to see everything because my view was obscured by the prison bars.

This might be a comment made by an attacker who infiltrates a network and is later caught. The comment might be made as he is trying to watch a prison-yard football game through his cell window (we can hope for justice—right?). Notice that the term *obscure* means to partially prevent viewing. Even the Merriam-Webster Online dictionary (found at www.webster.com) defines obscure as "shrouded in or hidden by darkness; not clearly seen or easily distinguished; not easily understood or clearly expressed; or relatively unknown." From this set of definitions, you can see that security through obscurity means to make the network less visible and not invisible.

SSID Hiding

One way you can limit the visibility of your wireless network is to hide the SSID. You are, in fact, not hiding the SSID so much as you just aren't shouting it out to the world any longer. The default for nearly all access points is to broadcast the SSID to the wireless network. This setting means that any device can see the SSID. Most access points also allow you to disable SSID broadcasting, which helps obscure your network. Figure 11.11 shows the

FIGURE 11.11   Disabling SSID broadcasting

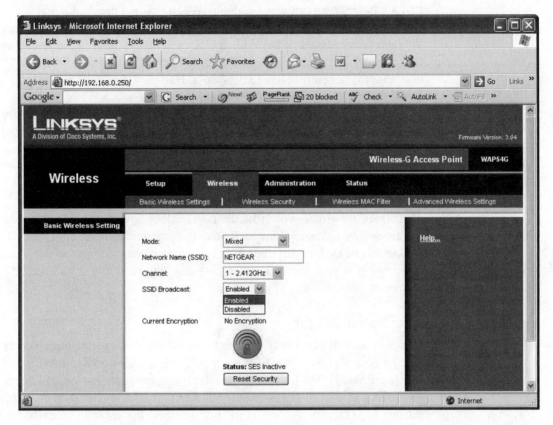

interface that allows you to disable SSID broadcasting in a Linksys WAP54G access point.

Disabling SSID broadcasting does not prevent a skilled attacker from getting the SSID of your network. Generally, consumer-grade access points do not truly let you disable SSID delivery. A skilled attacker can send specific packets onto the wireless air waves that make the access point respond with its SSID. Also, clients may send their SSID in unencrypted packets depending on other network configuration settings. For this reason, disabling SSID broadcasting is not considered a total security solution, as your network is not truly hidden (see why I say it is *obscured*?) from skilled eyes.

At the same time, disabling SSID broadcasting can prevent casual access attempts on your network. Recently, I was at an intersection in a small town near my home and my Pocket PC began beeping to alert me that a wireless network was available. When I pulled the Pocket PC out of my pocket (that's a good place for it, eh?), I noticed that the SSID was PO, and I was parked right beside a U.S. post office. While I did not access that network (which was not protected by encryption), I had to wonder how many others might have accessed it. Had they disabled the SSID broadcasting, this event would not have occurred.

In addition to disabling the broadcast of the SSID, you should change the SSID. If you disable the broadcast of the SSID, but do not change it from the default, hackers can simply scan for known SSIDs (like Netgear or Linksys) to try connecting. Use something that is not obvious. In other words, don't use your company or department name. Something along the lines of **B178CRX** usually makes a good SSID. Remember that this alone does not protect you from the best hacker; however, it does provide the needed evidence to show malicious intent from the beginning (the hacker had to hack to discover the network much less connect to it) as you can prove that your network is not an "open" network that anyone could mistakenly connect to.

Limiting Power Output

A second way of obscuring your network is by lowering the output power of your access points and client devices. Some devices do not provide this functionality, but for those that do, turning down the power can be an effective way of limiting cell size and, therefore, the ability from attackers outside your facility to connect to your network. For those devices that do not provide for output power adjustments, consider moving the access point to an area where it provides coverage for your users but is farthest from parking lots or other areas where a hacker might easily try to gain access.

AAA—Authentication, Authorization, and Accounting

A common principle in the world of information and computer security is the concept of *Triple-A,* also called "the three As," three-A, or written as "AAA." This concept suggests that a secure system should include authentication, authorization, and accounting.

Authentication

Authentication is the process that verifies the identity of a person or device. Authentication is later used by the authorization process to determine what the user or device should be allowed to access. There are three basic types of authentication: something you know, something you have, and something you are.

Something you know is information. The most common forms of authentication are passwords and PIN (personal identification number) codes. Because you can write this information down or easily give it to others, it is not considered the most secure authentication mechanism. Attempts at making passwords more secure include requiring longer passwords, requiring case-sensitive passwords, requiring the use of multiple character types (numbers, letters and symbols), and requiring frequent changing of passwords. If every user on the network abides by strict password rules such as these, and they never write them down, you might be able to provide an acceptable level of authentication for low security environments. Because you are not likely to achieve this, passwords are not generally used in medium to high security environments. For small businesses, they often are sufficient.

The next level of secure authentication is something you have. This might be a key or a smart card. These devices are generally considered more secure than passwords because you cannot "guess" a smart card and if a user gives his smart card to another user, he cannot be authenticated until he gets it back. This keeps many users from passing around the authentication device. The reality is that smart cards are generally more secure than passwords because most implementations require two-factor authentication. You insert the smart card and then enter a code to gain access. Because the card can be stolen easily, avoid an implementation that does not require a code.

The most secure level of authentication is usually granted to the something you are category. These are biometrics authentication devices. Today, biometric devices (particularly thumb scanners) are much less expensive than in the past, making them a common replacement for smart card implementations. Biometrics are considered more secure because you cannot give your thumb to another user (at the very least, it would be really painful). The reality is that many thumb-scanner authentication systems also require a password or PIN, providing two-factor authentication for greater security. To fool a biometrics system, you need to know more than you need to know to fool a smart card reader (you won't actually fool the reader, you just steal the smart card). If you are concerned about security and authentication, consider *three-factor authentication* (password, smart card, and biometrics). And in the most sensitive scenarios, you can even require multiuser three-factor authentication, but that goes way beyond what is needed in most environments.

Authorization

Authorization is the process of validating the right of an authenticated user to perform some action or access some resource. Authorization is usually provided through the use of *access control lists* (ACLs). An ACL contains a list of users or groups and the rights they have in relation to the associated network or resource. Properly configured ACLs go a long way toward providing the network security you need in a wireless or wired implementation.

Authorization is also the point where you consider the *principle of least privilege,* which simply states that an individual should not have any more capabilities on the network than are needed to perform the role she has been assigned. You should also consider the concept of *separation of duties.* For example, the person who can clear the accounting logs (the record of password resets and user account creation) cannot manage user accounts and the person who can manage user accounts cannot clear the accounting logs. This forces collusion between the two if an account password is changed (to access some resource as that individual) without a record of the change being maintained. Of course, to implement separation of duties requires the assistance of a trusted third party who can set up your environment in this way. If I configure all this myself, I can always go back and change it.

Accounting

The final element of the AAA concept is *accounting* (also known as *auditing* or *monitoring*). Accounting means logging the actions of users and devices on the network. Accounting can be centralized, as with a RADIUS server, or decentralized, as with the built-in logs in access points and vendor servers. The benefit of logging user and device activity is that you can view the logs later to determine what happened when a security incident occurs on your network. Another possibly greater benefit is that you can monitor the logs continually to detect security incidents as they are happening. You would use security log monitoring software to do this, otherwise it would take too much of your time to do it manually.

Data Confidentiality

Much of the data that traverses your network is sensitive. And although some of the data is not as sensitive, it still shouldn't be seen by unauthorized viewers. Protecting this data through encryption mechanisms provides for the security service of *confidentiality.* Providing confidentiality to data communications systems has become a top priority of many organizations, and most wireless vendors offer some mechanism you can implement to provide this service. Encryption has been available for many years and is a concept you should understand at a high-level if you wish to implement secure networks. You only need to understand encryption at an in-depth level if you need to program encryption algorithms or create new encryption algorithms altogether.

The process of converting data from its normal state to an unreadable state is known as *encryption*. The unreadable state is known as *ciphertext* (or *cipherdata*), and the readable state is *plaintext* (or *plaindata*). The normal way to encrypt something is to pass the data through an algorithm using a key for variable results. For example, let's say you want to protect the number 108. Here is an algorithm for protecting numeric data:

$$original\ data\ /\ crypto\ key + (3 * crypto\ key)$$

Using this algorithm with a key of 6, you come up with this:

$$108 / 6 + (3 \times 6) = 36$$

To recover the original data, you must know both the algorithm and the key. The formula for recovery is the reverse of the previous formula:

$$(36 - 3 \times 6) * 6 = 108$$

Any key fed into the algorithm generates a result; however, only the proper key generates the proper results. For example, if you take the key of 7 and pass it through the algorithm, you get the result 105, which is not correct. Needless to say, modern crypto algorithms are much more complex than this, and the keys are much longer, but this example gives you a good foundation for a basic understanding of how encryption works.

Encryption algorithms are used to secure the connection between wireless clients and access points in wireless networks. They are also used between wireless infrastructure devices such as wireless bridges. With wireless access points, encryption is often disabled by default and it is up to you to enable it. Because many IP-based protocols send information as clear text, it is important that you enable some kind of encryption to protect this information.

The two common types of encryption are *symmetric* and *asymmetric*. Symmetric encryption uses the same key to decrypt the data as was used to encrypt the data. This encryption is sometimes called *shared secret* encryption. Asymmetric encryption uses one key to encrypt the data and another key to decrypt the data. This is usually referred to as *public key encryption* because one key is known as the public key and the other is known as the private key. The term *public key infrastructure* (PKI) refers to the distribution and management of these public and private encryption keys.

You do not need to be a master of encryption technology to pass the Wireless# exam or to implement a small or medium-sized wireless network; however, you should consider becoming more familiar with encryption than the space here allows. I suggest the fine books *Applied Cryptography: Protocols, Algorithms, and Source Code in C, Second Edition* by Bruce Schneier (John Wiley & Sons 1996) or the *CISSP All-in-One Exam Guide, Second Edition* by Shon Harris (McGraw-Hill/Osborne 2003), the former being an in-depth resource on cryptography and the latter being an all-around review of security including excellent chapters on encryption.

Data Integrity

A concept closely related to confidentiality is *data integrity*. Data integrity provides for mechanisms to validate that data has not been modified during transfer. For example, you want to verify that a document transferred to you from another user was not intercepted by an attacker and modified before you received it. You perform this validation with data integrity algorithms.

These data integrity algorithms are usually called *hashing algorithms*. They are one-way mathematical algorithms that generate a fixed-length number regardless of the data size fed into the algorithm. The result of the algorithm is the *hash of the data* or the *message digest*. If the hash of a message is the same after a transmission as it was before the transmission, the data has not been modified maliciously or accidentally. The basic process used to verify the integrity of the data is outlined in the flow diagram shown in Figure 11.12.

FIGURE 11.12   Data integrity analysis process

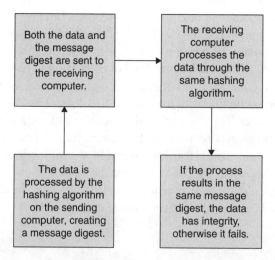

One protocol that supports data integrity and is often used in virtual private networks is IPSec. IPSec is the IP Security protocol used to provide security to IP-based networks. It allows for message confidentiality, integrity, and authentication (also referred to as *nonrepudiation* in this case).

Physical Security

A final general security principle that is absolutely essential to wireless networks is physical security. If an attacker can get inside your building or in the case of wireless networking, close to it, they can often gain access to your network. By providing physical security, you limit the potential for attack.

Some organizations place security cameras around and within the facility to provide centralized monitoring of access to the campus and building. Active monitoring helps prevent many wireless attacks such as eavesdropping and unauthorized access.

Secured entry ways are another physical security mechanism that may be useful. Employees and valid users scan a card (smart card or magnetic strip) to gain access to the facility. You could also use RFID devices that are distributed to employees to grant them access. These methods prevent unauthorized users from getting into the building.

You should also consider the physical security of your wireless network devices. I am continually amazed at how many hotels mount their access points on the walls in the hallways of the building. It would be easy to walk up to the device and steal it or the antennas without being noticed. The reset button is usually accessible as well, making it a simple task to reconfigure the access point to default settings. At best, this allows an attacker to stop users from getting Internet access through the AP, and at worst, it allows attackers to secure the AP so only they can use it. By placing the APs in secure closets or staff-occupied rooms, you prevent this kind of tampering.

WEP

Wired Equivalent Privacy (WEP) is the oldest standard for secure wireless communications in Wi-Fi networks. It is also the weakest and should be used only as a last resort. In this section, I explain how WEP works, why it is not as strong as other solutions, and how to get the most security from it if you are forced to use it.

WEP Functionality

WEP was designed to meet the requirements of the original 802.11 standard. This standard called for the following requirements:

- Reasonably strong encryption
- Exportable
- Efficient encryption
- Self-synchronizing
- Optional encryption

When you look at these requirements, it's clear that strong encryption was not the aim and not even required. The algorithm chosen was RC4 with a key length of 40-bits. Some vendors support longer encryption keys, but these implementations might not be compatible with other vendors' equipment— even if they support the same key length. The different vendors might have implemented the nonstandard key length of more than 40-bits in various ways. To ensure compatibility, you have to stay with the 40-bit key length or use all equipment from the same vendor.

Although I'm referring to the key as a 40-bit key, you'll see that it is actually 64-bits in many configuration interfaces. The 40-bits are used as the secret encryption key, and other 24 bits are used as an *initialization vector* (IV). Linksys APs often call it 40/64-bit or 104/128-bit encryption in an attempt to overcome the confusion.

The IV is a block of bits used in some cryptographic systems to allow for pseudo-random encryption keys. Rather than changing the entire key, only the IV changes at some interval. IV is also referred to as a *nonce* or a *number* used *once*.

You enter the encryption key manually at both the access point and the connecting client devices. You can't automatically manage encryption keys, and the keys do not change dynamically over time. Many devices allow you to generate or enter up to four WEP keys, and this has led to a lot of confusion on the part of implementers. The fours keys are not rotated in any way. The AP can respond to clients using any of the four keys, which means some clients use one key and other clients another. This allows you to reconfigure smaller groups of clients each time you change a single WEP key instead of the entire network and is particularly useful if a WEP key is compromised.

WEP Weaknesses

WEP is weak because of an exposure related to the 24-bit IV. You don't have to understand all the details of this weakness for the Wireless# certification or to implement a secure wireless network; just know that the WEP key can be hacked by an attacker in anywhere from a few minutes if the attacker has done much of the work before the attack to a few hours or days. In many smaller implementations with old hardware, this might not be a concern if you can't upgrade the hardware. However, because newer hardware supports WPA, you should use it instead of WEP when implementing new networks, as long as your clients also support WPA.

If you are using an AP that supports both WEP and WPA, you should know that one WEP client makes your network completely vulnerable—as if you have all WEP clients. APs can only be configured to use one or the other, which effectively limits your network security to the lowest security available. This is outlined in Table11.1.

WEP at Its Best

The reality is that the client devices used, and even the APs used, are not always in your control. For example, I was setting up a wireless network for the church I attend. Some of the members had PDAs that did not support WPA, and they wanted to access the wireless network. This forced me to use either WEP or no encryption at all for those devices. In this scenario, I used WEP as the older devices would not support WPA, but you can see how control was not necessarily in my hands even as the network administrator.

If you find yourself in this situation, you might consider using WEP but rotating keys periodically. Of course, this requires reconfiguring all

TABLE 11.1   WEP and WPA Security Combinations

Lowest Security	Highest Security	Resultant Security
None	WEP	None
WEP	WEP	Weak
WEP	WPA-Personal	Weak
WPA-Personal	WPA-Personal	Moderate
WPA-Personal	WPA-Enterprise	Moderate
WPA-Enterprise	WPA-Enterprise	Strong

your clients, but it might be worth it. You have to make that decision on a case-by-case basis.

Another common recommendation is to use two APs. Configure one AP to use WPA for your newer clients and another AP to use WEP. If they both provide access to the same network in the same way, it doesn't really improve security, but if you limit what the WEP AP provides, your network is more secure than with total WEP. Because they are in the same space, you configure each AP to use a different channel. You could then attach the WEP AP to a router or switch and filter traffic coming in through that AP to limit the network functionality.

Enabling WEP

To enable WEP, you access your AP, usually through the console during initial configuration. If you're using a consumer-grade or SOHO AP, you generally use a web-based interface like the one shown in Figure 11.13.

FIGURE 11.13   Entering WEP keys

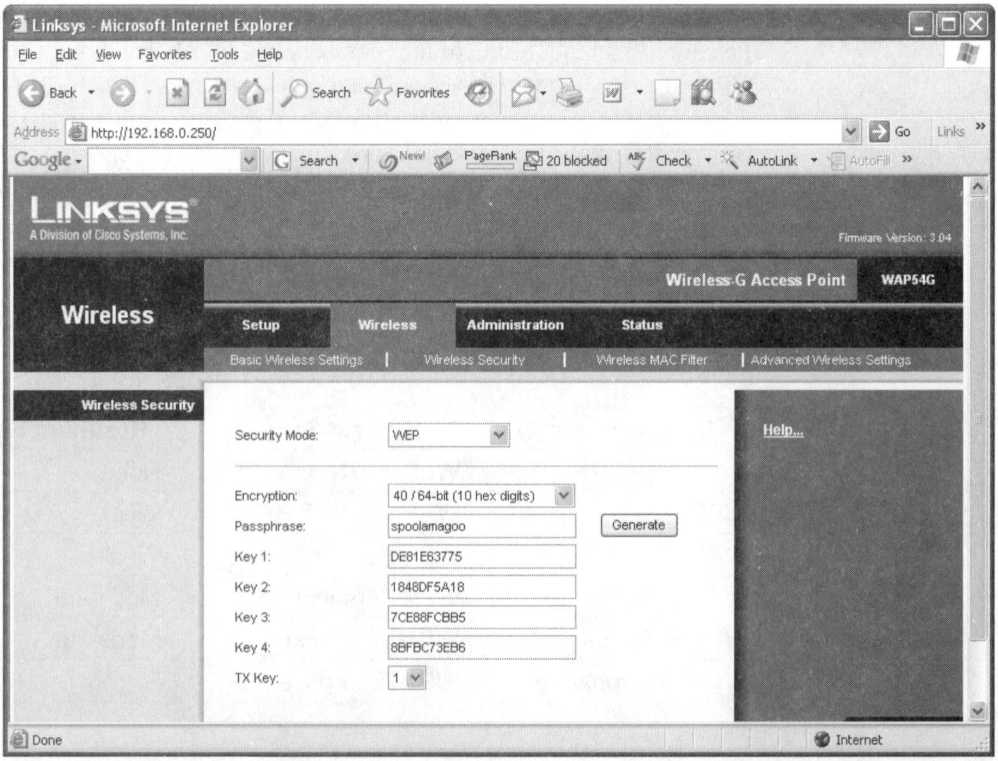

You can either enter one to four WEP keys manually or use a passphrase and have it generate the keys. If you're using compatible clients, you can enter the same passphrase on the client to generate the same WEP keys automatically. Otherwise, you have to type the keys into the interface manually.

There are two types of authentication in 802.11 systems, and they impact how WEP is used. The two types of authentication are *open* and *shared key.* Figure 11.14 shows the configuration for this setting. In the Linksys AP, you configure authentication on a different screen than the WEP settings. Remember this, because it's easily forgotten when configuring WEP and if set improperly can cause your environment to be even less secure.

If you must use WEP, set authentication to open and not shared key. Shared key sends a challenge to the client as clear text and the client must encrypt the challenge with the proper WEP key to gain access to the network. An attacker can intercept this challenge packet in the clear and then as it is sent back in an encrypted state, easily determine the WEP key because the attacker knows the clear text.

FIGURE 11.14   Configuring the authentication method for WEP

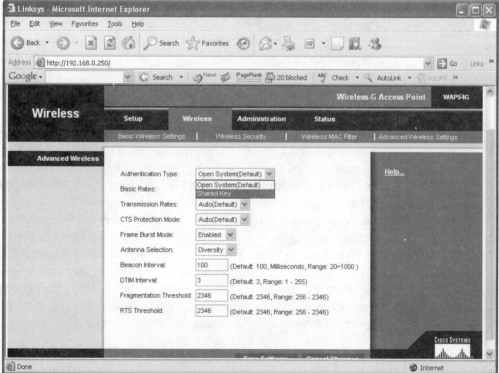

I cannot emphasize enough that you should not use WEP if you can use WPA or WPA2. That's why I'm saying it again with a caution callout. The only reasons for using WEP is having equipment that will not work with WPA/WPA2 and your organization—or some political interest—won't allow you to upgrade that equipment, or upgrading is out of your control because the equipment belongs to someone else. Otherwise, WPA/WPA2 is the way to go for small and SOHO businesses and organizations.

WPA/WPA2

To resolve the weaknesses in WEP while waiting for IEEE standards, the Wi-Fi Alliance created the Wi-Fi Protected Access (WPA) specification. Eventually, WPA2 (Wi-Fi Protected Access version 2) was released and is the preferred technology on newer wireless systems. In this section, I explain both WPA and WPA2 functionality and implementation procedures.

WPA

WPA comes in two basic versions: *WPA-Personal* and *WPA-Enterprise*. For this section, I focus on WPA-Personal, also known as *WPA-PSK (Pre-Shared Key)* or *WPA-Home,* as that is the technology used most frequently in small businesses and SOHO implementations as well as consumer home implementations. WPA-Enterprise requires a RADIUS server, and I cover that in the next section.

WPA Functionality and Benefits

WPA resolves the weaknesses of WEP by rotating keys frequently. It uses a function called *Temporal Key Integrity Protocol* (TKIP) to perform the key rotation. You can adjust the key renewal interval on most access points. For example, the Linksys WAP54G defaults to a 300-second interval. This frequent rotation overcomes the IV weaknesses in WEP that allows an attacker to get the WEP keys. Even if an attacker does acquire the WPA key, the key will have changed by that time, and the network is still secure.

With WPA, key size is increased to 128-bits, which makes it effectively impossible for an attacker to brute force the key in a reasonable amount of time. With the 128-bit keys and the key rotation, which you can configure to rotate (change) keys with every packet in some systems, WPA provides a much more secure environment.

In addition to these benefits, WPA provides the following advantages:

- The IV is doubled to 48 bits instead of 24.
- The key changes frequently enough so an attacker cannot gather enough "interesting" packets to acquire the key.
- WPA includes integrity checks (a way to detect tampering) through the *Message Integrity Code* (MIC) also known as *Michael*.
- WPA can be implemented on most hardware with a simple firmware upgrade if it is not available out-of-the-box.

WPA also adds the possibility of strong user authentication through RADIUS; however, RADIUS is not supported by WPA-Personal and is available only with WPA-Enterprise.

Enabling WPA

WPA is enabled in the same way as WEP only you do not have to enter four different keys and you do not actually see the keys. You usually enter a passphrase, and the AP uses algorithms to generate encryption keys from this passphrase. For this reason, your passphrase must be secure. Otherwise, an attacker can guess it. Don't use common things such as

- Your name
- Your pet's name
- Your city
- Your favorite sports team
- Your spouse's name
- The AP vendor name

The best practice is to use mixed-case alpha-numeric passphrases that are ten or more characters, making it more difficult to guess. Figure 11.15 shows the configuration interface for WPA-Personal on a Linksys WAP54G access point.

WPA2

802.11i is an IEEE standard defining greater security for wireless networks than the original 802.11 WEP specification. The Wi-Fi Alliance created

FIGURE 11.15 WPA configuration

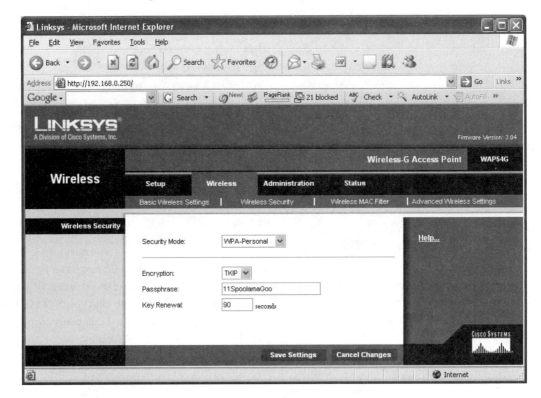

the WPA2 certification to verify the compatibility and interoperability of 802.11i-compliant devices.

WPA2 Requirements and Benefits

WPA2 cannot be applied to your network through firmware upgrades of existing hardware that does not support WPA2—even if the devices support WPA. The reason for this limitation is that WPA2 requires the use of *AES encryption*. AES is a computationally intensive encryption algorithm (in other words, it's a really complex algorithm that takes a lot of CPU power). The APs need a processor capable of handling the workload, which is only available as a hardware upgrade. You can't upgrade the hardware of most consumer-grade APs, so you have to perform an entire device upgrade. Today, most APs—even consumer-grade—have support for WPA2-Personal at a minimum and many support WPA2-Enterprise.

Some installations, such as for banks, government, and healthcare, require compliance with the U.S. and Canadian FIPS 140.2 standard. These environments can't use WPA, as it isn't in compliance; however, WPA2 does provide the needed compliance and can be used. FIPS 140.2 is used in environments that work with sensitive, but not classified, information.

Enabling WPA2

WPA2 is enabled in the same way as WPA. Simply select it in the APs configuration interface and provide a passphrase. If you're using a RADIUS server, you're implementing WPA2-Enterprise and this requires extra configuration.

RADIUS

The Remote Access Dial-In User Service (RADIUS) is a centralized authentication, authorization, and accounting service. You can implement RADIUS as a software solution on an existing operating system or as a hardware device plugged into your network. Many small and medium-sized businesses use software-based RADIUS servers because they already have the server software on which the RADIUS server runs. Figure 11.16 illustrates the use of RADIUS in a wireless implementation.

RADIUS servers provide three basic functions to your network:

- Authentication
- Authorization
- Accounting

RADIUS Authentication

Authentication can be against an internal database of the RADIUS server or an external database such as Microsoft Active Directory or Novell eDirectory. If you're using a Windows domain (Active Directory) and a Windows authentication service (IAS or Internet Authentication Service), the user's credentials, from her initial logon to the domain, are often passed through to the RADIUS authentication mechanism (IAS) automatically. IAS is Microsoft's implementation of a RADIUS server.

Many RADIUS servers also support the Lightweight Directory Access Protocol (LDAP). LDAP is used by Active Directory, but it is also used in some Linux implementations as well as other network directory databases.

FIGURE 11.16   RADIUS implementation

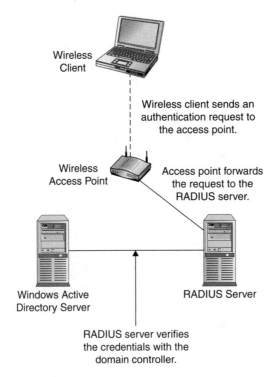

Wireless
Client

Wireless client sends an
authentication request to
the access point.

Wireless
Access Point

Access point forwards
the request to the
RADIUS server.

Windows Active
Directory Server

RADIUS Server

RADIUS server verifies
the credentials with the
domain controller.

If you have such a database and a RADIUS server that supports it, you can use it for wireless authentication.

RADIUS Authorization

Most RADIUS implementations have some form of authorization mechanism that determines what an authenticated user is capable of doing on the network or if the user can even access the network. This mechanism is often based on the number from which the user is dialing in or, in the case of wireless, the MAC address of the wireless NIC. RADIUS servers often use policy sets that allow for varying configurations for different clients. For example, a wireless client might require greater encryption than a PSTN dial-up client.

Possible parameters you can use to determine if a client should be authorized include

- Group membership
- VLAN identifiers
- The time of day
- The use of encryption levels
- Port and IP address filters that can limit what the user can access on the network

RADIUS Accounting

RADIUS servers also act as centralized accounting or auditing servers. They will usually store the accounting data in a log format that is either viewable by other systems or exportable to other systems. This allows you to analyze the logs using analysis software from network monitoring tools to Microsoft Excel. Information stored usually includes authentication accepts and rejects and possibly more details about the actions of the user on the network.

802.1x/EAP

802.1x is a port-based authentication mechanism that has been used in wired LANs for a long time. Though wireless networks have "virtual" ports (they are not physically plugged into an Ethernet port), they can still use the 802.1x authentication mechanism. extensible authentication protocol (EAP) provides the authentication mechanism used to unlock the port controlled by 802.1x.

802.1x

A port-based authentication mechanism such as 802.1x disables the port for all communications other than authentication until the client is authenticated. In a wireless network, the client device can communicate with the AP, but the AP does not allow access to the actual network (passing through the

APs Ethernet port) until the client has been authenticated. You can then use any number of authentication methods with your wireless network. In other words, you are not limited to 802.11 standards. You can allow open system authentication at the AP, but require 802.1x authentication before true network access is granted.

If you find yourself looking inside your AP for a setting to enable 802.1x and you can't find it, that's because it's usually referred to as a RADIUS server. Telling the AP to use a RADIUS server is usually synonymous with telling it to use 802.1x. The policies on the RADIUS server dictate the authentication mechanisms supported by the client.

EAP

802.1x is generally used with some form of EAP in a wireless network. There are many versions of EAP (hence the term *extensible* authentication protocol), and some versions require certificates. Some require a certificate for the server only, and others require certificates for both the client and the server. Table 11.2 outlines three common EAP types and supported clients as well as whether client or server certificates are required.

TABLE 11.2   EAP-Types Compared

EAP Type	Common Supported Clients	Certificate Requirements
EAP-TLS	Linux, MAC OS-X, Windows 9x, and NT-based systems (NT, 2000, XP, 2003)	Required for both server and client
EAP-TTLS	Same as above	Required for server; optional on client
PEAP	Windows XP	Required for server; optional on client
EAP-MD5	Most clients	No certificates; password-based; considered insecure compared to others

As the table indicates, EAP-MD5 is considered an insecure authentication protocol when compared with the others; however, EAP-MD5 does not require the use of a certificate on the server or the clients. If you want this simplicity, EAP-MD5 may be an option, but you are exposing yourself to the following security vulnerabilities:

- **One-way authentication** Only the client is authenticated—not the server.
- **Challenge passwords** The server sends a challenge string to the client as clear text and then the client responds with the hash of the text. This allows an attacker to intercept both messages and learn the password.
- **No per-session WEP keys** The WEP key is static and vulnerable to normal WEP weaknesses.

To avoid these vulnerabilities, consider using EAP-TTLS or PEAP, as they require a certificate only for the server and that certificate can often be generated without a full public key infrastructure (PKI), which requires the implementation of one or more certificate servers.

MAC Filtering—Strengths and Weaknesses

A security solution that has been available practically from the beginning of wireless LANs is MAC filtering. When you use MAC filtering, you configure the AP to allow only clients with specified MAC addresses to communicate on the network. This task is usually a manual one requiring that you enter each MAC address individually. For this reason, it is commonly used in home networks and SOHO or very small business implementations. The time it takes to enter all the MAC addresses manually is too restricting for larger environments.

In addition to the time constraint, most APs allow only a limited number of MAC addresses in the table. This limitation ranges from less than 10 in some consumer APs to more than 100 in some enterprise APs. Figure 11.17 shows the MAC address management interface in a typical AP.

As you can see in Figure 11.17, you can either *permit* client devices with a MAC address included in the table to access the network or *prevent* MAC

FIGURE 11.17 MAC address tables

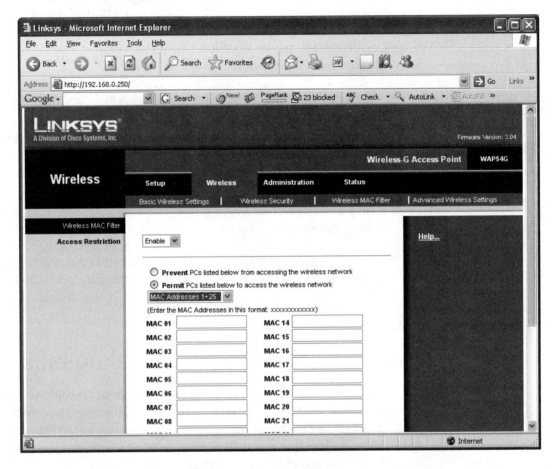

addresses included in the table from accessing the network. The deny option is useful if you detect you are under attack from an intruder and you know his MAC address; open the admin interface for the AP and prevent that MAC address from accessing the network.

MAC filtering can provide a false sense of security, however. Impersonating a valid MAC address (called MAC *spoofing*) is simple. The attacker configures his wireless NIC to use the MAC address of a valid user and then accesses the network with ease. These valid MAC addresses are discovered easily using a wireless packet analyzer. Figure 11.18 shows a typical dialog allowing the user to specify the MAC address of the wireless NIC.

FIGURE 11.18   MAC configuration

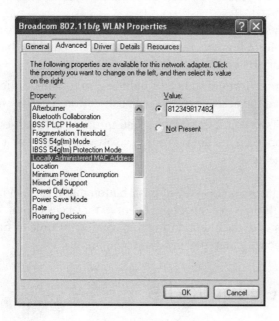

Push-button Security

Because of the insecure implementations of many wireless networks, vendors now provide simple push-button security mechanisms. Each vendor calls this technology something different. Here's an example of just two vendors' terminology used to refer to push-button security:

- AirStation One-Touch Secure System (AOSS), Buffalo Technology
- SecureEasySetup (SES), Linksys

Whatever its name, the client and the AP must support the technology in order for this to work. For example, the AOSS technology by Buffalo Technology only works with other AOSS devices. SES, by Linksys, is based on the Broadcom chipset's support for this function and clients with the Broadcom chipset in them can function with SES, though in some cases they can't and in others you need to install newer drivers.

The basic process of push-button security is as follows:

1. Push the security configuration button on the access point and hold it for a few seconds (the time to hold it and the button's name will vary by vendor).
2. Some form of indicator light begins to blink or light up to indicate that the access point is in "push-button security" mode.
3. Go to your client device and initiate the "push-button security" mode on the device (either a software setting or a literal button on the device).

Most access points stay in push-button mode for 2–3 minutes, giving you enough time to connect the client to the access point. The access point negotiates with the client during this window of time to find the greatest level of security that they have in common.

Virtual Private Networks

A virtual private network (VPN) allows for secure communications across insecure mediums. VPNs are useful in wireless networks as the wireless medium is inherently insecure. They are also useful for internal wireless connections to the wired network or for securely accessing services across the Internet in public hotspots. In this section, I explain what a VPN is and give some examples of useful scenarios where VPN technology can be utilized.

VPN Functionality

While the acronym VPN stands for *virtual private networking,* you might think of the technology as *encrypted public networking.* A secure VPN connection tunnels encrypted data across an insecure connection. For example, you connect to the Internet (an insecure connection) and then use a VPN protocol to connect to a corporate server at work (a secure connection). VPN connections can be many-to-one or one-to-one.

Many-to-One VPN

In a many-to-one scenario, you have one VPN server that many VPN clients connect to. This scenario is common when you have mobile workers who need to access the corporate network. They connect to their Internet service

FIGURE 11.19   Many-to-one VPN

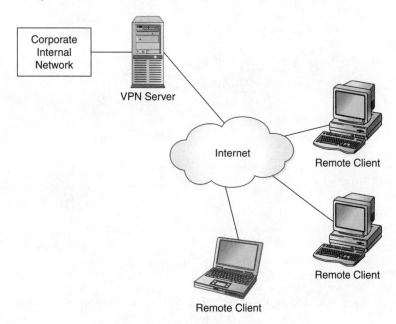

provider (ISP) and then create a VPN connection across the Internet to the corporate network. This is illustrated in Figure 11.19.

One-to-One VPN

In a one-to-one VPN implementation, you create a VPN-based WAN link between two networks. For example, you have a site in Atlanta, Georgia, and another in Washington, D.C. If you have high-speed Internet connections at both sites, you can create a link between them using VPN technology. Once the link is established, data can be routed through the connection as if there were a physical wire running between the two sites. Figure 11.20 illustrates this network configuration.

VPN Tunneling

The tunnel created by a VPN connection is, of course, not a literal tunnel across the public network. At each end of the VPN connection, all traffic destined for the other end is encrypted before it is sent. When the receiving end receives the data, it is decrypted. In the case of a one-to-one VPN connection,

FIGURE 11.20   One-to-one VPN

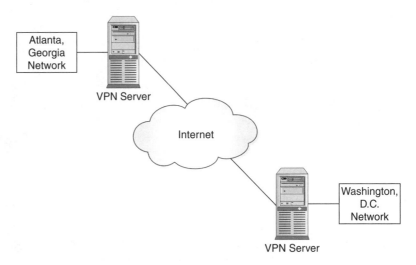

the data is unencrypted (unless an additional encryption standard is used on the local network) as it travels the local network on its way to the VPN connection. The data is then encrypted and transferred across the VPN connection (this is called *tunneling*) and decrypted at the other end. Now, the data travels unencrypted on the destination network.

The tunnel, once created, is "transparent" to the applications running on your computer. The applications do not see it as an encrypted connection—they just see a connection. VPN connections reduce actual throughput even further than the wireless management overhead by itself, in many cases 25 percent of the data rate or lower.

VPN Protocols

There are three common VPN protocols in use on networks today: the Point-to-Point Tunneling Protocol (PPTP), the Layer 2 Tunneling Protocol (L2TP)/IPSec (IP Security), and the Secure Shell (SSH) protocol.

PPTP is an easy-to-implement solution, but it also provides the lowest level of security. If you are configuring a VPN connection into a sensitive network, you shouldn't use PPTP. It's an acceptable solution for home wireless implementations if you are using it to secure the connection between the wireless client and your network. However, WPA is much easier to implement and provides better security. Some consumer-grade devices come with PPTP servers built in and may be used for remote access to your private network.

L2TP is a more secure, and also more complex, protocol than PPTP. The most important thing to remember is when you use L2TP, you need to use IPSec in conjunction with it to provide encryption to the tunnel. L2TP establishes the tunnel, and IPSec policies dictate the encryption rules. In a Microsoft environment, L2TP and IPSec is much more difficult to configure than PPTP; however, if you require the security they provide, you need to master these configuration challenges.

SSH is a little different than the previous two, in that it is implemented within an application. The most popular and secure version of SSH is SSH2 (Secure Shell version 2), and it is often used to secure FTP and Telnet traffic. By default, FTP and Telnet send their authentication packets as clear text. On a wireless network without encryption, this is a huge problem. You can either enable encryption or use an SSH-compatible FTP or Telnet client and server.

Even on a wired network, it is dangerous to use standard FTP or Telnet as an administrator. Though it may be more difficult to intercept than it is on the wireless LAN, data can be intercepted on the wired network. The best practice is to use secure channels any time you perform administrative functions. Use SSH-compatible admin tools or create a VPN connection in which you perform the administrative functions.

VPN Applications

The most common implementation of VPN technology, as it relates to wireless LANS, is in public hotspots. Public hotspots generally use unencrypted communications with wireless clients because it allows for simpler configuration. Imagine if users who wanted to connect to the hotspot had to configure WEP keys or WPA passphrases. They would be required to go to a service desk and acquire the needed information. Then they would have to reconfigure their wireless client to use these settings. The complexity would keep many novice users from taking advantage of the hotspot and would reduce the benefits of providing the service in the first place.

Because these hotspots are left "wide-open," you should consider some means of securing your communications. One effective technique is to create a VPN connection to your business network and then browse the Internet through that connection. This rather interesting solution is illustrated in Figure 11.21.

FIGURE 11.21   VPN connection protecting hotspot communications

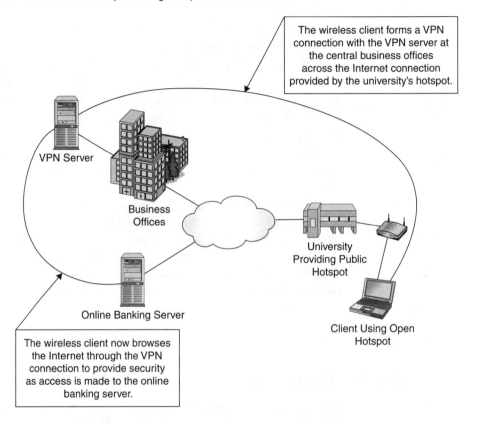

The wireless client forms a VPN connection with the VPN server at the central business offices across the Internet connection provided by the university's hotspot.

VPN Server

Business Offices

University Providing Public Hotspot

Online Banking Server

The wireless client now browses the Internet through the VPN connection to provide security as access is made to the online banking server.

Client Using Open Hotspot

In the scenario depicted in Figure 11.21, the wireless client first connects to the Internet through the unsecured public hotspot provided by the university. This connection uses no encryption or authentication. Once the connection is established, the user initiates a VPN connection to the VPN server attached to the business offices network, which is on the Internet. This connection uses encryption and authentication. The user's data is now completely routed through this VPN tunnel and passes back out to the Internet from the business offices to the online banking website. This provides the extra level of security a user needs when connected to an open wireless network.

Another use of VPN is for internal connections to the wireless network. If you don't want to implement a RADIUS server, but you want to provide secure access for your wireless clients, you can use a VPN service. Figure 11.22 illustrates this concept. As you can see,

FIGURE 11.22   Wireless VPN-based client access

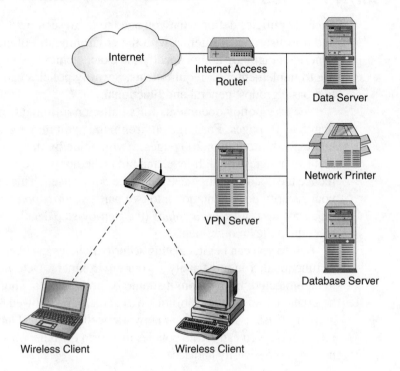

the wireless AP is connected to a network with only one device on it—the VPN server. The VPN server is then connected to the regular network and routes packets between VPN clients and the regular network. Because the only way to get through the VPN server to the regular network is to create a VPN connection with the server, all wireless clients must run a VPN session if they want to utilize the network.

Security Policies and Plans

Now that you've learned about the different security threats and protection mechanisms, you need to put them into practice. While you could just start implementing security tools, this usually leads to a complicated and hard-to-manage implementation. A better route is to create security policies and plans to use to secure your environment. This way, you've documented the general requirements of your environment and the specific tools that you are utilizing to meet those requirements.

Security Policies

Security policies define what you need to do to secure your environment and how users must interact with the environment. Policies are usually generic in that they do not specify the exact technology or steps you will use to implement their requirements. Security policies can be divided into two basic groups: general and functional.

Security policy documents for smaller environments may be no more than 5 to 10 pages. For large environments, you may require a three-ring binder with more than 200 pages. If you abide by the guideline that says security policies are high-level and not technology-specific, you can usually reduce the documentation needed in the policy itself. This effectively divides your security documentation into two parts: *security policies* (the high-level requirements) and *security plans* (the step-by-step details of how you will meet the policy requirements).

Before you can begin creating security policies in either category, general or functional, you must analyze your environment. Determine what needs to be protected, from whom it should be protected, to whom access should be granted, and what capabilities will actually be allowed. This process is all part of risk assessment and network needs analysis. Once you have this information, you can create policies that form the blueprints for how you will provide both security and access.

General Policies

When determining if a policy is functional or general, ask this question: Does the policy reference a function performed on the network? If the answer is yes, it is probably a functional policy. If the answer is no, it is a general policy. General policies often impact how functional policies are implemented. For example, you might define a general policy that states that all data must be classified as either public, private, or classified. While not providing a direct function to the network, this general policy is the foundation on which functional policies are built.

Items to consider for general policies include:

- Data classification
- Threat definition and identification
- Whether audits will be performed and how often
- Asset evaluation procedures

Functional Policies

Functional policies define how a technology must function in order to be used in your network. Do not confuse this with how a technology is configured or implemented. These are two different things. The former is a policy, and the latter is a plan or procedure. Here are some examples of functional policies:

- All wireless devices used in our environment must support WPA-Personal as a minimum level of encryption.
- All wireless routers used in our environment must support VPN pass-through for wireless clients, including both PPTP and L2TP/IPSec pass-through.
- All users accessing classified data must use VPN tunnels to access the data whether they are on wireless or wired clients to prevent eavesdropping when the data travels the wired LAN.
- Passwords must be at least six characters in length and be alphanumeric and case-sensitive, having at least one uppercase and one lowercase letter.

These policies do not specify how these requirements will be met, only that they must be met. You can begin to see the benefit of this kind of security documentation. Selecting equipment is easier because you have criteria to compare to determine if the equipment meets your needs. For example, if you are considering an AP from a particular vendor, but it only supports WEP encryption, you mark it off the list instantly because it does not meet the first functional requirement listed.

Another benefit of creating this kind of policy is that it acts as a tool for user education and weighted decision making. What I mean by weighted decision making is that you have more weight behind your technology decisions because management usually signs off on the policies.

 In fact, it is essential to get management to sign their approval on the dotted line. Without their signature of support, the policies will actually mean very little, and you will run into situation after situation where users want to do something disallowed by the policies, and you have no weight because the management staff did not sign off on the policies in the beginning. I encourage you to get a literal signature from the managers, but at the very least, get their verbal consent.

You should consider creating policies for the following items and possibly more depending on your environment:

- Physical security
- Authentication requirements
- Internet access
- Email use
- Viruses, worms, and Trojan Horses
- Encryption
- Network administration
- Wireless access

Security Plans

Security plans provide the instructions for implementing specific technologies to comply with your security policies. Security plans are procedural and are often called security procedures. Depending on the needs of your environment and security management staff, security plans can be very detailed (step-by-step) or high-level (turn this on and that off on this device). Here's an example of a security plan for installing a Linksys WAP45G access point. This plan is in line with the security policies listed earlier in this section.

1. Unpack the Linksys WAP54G access point and connect an Ethernet cable to the Ethernet port on the access point.
2. Connect the other end of the Ethernet cable to a laptop or desktop computer that is not connected to the corporate network.
3. Configure the IP address of the computer's Ethernet NIC to 192.168.1.40 and the subnet mask to 255.255.255.0. (This IP address allows you to connect to the Linksys device's web-based configuration interface as the WAP54G defaults to an IP address of 192.168.1.245—you can use any IP address in the 192.168.1.x network other than the 245 address.)
4. Power on the Linksys device by plugging the power cord into a power outlet and wait 90–120 seconds.
5. Open the web browser on the computer and point it to 192.168.1.245.

6. You should see a logon screen. Leave the User Name field blank and enter the Password of **admin** and click OK.

7. You should now see a web-based administrative interface. Click the link that says Wireless on the top menu.

8. Click a new link that says Wireless Security.

9. Click the Security Mode drop-down combo box and select WPA-Personal.

10. Type the passphrase communicated to you by the network administrator in the Passphrase field. (NOTE: If you do not know the passphrase, contact the network administrator at x3947.)

11. Click the Save Settings button.

12. Wait for the access point to apply the settings, and when it is ready, continue with the next step.

13. Click the Administration link in the menus.

14. Enter the password **z7Bhr609** into the Password fields to change the administrative password and click the Save Settings button.

15. Wait for the access point to apply the settings, and when it is ready, continue with the next step.

16. Click the Setup link in the menus.

17. Click the new link called Network Setup.

18. Enter the IP address settings provided by the network administrator. (NOTE: If you do not know the network settings, contact the network administrator at x3947.)

19. Once the access point finishes applying the changes, configuration is complete. You can now connect the access point to the Ethernet port on the production network where it is to be placed.

This example is a very detailed security plan for a specific device. You can see that these instructions could be used for every Linksys WAP54G you install in your environment. In some cases, this is a baseline security configuration, which means that this is the minimum required configuration for the access point to be installed on your network. Some of the access points might require additional configuration, such as WPA-Enterprise instead of WPA-Personal; however, the previously listed policies indicate a minimum of WPA-Personal, which is provided by this security plan.

FIGURE 11.23   Saving the configuration to a file

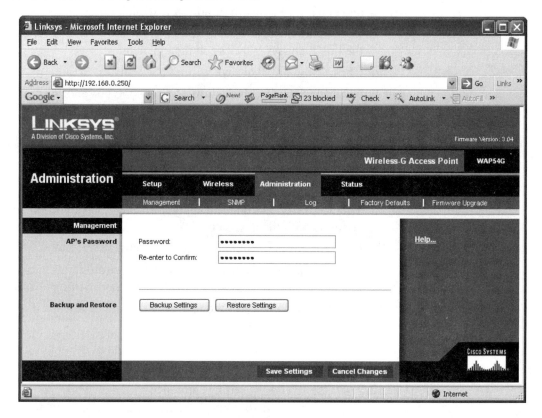

One additional benefit of modern network devices is the ability to save configuration settings to a file. Figure 11.23 shows the screen where you can do this with a Linksys WAP54G access point. As you can imagine, this makes creating the security plans much simpler. You configure one access point and then save the configuration settings. In the future, you apply these configuration settings to any new WAP54G access point and then quickly change the device name and IP address settings to customize the device. Saving the configuration not only speeds up the configuration of new devices, but also reduces the likelihood of a configuration oversight.

Some access points may support remote configuration through SNMP or some other centralized management tool. With these devices, you can plug them into the network and either wait until they are detected by the

management suite or enter them immediately into the management software to
have them configured automatically. Windows operating systems do not ship
with SNMP management software, but there are many available management
applications for this purpose.

Summary

There are many different tools and methods that you can use to secure
your wireless networks. In this chapter, I provided the needed information
on security threats and vulnerabilities as well as protection measures you
can use to defend against them. You learned about encryption technologies
such as WEP, WPA, and WPA2 as well as more advanced tools such as
802.1x and virtual private networking. With this knowledge, you can create
effective security policies and plans for any home, SOHO, or small business
environment.

Key Terms

- ☐ **802.1x/EAP**
- ☐ **attack surface**
- ☐ **cracker**
- ☐ **Denial of Service**
- ☐ **encryption**
- ☐ **hacker**
- ☐ **hijacking**
- ☐ **MAC filtering**
- ☐ **push-button security**
- ☐ **RADIUS**
- ☐ **rogue access point**
- ☐ **virtual private networking**
- ☐ **war driving**
- ☐ **WEP**
- ☐ **WPA/WPA2**

Review Questions

1. Attack surface reduction refers to what practice of network security?

   A. Reducing the length of the wireless connections on your network

   B. Reducing the number of entry points to your network

   C. Reducing the length of the wired connections on your network

   D. Disabling the wireless nodes on your network

2. Why is securing the wired entry to your network an important part of wireless security?

   A. Because the wired network is insecure by default

   B. Because the wired network provides a way to access the wireless network while avoiding the use of the access point

   C. Because the wired network provides a way to access the access point's configuration interface

   D. Because the wireless network cannot function on an insecure wired network

3. All types of attackers provide an equal threat to all networks.

   A. True

   B. False

4. Wireless networks come secure out-of-the-box.

   A. True

   B. False

5. You cannot implement a system and assume that it will remain secure without intervention on an ongoing basis.

   A. True

   B. False

6. You are preparing to perform data flow analysis for the data your wireless users will transfer on the network. You plan to consider the entry point of the data, the live storage point, and the backup storage point. What other part of the data flow should you consider?

    A. None, you have covered all the bases

    B. OSI layer communications

    C. Keyboard entry

    D. Network traversal

7. The wireless users in Building A have been calling the help desk for the past hour saying that they cannot use the network. You have verified that you can ping the Ethernet IP address of the access point in their area and the servers they access are all functioning properly. Based on this preliminary analysis, you suspect that a network attack might be under way. What kind of attack would cause these symptoms?

    A. Denial of Service

    B. War driving

    C. Social engineering

    D. Eavesdropping

8. You notice a car parked in the parking lot just outside your building. The individual sitting in the car has a laptop open and he seems to be typing on the keyboard. You check your network and everything seems to be functioning properly and no unauthorized devices have been connected. If the person is attacking your network, what kind of attack are they likely to be performing?

    A. Denial of Service

    B. War driving

    C. Social engineering

    D. Eavesdropping

9. When an attacker calls an unsuspecting user or administrator and gains information about the network, what type of attack is this?

   A. Social engineering

   B. Rogue access points

   C. Hijacking

   D. Unauthorized use

10. You notice a device sitting on the desk of a user that looks like a computing device, but you know it has not been authorized by the IT group. What kind of security vulnerability might this represent?

   A. Social engineering

   B. Rogue access points

   C. Hijacking

   D. Unauthorized use

11. Defense-in-depth provides for greater security than one point of security. It is also referred to by another name. What is that name?

   A. Deep security

   B. Strong security

   C. Layered security

   D. Multiform security

12. You have installed ten access points to cover a factory floor. In each access point, you have disabled the broadcast of the SSID. This is an example of what general security principle?

   A. AAA

   B. Data confidentiality

   C. Data integrity

   D. Obscurity

13. When you enable WEP, many devices support the use of a passphrase to generate a number of WEP keys automatically. How many WEP keys do these devices usually generate from the passphrase?

    A. 1

    B. 2

    C. 3

    D. 4

14. WPA was implemented by the Wi-Fi Alliance to overcome the weaknesses found in an earlier encryption protocol. Which of these is a weakness overcome by WPA?

    A. Static keys that do not change

    B. Weak passwords

    C. Incompatible passphrases

    D. Hijacking

15. What is the most secure wireless protection among the listed items if you were to choose just one?

    A. WEP

    B. WPA2

    C. MAC filtering

    D. SSID hiding

16. In order to use WPA-Enterprise, you need what kind of server?

    A. Windows

    B. Linux

    C. RADIUS

    D. Firewall

17. You are considering the use of push-button security to secure your environment. What is an important consideration of this type of security?

   A. It does not support WPA.

   B. You usually need hardware from the same vendor.

   C. You usually need hardware with the same version of WEP.

   D. It does not support VPN pass-through.

18. You are the network administrator for a small company. The company does not handle any sensitive data, but the manager of the marketing group says she wants to access the network from her house. She has a high-speed Internet connection, and your company has a high-speed-business-class cable connection with five static IP addresses. You are currently using only three of these addresses. You want the simplest solution with weak to moderate security as security is not your chief concern. What technology should you use? Choose one.

   A. A wireless router

   B. A VPN server at the office using PPTP and a VPN client at the marketing manager's house

   C. A wired router

   D. A VPN server at the office using L2TP with IPSec and a VPN client at the marketing manager's house

19. You happen to look at the "connected devices" interface of your wireless router and see that a client is connected with whom you are not familiar. What could you do to prevent this client from accessing the network in the future?

   A. Enter the MAC address of the client and set the MAC filter mode to Prevent.

   B. Enter the MAC address of the client and set the MAC filter mode to Provide.

    C. Enter the IP address of the client and set the IP filter mode to Prevent.

    D. Enter the IP address of the client and set the IP filter mode to Provide.

20. There are two basic kinds of security policies you should create for your network. What are they?

    A. Acceptable

    B. General

    C. Functional

    D. Unacceptable

21. All versions of EAP (extensible authentication protocol) require the use of certificates, so you need a certificate server and a PKI to use it.

    A. True

    B. False

22. What is the difference between a security policy and a security plan?

    A. A security policy defines how to configure specific technologies and a security plan defines high-level requirements for security.

    B. A security plan defines how to configure specific technologies and a security policy defines the high-level requirements for security.

    C. A security plan is required while a security policy is optional.

    D. A security policy is required while a security plan is optional.

Review Answers

1. **B.** Attack surface reduction (ASR) is the process of reducing the number of entry points to your network. While disabling all wireless nodes would be one way of doing this, this act is not total network ASR, and you cannot do this and achieve ASR for your wireless network because it would no longer exist.

2. **C.** Because you can access the web-based configuration interface of most access points through either the Ethernet or wireless interface, the wired interface should be secured. Many administrators disable the wireless web-based management interface, but this is not enough if the wired interface is not secured.

3. **B.** False. Some networks are more likely to be a target of corporate espionage than others. These attacks are more likely to be performed by skilled attackers where unskilled attackers would not be able to circumvent basic security defenses.

4. **B.** False. Wireless networks usually come "wide-open" out-of-the-box and you must secure them. Even those that come presecured, usually use WEP, and it is insecure by modern standards.

5. **A.** True. You must maintain the security of your network because new threats and vulnerabilities are created and discovered—sometimes on a daily or weekly basis. While home users might be able to get by with a security update every few months, business users need to update monthly or even weekly.

6. **D.** You should also consider network traversal. This is the path the data travels as it goes from the entry point to the live storage point. There may be wired and wireless paths along the way and you should consider both for security purposes.

7. **A.** Denial of Service attacks present these symptoms. The Ethernet port is available because it does not use RF communications. If an attacker is using an RF signal generator in the area, the wireless portion will be down, but you will still be able to ping the Ethernet port of the access point.

8. **D.** Eavesdropping is the most likely candidate. If the attacker were performing a DoS attack, your network would not function properly. The attacker is probably not war driving because they haven't bothered to associate with your network. When attackers eavesdrop, they pull packets of the RF air waves without associating with your access point. The only indication that they are doing it is that you see them in the car with their laptop open.

9. A. Social engineering is the process of taking advantage of human weaknesses. The attacker attempts to manipulate the unsuspecting individual into giving him information she should not be giving out.

10. B. This is likely a rogue access point. Access points come in many form factors and some are as small as two or three credit cards stacked on top of each other.

11. D. Layered security, or defense-in-depth, provides for greater security because the attacker must penetrate multiple layers to get to your network. An example of layered security is to install a firewall between the Internet and a DMZ (demilitarized zone) in your company's network and then another between the DMZ and the corporate network. The attacker must penetrate two firewall layers to get into the network.

12. D. Obscurity is the act of making your network less visible to attackers. While disabling SSID broadcasting does not make it impossible for an attacker to discover the SSID, casual passersby will not see the network.

13. D. Most devices generate four WEP keys from the passphrase.

14. A. Static keys that do not change are an inherent weakness in the WEP implementation. WPA overcomes this weakness by implementing key change at intervals specified by the implementer.

15. B. WPA2. WEP is less secure than WPA2, and MAC filtering can be easily circumvented. SSID hiding should be considered for legal reasons and to prevent casual mobile connections, but it is not as secure as many people believe.

16. C. A RADIUS server is needed to use WPA-Enterprise. The RADIUS server provides centralized authentication, authorization, and accounting for the wireless network.

17. B. Because of the proprietary nature of this kind of solution, you may need to select hardware from the exact same vendor for all of your equipment. While this requirement may change over time, it is the current situation.

18. B. In this scenario, you install a PPTP-based VPN server at work because it provides security in the weak to moderate range and is simple to set up. The L2TP solution is more complex and the wired or wireless router would not necessarily provide you with a VPN connection.

19. A. By filtering the MAC address and setting the filter to Prevent, you disallow that MAC address from connecting in the future. This is not completely secure as the attacker can change the MAC address on the client; however, it is an excellent solution if an office worker in the building next door has connected. They probably don't know how to change the MAC address of their wireless NIC.

20. B, C. The two broad categories of security policies are general and functional. You might define acceptable and unacceptable use of the network in these policies.

21. B. False. Not all versions of EAP require the use of certificates. EAP-MD5 uses no certificates, but it is not considered secure. EAP-TTLS and PEAP require that a certificate be available for the server, but not the client. This optional client certificate means it can be implemented without a certificate server or PKI.

22. B. Security policies are high-level requirements for security in your environment, and security plans are procedures for implementing specific technologies.

Installing, Troubleshooting, and Optimizing Your WLAN

Wireless# Exam Objectives Covered:

❖ Identify proper procedures for installing and configuring common WLAN applications

- Small Office, Home Office

- Extension of existing networks into remote locations

- Building-to-building connectivity

- Flexibility for mobile users

❖ Identify procedures to optimize wireless networks in specific situations

- Hardware placement

- Hardware selection

- Identifying sources on interference

- Network utilization

- Appropriate security protocols

❖ Recognize common problems associated with wireless networks and their symptoms, and identify steps to isolate and troubleshoot the problem. Given a problem situation, interpret the symptoms and the most likely cause. Problems may include

- Decreased throughput

- No connectivity

- Intermittent connectivity

- Weak signal strength

- Device upgrades

This chapter provides you with the knowledge and skills you need to plan, implement, and maintain wireless networks using Wi-Fi technology. You'll learn to perform a site survey and what tools are needed to complete one. I walk you through the installation and configuration of multiple wireless devices, including both clients and infrastructure devices used in wireless networks. You'll also learn the step-by-step procedures used to maintain a wireless network and how to troubleshoot and repair common wireless network problems.

This chapter is divided into five main sections:

- Understanding Site Surveys
- Performing the Site Survey
- Implementing the Network
- Maintaining the Network
- Troubleshooting the Network

Understanding Site Surveys

A site survey is an investigation of the organization's needs, the behavior of RF signals in the organization's facilities, any inference sources, the availability of power and Ethernet connections, and an analysis of any legal issues that may require specific wireless configurations. From this survey, you create a document describing how the wireless network will be configured to provide for the needs of the organization.

Small networks, such as SOHO implementations and small businesses, should still perform a site survey. The survey won't be as intensive, but it is still essential to be an effective wireless installation. The reality is that you have to do a site survey. The question is, do you perform the survey before installation and therefore have a smoother installation process. If you decide to "analyze as you go," expect to encounter problems—in even the simplest of networks. A preinstallation site survey also leads to a faster installation.

During the site survey, you meet with key users of the network to determine their needs. I've seen many network and systems implementations end in complete failure because users were not involved in the beginning. Their involvement often reveals needs and problems you wouldn't know about otherwise so you can plan for them and even prevent them in many cases before beginning the installation. In the end, the purpose of a site survey is to ensure that your installation plan meets the needs of the wireless users.

To perform a fully effective site survey, you should include the following analysis areas:

- User needs
- RF behavior
- Interference discovery
- Hardware selection and placement
- Existing networks and systems

Before you begin the actual site survey, make sure you have the proper tools to achieve the task. I cover the tools needed for your site survey kit first and then investigate the analysis areas involved in the survey itself.

Site Survey Toolkit

Your site survey toolkit provides you with all the tools you need to accomplish the survey and document your findings. Following is a list of items that are usually included in a site survey kit:

- Laptop and/or PDA
- Wireless NIC
- Access points and bridges
- Battery power source (UPS)
- Site survey software
- Note-taking implements
- Blueprints or floor plans
- Network diagrams
- Indoor and outdoor antennas
- RF cables and connectors
- Binoculars and two-way radios
- Standard toolbox and tools
- Carrying cases and/or carts
- Digital camera
- Distance measuring wheel

While advanced RF engineers installing enterprise WLANs may need more than what's listed here, this collection should suffice for smaller installations and many larger implementations as well. Let's look at each of these items and their purpose.

Laptop and/or PDA

A laptop computer is much better for most site surveys than a desktop because it is more mobile, and a PDA may be better still. You have to decide if the applications running on the final wireless network are sensitive to wireless signal strength because of bandwidth requirements or if the existence of the signal is all that matters. The reason for this distinction is the simple fact that most PDAs do not have the same antennas that laptops have available and therefore PDAs might give a very different result than you get with more powerful equipment. Another possible issue with PDAs is the fact that many of them only support 802.11b because of battery life constraints. If you plan to use 802.11a or 802.11g, these devices won't work for your installation. They might provide a reading of RF signals, but you can't measure dynamic rate shifting as it would apply to 802.11g as you get farther from the access point.

You use the laptop or PDA to measure signal strength as you walk through the building. You report on signal strength, the noise floor, and the signal-to-noise ratio as well. This helps determine how many access points you need and their location.

In addition to the laptop itself, consider bringing extra batteries. Most laptops only operate for two to three hours—or even less when running the Wi-Fi card. By bringing an extra battery along, you can swap it out and keep working instead of taking a break and waiting for it to recharge. Of course, you could also carry two or three laptops with you, but that's much more expensive than bringing extra batteries.

When selecting the laptop for the site survey, choose one with both USB 2.0 and PCMCIA/CardBus slots, so you can connect different types of cards for various scenarios. While some CardBus cards support 802.11a, b, and g, most of them are either 802.11a or 802.11b/g. The same is usually true for USB adapters. An additional benefit of using USB or CardBus devices is that you can acquire devices that support external antennas, which allows you to test using different dBi gain antennas connected to the client as well as the access point.

Wireless NIC

The second essential tool you need is a wireless NIC. You simply cannot perform a site survey without a laptop or PDA, wireless NIC, and access points. These major devices determine how the wireless network will perform in the client's or your organization's facility. Even the smallest environment requires these devices.

Some technicians suggest using Wi-Fi finders to see if there is an RF signal; they believe that this practice is "good enough" for small networks. While I agree that this practice allows you to verify if you have an RF signal, it does not provide you with the extra information, such as the data rate at which you are connecting or the actual throughput readings, that a full wireless packet analyzer and laptop with wireless NIC does. Another problem with the Wi-Fi finders is that you cannot adjust the power output level to determine requirements for reaching the access point and troubleshooting possible near, far, or hidden node problems. For these reasons, I caution against assuming you can perform a successful site survey with an access point and a Wi-Fi finder. Perhaps in the future, Wi-Fi finders (hotspot detectors) will give more information and can be used in this way, but for now the laptop and wireless NIC are probably best.

When deciding on the wireless NIC to use for your site surveys, you want to consider a number of important factors. First, the card should support the technology you intend to use. Some wireless NICs are actually a/b/g, meaning they support all three 802.11 standards common today. If you can use this kind of card, it might provide all you need for any situation you find yourself in. Second, the card should support external antennas, if possible, so you test with different dBi gain and directional antennas to measure the impact on the wireless link. Third, you absolutely must make sure the card or cards you select work with the wireless site survey software you want to use. If you plan to use a generic tool such as NetStumbler, you will probably be fine with any NIC, but if you want to use an advanced packet analyzer or site survey application, you must verify compatibility.

Access Points and Bridges

The third essential tool is an access point. You place the access point in various locations with different orientations to find the best places for access points to achieve coverage in the areas required. You probably want to choose a small form factor access point that supports external antennas.

However, you do not want to use a pocket access point because they don't provide external antennas and they don't have a "real-world" range. In other words, you end up thinking you need more access points than you really do. Pocket access points usually have a range of 50–100 feet of good reception whereas a standard access point has a range from 100–300 feet or more. As you can see, there is a tremendous difference between them.

Many site survey engineers take a second laptop with them and connect it to a small switch connected to the physical Ethernet port on the access point. They then transfer data to and from the laptop to determine actual throughput readings. Another option is to carry a small NAS (network-attached storage) device that you can easily connect to the switch and then connect the AP to the switch and use this configuration to test throughput. Of course, you need power for the switch, the NAS, and the access point. Figure 12.1 illustrates this concept for throughput testing.

One advantageous feature for site surveys is variable output power, so you can test coverage patterns and communications distances without needing to swap antennas continually. For example, you could use a 7 dBi gain omni-directional antenna with an access point having an output power of 20 mW. This gives you an effective output power of approximately 100 mW. Then, you could use a 5 dBi gain antenna to achieve an output power of between 60 and 70 mW. However, you could also use an access point that has the ability to vary the output power from 20 mW to 100 mW without swapping antennas.

In addition to access points, you need to take wireless bridges with you if you plan to test any bridged connections. For example, if the organization wants to link two buildings separated by 75 feet with wireless bridges, you need two bridges and the proper antennas to test for the best placement of the devices. With both the bridges and the access points, you might want to carry alternate antennas to test for the possible coverage patterns they provide.

FIGURE 12.1   Throughput test configuration

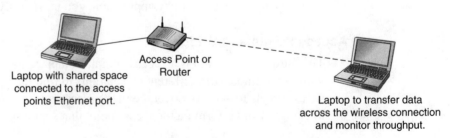

Laptop with shared space connected to the access points Ethernet port.

Access Point or Router

Laptop to transfer data across the wireless connection and monitor throughput.

Battery Power Source (UPS)

If you are an employee of the company where the site survey will be performed, you probably know where power sources are located and you may not need charged UPS systems or battery packs with DC-to-AC converters. If you are a consultant going in to a company to perform the site survey, you might find these devices very helpful. You won't have to worry about power outlet locations when testing for RF coverage. Of course, when implementation time comes, if there are no outlets where you determine the access points should be placed, you'll need to install power outlets or run an Ethernet cable and use Power over Ethernet to power the device.

If you are testing a small environment, such as a 20 × 40 foot office, for example, you might be able to get by with a laptop running a software-based access point and another laptop acting as the client. This setup allows you to test for interference and RF coverage without needing batteries or any other power source for an access point.

Site Survey Software

Wireless site survey software falls into three main categories:

- Dedicated site survey software
- Wireless protocol/packet analyzers
- Wireless finder software

Using dedicated site survey software, you can usually import a blueprint of the building and then map your findings to the blueprint on-the-fly as you are working. This feature is very useful, but site survey software is so expensive that most small businesses do not benefit from its use. If you are a contractor or consultant, you might want to invest in this software as you will be performing site surveys for many locations over time.

In many cases, site survey software provides predictive modeling features. If you know the material types for walls, ceilings, floors, and other environmental objects (such as windows and doors), the software can determine optimal placement of antennas and other wireless devices with an acceptable level of accuracy. Because things often change between the site survey and the actual implementation, always test the results you get after the installation to be sure nothing has changed, warranting a different device placement scheme.

The wireless protocol analyzer is a packet analyzer that allows you to see the traffic traversing the wireless networks in "earshot." Use this to determine if interference is active or passive; in other words, active interference from a nearby wireless network or passive interference from a motor or microwave oven. These tools can also show you the actual throughput of applications on the wireless network and verify that encryption settings are working properly.

The third category of software is wireless finder software. The most well-known tool in this category is the NetStumbler application. This freeware tool, which also comes in a PDA version called MiniStumbler, shows you the wireless networks in an area and is used often by war drivers, as discussed in the previous chapter. Because the tool shows the noise floor, signal strength, and signal-to-noise ratio, it can be very useful for site surveys.

Note-taking Implements

We live in a computerized world, but in reality, when walking around a facility performing a site survey, a pad and pen or pencil seem to work best for taking notes. Some technicians use Tablet PCs with Wi-Fi gear installed to perform site surveys. This gives them a wireless client and their pad, pen, grid paper, and even Visio software all-in-one. If you choose to use a Tablet PC, be aware that the wireless NICs that come installed from the factory are seldom best for performing site surveys; however, you can usually disable the internal NIC and install a PCMCIA or CardBus NIC to serve the purpose fine. The Orinoco Gold card, shown in Figure 12.2, is an excellent card for site surveys if you do not need an external antenna.

FIGURE 12.2   Orinoco Gold 11a/b/g ComboCard

Blueprints or Floor Plans

Having blueprints or floor plans is essential when working in medium and large facilities. Full blueprints show the locations of power outlets, and you map out the RF cells and device placements right on the plan. Another advantage of mapping the installation directly on the floor plan is it's easier for decision makers to understand your proposals. Because they're familiar with the layout of their buildings, they're more likely to grasp your message when looking at the device placements and RF cell sizes overlaid on the floor plan.

Some intelligent site survey software programs provide predictive modeling for wireless implementations. If you can define the wall materials, ceiling materials, and other environmental factors, the software can predict, within a certain level of accuracy, where you should place the access points and how to configure them in terms of output power, antenna types, and so on. While this software is seldom perfect, it can be a tremendous timesaver and often yields results that require only minor changes during actual implementation. Because of cost constraints, this software is not likely to be available for smaller projects, however.

Network Diagrams

If you're the network administrator of the company where the wireless site survey is to be performed, you likely have these network diagrams. (You have documented your network, right?) As a consultant or contractor, ask for them to be emailed to you before the site survey, if possible. When a client does not have a network diagram, make sure they have one—of at least the wireless portion of the network—when you leave. As you upgrade and troubleshoot the network in the future, diagrams will be useful to the organization.

Indoor and Outdoor Antennas

You'll need various antennas to test different configurations. Compare the results of two or three different omni-directional antennas and consider testing directional antennas for indoor and outdoor scenarios.

Omni-directional antennas allow you to test with different dBi gain antennas to provide the needed coverage and nothing more. Remember that a higher dBi gain antenna "flattens" the RF output so it goes farther, but it does not reach as high or as low (above and below) as a lower dBi antenna. If you're using an omni-directional antenna to provide coverage for multiple floors in a building, you may need to use lower gain antennas.

Actual results show that 7 dBi and lower antennas do not have tremendous impact on vertical coverage; however, the 12 dBi omnis often have a huge impact on vertical coverage. Remember that the position directly above or below an omni-directional antenna often has a lower signal strength than a position some distance away horizontally.

Directional antennas help when testing point-to-point links or alternative coverage options. For example, you can test the results of an omni-directional antenna placed in the center of a coverage area and then test the results with a semidirectional antenna placed on the outer perimeter of the coverage area and pointed inward. This helps you determine if the omni- or the semidirectional antennas serve your purposes better.

When creating point-to-point links, use semidirectional or highly directional antennas depending on the distance of the link. For most point-to-multipoint links, use one high-powered omni-directional antenna and two or more semidirectional or highly directional antennas.

RF Cables and Connectors

Because you provide all the equipment used for the site survey, you should know all the RF connector types (RP-TNC, RP-SMA, MC, and so on) that you will need. Be sure to take some extension cables as well. Extension cables can be very useful in adjusting the location of the antenna instead of the access point to determine optimal location of the access point and antenna combination in the final implementation.

Binoculars and Two-way Radios

If you are creating links between buildings that are more than 150 to 200 apart, take binoculars and two-way radios with you. An assistant can be on the other end of the link and you can give instructions for antenna positioning over the radio. Make sure the two-way radios are not using an interfering frequency such as 2.4 GHz.

Standard Toolbox and Tools

Standard tools are part of any site survey toolkit. Bring a toolbox full of basic tools such as pliers, screwdrivers, hammers, hex wrenches, and so forth. These tools come in handy when you need to gain access to enclosures that are permanently fastened to the wall, ceiling, roof, or floor of the facility. Make sure you include some industrial ties in this toolbox, too; they're helpful for temporary placement of access points and antennas to poles and other mounting locations.

Digital Camera

Have you ever gotten back to your office after visiting another site in your organization or the site of a customer only to wonder, "I think there was an available power outlet in that office"? If you have, you are not alone. Bring a digital camera with you and take pictures of any areas where you will be installing equipment.

 Here's a great tip I learned from shooting video for computer-based training programs (I'm afraid I don't have the looks for Hollywood): Take a dry-erase board with you and write the purpose of the photo on it. Then, take a picture with the dry-erase board in it. You can use a small 8.5 × 11 sheet of board. It saves you a lot of headaches down the road. Imagine looking at three different pictures of similar rooms and trying to remember which is which. To make your life simpler, use this dry-erase board trick and all your digital images will be labeled in the picture itself.

Distance Measuring Wheel

The final must-have tool in your kit is a distance measuring wheel or, at least, a tape measure to measure distances for determining where dynamic rate shifting occurs and the cable lengths needed. Remember the old rule: measure twice, cut once. This adage is even more important when going offsite to perform an install because you can waste a lot of time if you have to make multiple trips away from the facility.

Carrying Cases and/or Carts

As you can see, you have a lot of equipment in your site survey toolkit. You probably won't use all of it on any single site survey, but you'll use some of it on every site survey. Having what you need when you need it is a big timesaver. I know a construction contractor who never seems to have what he needs when he goes onsite to do a job. When he runs into the first thing he needs, he goes to the store to get it and then heads back to work. A little later, he needs something else requiring another trip to the store. Of course, this is not very efficient and the same is true for your site survey. So, gather all the tools you need and use a good carrying case or cart to help you lug it from place-to-place.

Discovering User Needs

According to research performed by the Standish Group in their CHAOS Report, one of the top factors in the success of any IT project is user involvement and a clear definition of requirements. After having installed and consulted on the installation of many wireless networks, I can assure you that it is just as true of infrastructure-based projects like wireless and wired networking as it is of programming-type projects, which was the main focus of the Standish Group study. Determining the needs of your users includes the following elements:

- Perform a business process analysis
- Determine technical requirements of users
- Determine security requirements of users
- Perform a feasibility analysis

Business Process Analysis

A *business process* is a set of logically or sequentially related business activities that combine to deliver something of value to a customer, which, in turn, provides value to the organization. Business processes may cross departmental boundaries and, therefore, may cross network segments. Departmental employees generally work together in an area and that area is usually a single network segment connected to other segments, and therefore other departments, by routers. Larger organizations can have multiple IP subnets for a single location that might house only one department. The point is that business processes are likely to be impacted by the combination of your wireless and wired LANs and WANs.

Because these processes are impacted by the performance of the network, you should analyze them to determine how employees use the network. For example, a sales professional enters data into a database related to a sale that a shipper in the shipping department then accesses to deliver the products. The customer service staff will access this data for a follow-up call 48 hours after scheduled delivery to determine if the product arrived at the destination to the customer's satisfaction. This is considered the last step in the sales process. In this process, there are three points of network contact, but understanding what happens before and after that network contact tells you if wireless technology can help improve the process. For example, the shipper might be able to ship products faster if he carries a wireless Pocket PC that beeps when a new order needs to be

FIGURE 12.3   Business process diagram

Sales Person Enters the Sale
Into the System

Shipper Processes Order

Customer Service
Verifies Satisfaction

prepared for shipment. If he currently checks for new shipments once every two hours, adding wireless technology might provide an advantage.

It often helps to document the flow of business processes in a way that provides a visual representation of the actual process. You can do this with Visio and other flow diagramming tools. Figure 12.3 shows a business-process flow diagram based on the information in the previous paragraph. You can actually "see" how the business is accomplished and this often triggers ideas for improving that process.

Technical Requirements

When investigating the technical requirements for the wireless network, consider the following components:

- Applications and the bandwidth required
- Maintenance tasks and the bandwidth required
- Response times needed for satisfactory results
- QoS requirements
- Number of clients
- Support for older clients

Applications and maintenance tasks both require bandwidth on your wireless networks. Applications sometimes require continual bandwidth and sometimes require bursts of bandwidth. For example, when running an application on a terminal server from a client, communications are continual because this environment sends screens to the client and keystrokes and mouse movements and clicks to the server where processing actually occurs. On the other hand, when running Microsoft Excel on a client computer and saving data to the network, a burst of bandwidth is required when the user saves the data to the network and very little bandwidth is needed at other times. Determining the sustained and maximum bandwidth demands are important factors in these situations.

Applications also require different response times and QoS guarantees. A VoIP implementation is very intolerant to delays while a user browsing a website is not as demanding. If you need to support QoS-type applications, such as VoIP, be careful to select the appropriate equipment with the needed features.

The final technical requirement covered here is that of the clients. You need to know how many and the types of wireless clients required in each coverage area. If you must support older clients or PDAs, they might support only 802.11b and this impacts the newer clients running 802.11g devices. Consider dedicating one or more access points to the 802.11b clients and a separate pool to the 802.11g devices.

Security Requirements

Another important area to investigate is security requirements. Different environments demand different levels of security. When investigating security requirements, consider these issues:

- What level of confidentiality is needed?
- What level of throughput is needed (this helps determine what level of encryption to use as encryption adds overhead and reduces throughput)?
- What kind of authentication must be used?
- Do you need to support multiple forms of authentication for different users?
- Do you need a wireless intrusion detection system?
- Does the site have existing wireless devices that support older standards only?

Feasibility Analysis

The final part of analyzing users' needs is to determine if their needs are possible within the budget constraints of the organization. Nearly anything is possible, but that doesn't mean it's feasible. Feasibility analysis includes answering the following questions:

- Does the technology exist that provides for the users' demands?
- If it does exist, can you combine technologies to meet these demands and also provide all other needed services?

- Can you provide the needed security while implementing all the users' needs?
- Is the budget available to accomplish what is being asked of you?
- Is there a measurable or perceived return on investment (ROI) from the implementation?

If you can answer these questions affirmatively, you're on your way to a successful wireless implementation before you have even started analyzing how the RF signals act in the organization's facilities. If you cannot answer them affirmatively, expect problems and be aware of a high probability of failure for your project. In the end, you may implement a wireless network service that makes you proud, but if it doesn't provide for users' needs, they won't share your feelings. Determine the users' needs and do your best to make them a reality. Don't over promise, however, and then under deliver. It's better to tell the user something is not possible in the beginning and have them approve going ahead anyway than to tell them you can "probably" get it done and then fail later on.

RF Behavior

RF signals can surprise you. If you work in a single organization and are responsible for their wireless network implementation, it's essential to test the behavior of RF in your facilities. Even engineers who have performed wireless installations in dozens of facilities are often surprised by what can cause RF reflections and degraded signal strength in a production environment. While over time you may gain an intuitive ability to determine how RF will behave in any given environment, it's best to test every time. There may be "hidden" RF generating motors and devices that no one in the facility is aware of and only a full RF test of the facility reveals.

You can usually get the information you need by setting up an access point in an area and then determining if it gives you the coverage you expect for that area. Document your findings and then move the access point to the next location where you need a wireless cell. Continue to do this until you have blanketed the facility with your tests and determined—by actually placing the wireless equipment—that the devices behave as you need. In some areas, you may have to move the access point or antenna to modify the results you are getting. Sometimes a shift of a few inches can make all the difference.

This doesn't mean you can't plan ahead to determine where you think access points should be placed to provide the needed coverage. If the organization can give you floor plans before the site survey, you can insert access points in the diagram where you think they're needed based on standard behavior. When you get to the facility, test based on this preliminary configuration and then modify as you go. Assuming the floor plans or blueprints list the locations of elevators and break rooms (microwave ovens), you can at least take some placement precautions in advance.

Interference Discovery

Interference discovery is a very important part of a site survey. Because Wi-Fi equipment uses the unlicensed frequency bands, other businesses or homes might be using Wi-Fi equipment in a nearby location. This is highly likely in large cities and less likely in rural areas; however, you can't assume there are no other Wi-Fi networks just because you're in a rural location.

In a worst-case scenario, you have so much Wi-Fi traffic around you in the 802.11b/g and 802.11a frequencies that you cannot install a standard Wi-Fi network that functions effectively. While it is possible for you to negotiate with your neighboring businesses and home users, because the frequencies are unlicensed, you might not be able to get them to change their networks. Wi-Fi space is on a first-come, first-served basis.

If you can't work with your neighbors to adjust the channels used, you might be able to get them to turn the power output down on their access points. Perhaps they have the settings at the default and it might be more than they need. Educating them on the possible ways to "play nice" is often enough to get the change made.

RF interference does not come from other Wi-Fi networks alone. You should also consider the possibility of interference from 2.4 GHz phones, microwave ovens, and elevator motors. All these can cause problems for your network; investigate fully to determine if they actually cause any measurable interference.

Hardware Selection and Placement

Only after you've determined the needs of users and the behavior of RF signals in the facilities can you select the best equipment for the job. This allows you to ensure the access points selected include the security and capabilities needed by the organization and replace the factory antennas with alternatives, if needed. You can also select the appropriate mounting hardware, Power over Ethernet equipment (when needed), and other items to complete the installation.

For outdoor installations, you need to acquire the appropriate enclosures and mounting poles or towers. The access point is often located inside an outdoor enclosure with the antenna mounted to the outside of the enclosure or to a pole at a nearby location. If the pole or tower is a great distance from the access point, you may need to install an amplifier in the path to the antenna to make up for signal loss in the cable.

When selecting equipment, remember that all Wi-Fi hardware is not created equal. Just as any other computing devices, access points run software and some software programs run better than others. You can have two access points, both supporting the same 802.11-based standard, that provide very different performance. Some have greater range with lesser throughput while others have lesser range with greater throughput. You're responsible for determining the right device for the users' needs in each installation.

Existing Networks and Systems

The final element of the site survey is the analysis of existing networks and systems. Knowing what users are accustomed to can help you satisfy those users in a wireless world. If they currently use 10baseT network configurations, a wireless network likely presents no apparent difference to them. However, if they are currently on 100MB or GB speeds, the wireless results will be noticeably different.

The newer MIMO technologies being produced today have the potential of coming close to 100 Mbit Ethernet. They're still slower, in my tests, but close enough that most users do not notice the difference unless they're transferring really large files frequently. The problem with this technology is that many vendors implement it differently because the standard (802.11n) is not yet complete. Once the standard is finalized, this technology should be available in a standard implementation that works across vendors.

Other factors to consider regarding existing networks and systems include Ethernet connection locations, current network utilization, expandability of existing computers, and the applications in use and planned.

Ethernet Connection Locations

You need to connect access points, wireless bridges, wireless routers, and other wireless devices that are network connected to an Ethernet port. To do this, you need to know where the existing Ethernet connections are located and how many, if any, are available. It is not uncommon for a wiring closet to have three or four 24-port switches with all the ports being used. You may need to install a new switch in order to have a port for the wireless device or devices.

 Don't think that your work as a wireless engineer means you don't have to work with standard wired equipment. At some point, most wireless networks touch the wired world in some way—usually at the backbone of the internal network or at the Internet connection (WiMAX could change this part soon). In any case, you need to be familiar with routers, bridges, switches, and other devices from the wired side of the network as well.

One of the easiest ways to keep track of where you need to provide an Ethernet connection versus where a connection already exists is on the floor-plan map of the facility. When you diagram the location of wireless devices, go ahead and note whether an Ethernet port or power outlet is available in that area. This one document is a source for determining all the hardware you need to provide and budget for to perform the install.

Current Network Utilization

A second important element related to the existing network is current utilization. Assuming the current network continues to exist, which may or may not be the case, you must consider what your wireless network will add to that utilization. In some cases, an equal number of users stop using the wired network as those who begin using the wireless network. In effect, this nearly cancels out any bandwidth changes. The reality, even in these circumstances, is that those users who were not originally slated to utilize the wireless network often get wind of it and start accessing it with their Pocket PCs or laptops as well. Before you know it, network utilization has reached a ceiling and users are beginning to complain about performance.

As a general rule, if the existing network is at 75–80 percent utilization, consider segmenting the network or upgrading to a faster medium and device set on the wired side before installing the wireless network. You may not have to do this on all segments. In some cases, changing the segment where the wireless devices attach suffices. Even if network utilization is lower than

75 percent, it's important to consider how the new wireless network and devices impact it.

Wireless devices can be accessed in users' workspaces, and they can also be accessed in a mobile fashion. This "nature-of-the-beast" often causes network utilization to climb higher than the administrative staff expected. Once users discover that they can take their laptop to the conference room and work during the meeting, they do it en masse, which causes network utilization to climb higher than it was previously because more users are accessing the network at any given time. In the past during meetings, users stopped using the network, which freed the network for other users who weren't in meetings. The wireless network could change all that.

Expandability of Existing Computers

An equally important factor to consider is the expandability of existing computers. I still encounter networks with computers that have no USB ports and only PCI slots for expandability. This means that I'm forced to use PCI adapters for the wireless network. While this isn't a problem, the computers are older and don't process wireless networking as well as wired and it takes longer to set them up—because older computers take longer to set up—and you have to take them apart. Factor this into the cost of implementing the wireless network.

Laptops often come with wireless capabilities built in; however, the older wireless-capable laptops only support 802.11b, which means they do not perform like newer 802.11g cards and they aren't compatible with any MIMO technologies. For this reason, you might want to upgrade these laptops with newer wireless cards. First, disable the built-in wireless device and then install the new one. This can take time, but most laptops can use USB devices or PCMCIA/CardBus devices that install rather quickly and perform very well.

When selecting wireless devices for desktop computers, keep in mind the location of the antenna. Most PCI cards have an antenna connected directly to the back of the computer. Computer units are often placed under the users' desks, however, and this can reduce the ability of the wireless card to communicate. Purchase an external antenna with a cable long enough to reach the top of the users' desks to allow for effective communications and overcome any problems created by having the antenna so low and close to the computer.

Applications In Use and Planned

The final element to consider is the application set on the network. Some applications use the network intensely and others use the network very little or not at all. Often, newer versions of applications consume more bandwidth as the applications add new features, but at other times they consume less.

At the time of this writing, Microsoft is beta testing their new version of Microsoft Office, which is called Office 12 (at least for now). According to preliminary studies, the new Office file format, which now uses XML instead of proprietary formats, is up to 90 percent smaller in data size. Even if the final product reduces file size by only 50 percent, can you imagine the impact on network bandwidth? Many companies have more than 1GB of Microsoft Office data traversing their network daily (and these are small to medium-sized companies). Cutting that in half would have a tremendous impact on network utilization. This is just one example of how newer technologies sometimes reduce the bandwidth consumed on the network.

When considering applications, look at bandwidth consumption per second or minute of use and how many users access the application at a given moment. Consider the scenario where at any given moment, an application consumes approximately 20 Kbps and 20 users on the same network segment are working in the application. This means the application requires at least 400 Kbps to operate effectively. If you discover 25 such applications are used at the same time on the network, bandwidth increases to 10 Mbps. This estimate doesn't factor in network management processes, such as DHCP, DNS, WINS, network monitoring, and so on, that consume bandwidth themselves separately from the applications.

Performing the Site Survey

Now that you understand the basic components of a site survey and the tools needed to perform one, I'll walk you through a typical site survey for a small business. In most small businesses, the primary focus is on reducing interference sources because the space being covered is usually relatively small. Site surveys for larger installations are more complex than what is described here.

The basic process of performing the site survey for a small business can be broken into three main steps:

1. Get an overview of the organization
2. Perform the physical site survey
3. Document your findings

Get an Overview of the Organization

An organizational overview consists of understanding where the organization is currently, where they hope to go, and what their intentions are for the wireless network. You'll interview managers and users and gather the appropriate documentation. I suggest providing a summary of this information to the decision makers before performing the physical site survey. This verifies that your understanding is correct and provides an opportunity for the decision maker to change the intended plans.

Interviewing

Understanding the organization's business processes is an essential first step. Interview the management staff for each department impacted by the wireless network to determine their current processes and future needs. You may also want to sample survey some of the end users of the current network and future wireless network. Determine what applications they run, how they obtain the information they enter into the applications, what their primary responsibilities are, and any other information that helps you better plan the wireless network.

Interviewing methods vary, but here are a few techniques you can consider using:

- Focus groups
- One-on-one meetings
- Surveys
- Observation

While all of these techniques can reveal beneficial information, I've found observation to be effective and often essential. Have you ever had someone ask you how you do a certain portion of your daily work? If you have, you probably found it difficult to recall every step along the way.

The users of the future wireless network are going to have the same difficulty. By observing their actions, you ensure that the steps you are documenting are the actual steps taken to perform the work.

Gathering Documentation

Next, you want to gather blueprints and floor plans for pre-evaluation and for documentation use later on. In addition, acquire any available network diagrams. These might show the services running on the network, which helps you determine bandwidth needs for the wireless network. They can also be used to discover available Ethernet ports if they are sufficiently detailed. Figure 12.4 shows a simple network diagram for a small business network.

This diagram does not provide any information on available ports in the switches or routers, which is not uncommon, but at least you know where the devices are located. You can also discover bandwidth needs based on the fact that there is a SQL Server and three file servers. You need to ask the network administrator how heavily the SQL Server is used and how often the file servers are accessed.

FIGURE 12.4   Network diagram for small businesses

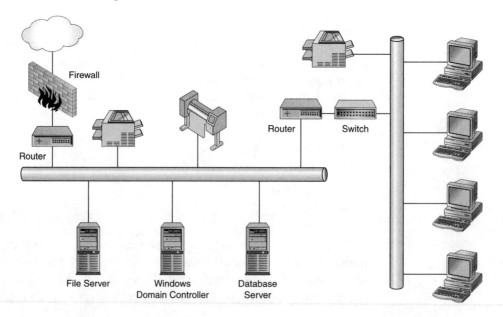

Perform the Physical Site Survey

When performing the physical site survey itself, you're likely to encounter other wireless networks in the same area. It's not uncommon to see information similar to that in Figure 12.5 when using NetStumbler to perform an existing wireless network analysis.

If you're surrounded by organizations using all three channels for 802.11b/g in an area, you might need to plan for an 802.11a implementation. An 802.11a network is more expensive, and for this reason, you might choose to attempt negotiations with the organizations surrounding the intended implementation area. Figure 12.6 illustrates a scenario where you might be able to negotiate a modification of settings in another organization's implementation.

In this figure, the organization north of your facility is using 802.11g devices on channel 6. The organization south of your facility is using 802.11g devices on channel 11, and the organization east of your facility is using 802.11g devices on channel 1. In reality, the distance between the facility on the east and the north is far enough (more than 200 meters or roughly 656 feet) that they could both utilize 802.11g devices on the same channel. This frees a channel for your environment. There would be no extra cost to the neighboring organizations, and in effect, you only have to get one of them to make the change.

FIGURE 12.5   Multiple existing networks

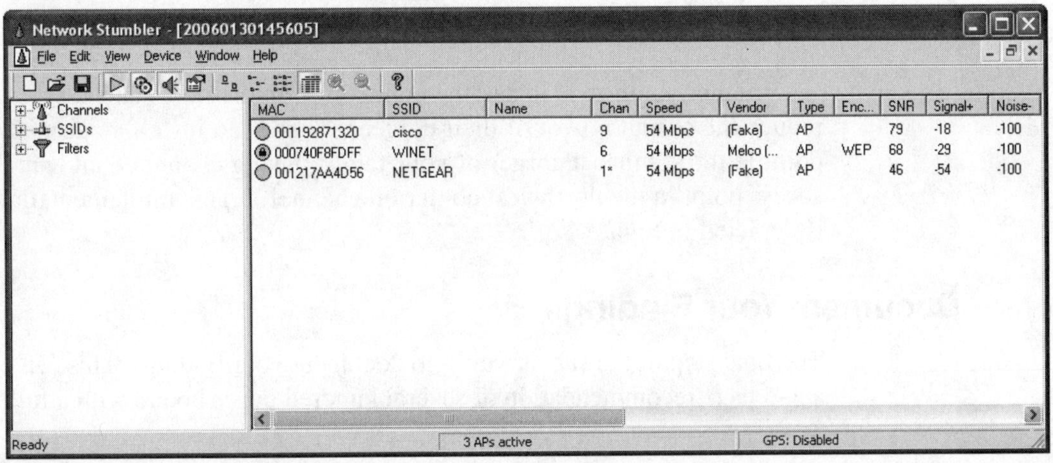

FIGURE 12.6   Negotiation scenario

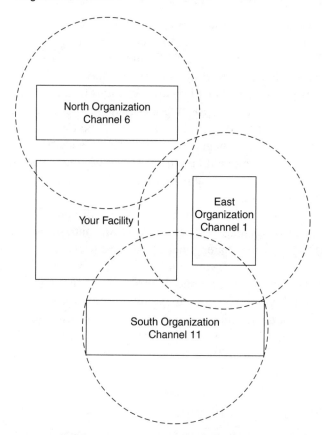

Another solution is to ask the companies on the north and east to reduce the output power of their devices. Then, you install an access point in the southeast corner of your facility using channel 6 and an access point in the northwest corner on channel 1. This implementation is depicted in Figure 12.7.

Document Your Findings

The final step of the site survey is to document your findings. This can be a 3–5 page recommendation or several hundred pages bound with a full

FIGURE 12.7   Implementation after adjusting power levels

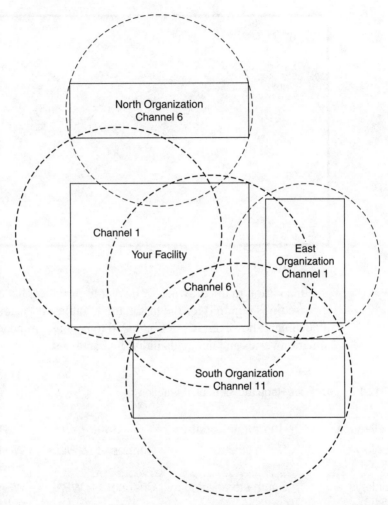

installation and maintenance plan. In most cases, you can provide rough sketch drawings, similar to the one in Figure 12.8, that will suffice for small businesses. You can take this drawing back to the office and re-create it using Visio or another diagramming tool for the client presentation.

FIGURE 12.8   Site survey drawing

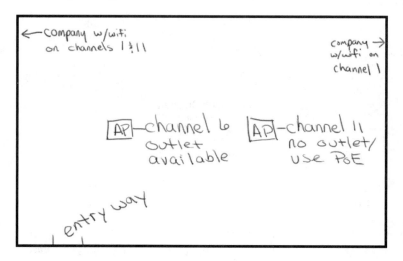

In addition to the drawing, you want to provide a list of devices and their settings required for the installation. Table 12.1 is an example of such a document; however, it's not intended to be a recommended list. Each situation varies and demands individual analysis.

TABLE 12.1   Devices Required for Implementation

Device	Installed Location	Settings	Requirements
AP (Linksys WAP54GP)	North closet	Channel 6, WPA	WPA, variable output power, PoE
AP (Linksys WAP54G)	South storage room	Channel 11, WPA	WPA, variable output power
AP (Linksys WAP54G)	Front office	Channel 1, WPA	WPA, variable output power
Router (Linksys WRT54G)	IT center	Channel 11, WPA, VPN Pass-through	WPA, variable output power, VPN pass-through
35 PCMCIA Cards (Linksys WPC54G)	Throughout facility	Based on location	WPA, 802.11G

Implementing the Network

This section provides you with an in-depth understanding of how to implement a wireless network by taking you step-by-step through an actual demonstration. To help you understand the reason for each set of tasks, study the diagram shown in Figure 12.9. This diagram of the facility shows the intended location of infrastructure devices and which devices will be used at the different locations in the facility.

In this example implementation, you're using Linksys WAP54G access points, which are a good choice for most small business uses. You'll also use one Buffalo Technology Air Station wireless router with PPTP VPN end-point functionality. This router allows for remote client connections to the organization's network. Existing wired clients use a standard 16-port switch and one wired server as a file-and-print server. You'll connect a new 8-port switch into the existing 16-port switch to provide the needed Ethernet ports.

The technology used in this chapter is just a sampling of the technology available today and should not be taken as an implication of its superiority over other technologies. Evaluate every situation independently to select the best solution.

FIGURE 12.9   Infrastructure device locations

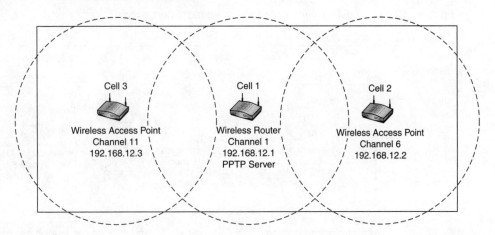

The organization in this example scenario has four goals:

- Provide wireless connectivity for all future client devices.
- Provide sufficient bandwidth for typical business applications such as saving Microsoft Office documents to the server, email, and web browsing.
- Allow for remote VPN connections to the corporate network for select users while providing acceptable levels of security for a low risk implementation.
- Provide acceptable security without the need for continual modifications of configuration settings.

Installing the Infrastructure

The first step to installing the wireless infrastructure is to install the new 8-port switch. This device provides the needed ports to connect the wireless access points to the existing wired network. The existing 16-port switch is located near the center of the facility, as shown in Figure 12.10. Plug the 8-port switch directly into the 16-port switch, and because all 16 ports are in use, unplug one Ethernet cable and then plug it into the 8-port switch to provide continued support for the wired device. This leaves 6 available ports in the new 8-port switch of which 4 are required for your implementation.

FIGURE 12.10   Existing wired network with added 8-port switch

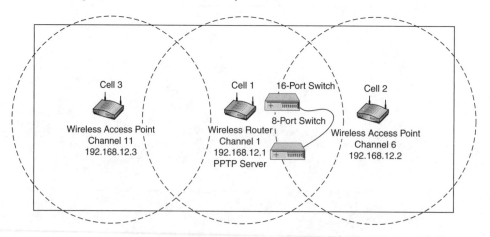

TABLE 12.2   Infrastructure Devices, Channels, and Configuration Specifics

Device	Channel	Specific Configurations
Wireless router	1	PPTP server, WPA, Internet routing, SSID (WINET)
Access point 1	6	WPA, SSID (WINET)
Access point 2	11	WPA, SSID (WINET)

To successfully install this wireless network infrastructure, which consists of two wireless access points and one wireless router, perform the following configuration steps:

1. Configure and install the router.
2. Configure and install the access points.
3. Test the implementation.

Table 12.2 lists the primary configuration settings for each of these infrastructure devices to guide you through the installation and configuration of each device.

Configure and Install the Router

This example implementation uses a Buffalo Technology Air Station WZR-RS-G54 broadband router (see Figure 12.11). This device provides a VPN PPTP server without the need for extra software on other devices such as a Windows server running Routing and Remote Access Services. Internet access is also provided through this device, and it provides DHCP services to the network. As an 802.11g standards-based device, it offers 54 Mbps data rates for the wireless network in the coverage cell referenced as "cell 1" in Figure 12.9.

The first step to installing this device is to configure the settings in the wireless router. For security purposes, do not connect the device to the existing network. To configure the device, connect an Ethernet cable to the available port on the router and then connect the other end of the cable to a laptop computer. This device defaults to an IP address of 192.168.12.1, so you configure the IP settings on the local laptop to reflect those in Figure 12.12.

FIGURE 12.11 Buffalo Technology WZR-RS-G54 wireless router

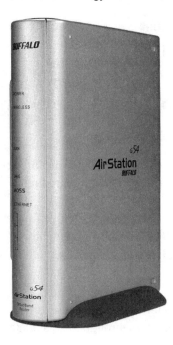

FIGURE 12.12 IP Settings on laptop to configure Buffalo Air Station

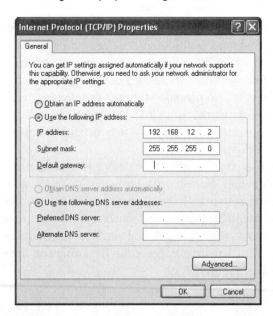

Now that the laptop has the appropriate IP configuration, you can access the configuration interface on the wireless router. To do this, open the web browser and connect to the IP address of 192.168.12.1. A logon dialog appears. Enter the user name of **root** and leave the password field blank, as this is the default. When you click OK, you see the configuration interface in Figure 12.13.

As you can see in Figure 12.13, this device supports DSL or cable Internet connections. In fact, the cable Internet connection is really just a standard router interface using Ethernet, so you could use this device to route between two internal network segments; however, this is not the intended purpose of the device and dedicated routers designed for that purpose perform better.

FIGURE 12.13   Air Station configuration screen

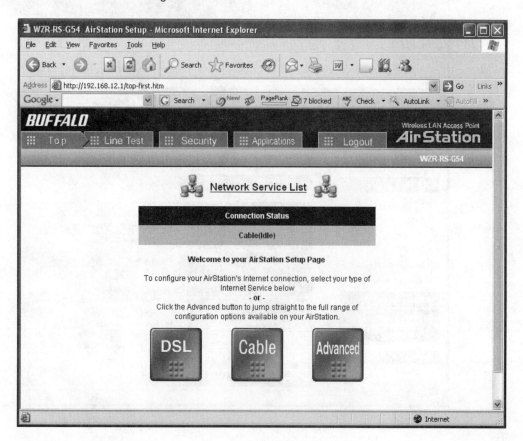

Because the network has very specific configuration needs, click the Advanced button to go to a configuration interface that allows you to enter everything manually. If you understand these settings, this interface is preferred. Though many wireless routers and access points provide wizards and automated configuration tools, you generally want to perform manual configurations for greater control over the end results and a level of certainty that the device is configured properly.

The initial configuration screen, shown in Figure 12.14, allows you to configure the SSID, wireless channel, and other settings. The device uses channel 1 and a SSID of WINET. After entering these settings, scroll down and click the Apply button.

FIGURE 12.14   Configuring the SSID and wireless channel

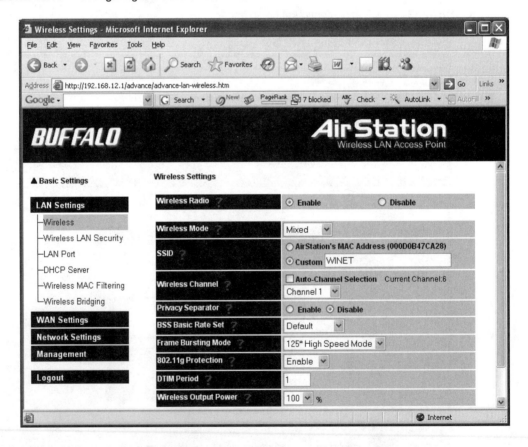

Next, you configure the security of the device by changing the default logon password to something other than blank and configuring WPA for use on the local wireless network. From the screen shown in Figure 12.14, click Wireless LAN Security from the menu on the left. Click the TKIP radio button and enter a WPA-PSK key of **911080703,** and then click the Apply button. The default logon password used to access the configuration interface is in a different location, so navigate to the Management link in the menu on the left side of the screen. Click Change Password and then change the password to something other than blank.

Since this device will provide DHCP services to the wired and wireless LANs, you need to configure the DHCP server settings next. Access these by selecting LAN Settings and then DHCP Server from the left menu. The screen shown in Figure 12.15 allows for configuration of DHCP.

FIGURE 12.15   DHCP settings

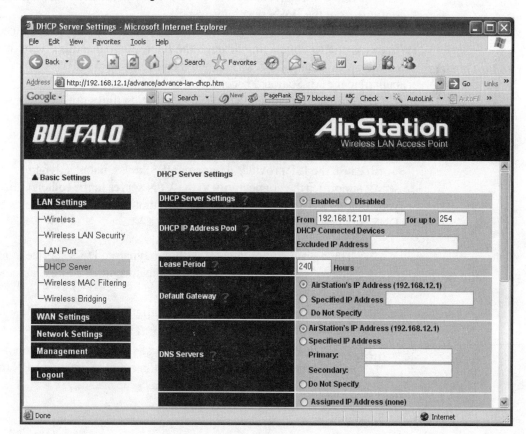

As indicated, configure the IP address pool to include the addresses from **192.168.12.101** to **192.168.12.254**. This provides plenty of IP addresses for the network, since there are far fewer than 154 devices to receive dynamic IP configuration. The nondynamic devices, which use static IP addresses, include addresses from **192.168.12.1** to **192.168.12.100**.

 If the environment in which you were implementing this wireless network included a Microsoft Active Directory network, you would probably be hosting both the DHCP and DNS on a Microsoft server. In this case, the devices function in a workgroup configuration. The Buffalo Air Station acts as the DHCP and DNS server for the network as well as the default gateway, or router, out to the Internet.

Because the small network you're installing uses an ISP that provides dynamic IP addresses only, you do not have to configure the WAN settings. This device comes preconfigured to receive dynamically configured IP settings from the WAN port interface.

The final step is to configure the device to support PPTP VPN connections from the clients connecting through the Internet. To use this effectively, configure a dynamic DNS service and then configure the PPTP server that is built in to the Air Station device.

To configure dynamic DNS, click the WAN Settings option on the left and then select the Dynamic DNS option. Figure 12.16 shows the configuration screen for dynamic DNS. Before these settings will work properly, you must create an account with DynDNS.

Because the ISP provides a dynamic IP address, using a dynamic DNS server simplifies the connectivity to the VPN server in the router. Otherwise, you couldn't save a permanent VPN configuration setting file. The dynamic DNS services work like this:

1. The device communicates with the dynamic DNS service at regular intervals to inform the service of the current IP address associated with a particular domain name.

2. The clients that wish to connect configure their VPN client software to connect to the domain name.

3. The dynamic DNS service dynamically resolves the domain name to the current IP address, allowing the client to create a VPN tunnel.

FIGURE 12.16   Dynamic DNS configuration

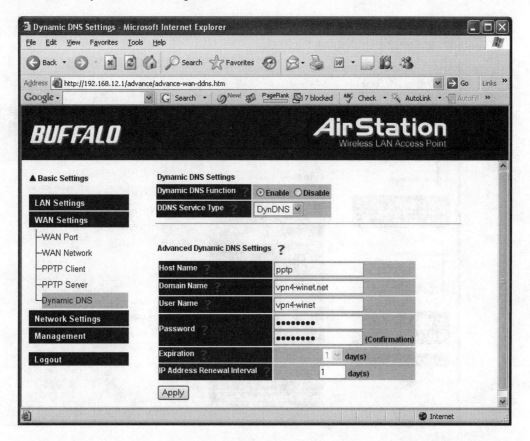

Now that you've configured dynamic DNS, you can configure the final setting for this router: the PPTP server. Click the PPTP Server option on the left menu, as shown in Figure 12.16. Because the Buffalo Air Station supports only PPTP VPNs internally, the configuration is simply one of deciding to enable the service and what encryption levels to use. As shown in Figure 12.17, allow only the highest encryption and authentication level for this system.

The router is now configured and secured, and you can connect to the wired infrastructure. The device comes with a built-in antenna that lacks communication range. For this reason, you'll connect an external antenna to the MC antenna connector. When connecting to an MC connector, be very careful as they are among the easiest to damage. With the 7 dBi

FIGURE 12.17 PPTP server configuration

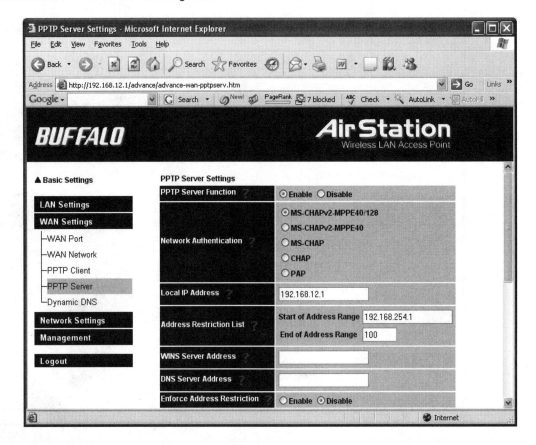

antenna connected to the device, plug the Ethernet cable into an available switch port and plug the power cable into an outlet and the device is live on the network.

This device uses a PPTP VPN protocol, which has received much press for being insecure. However, for moderate security needs, the service suffices. This implementation does not require high levels of security, so PPTP serves the needs of the organization. Also, note that the device is located in the switch closet, so there's no need for extension cables or repeaters between the device and the switch port.

Configure and Install the Access Points

Both of the access points are configured identically with the exception of the IP address and wireless channel. For this reason, I'll walk you through the configuration and installation of only one access point in detail. You'll use the Linksys WAP54G access point for this exercise.

You configure the access points in much the same way as you do the router. First, connect the access point to your laptop, and then configure the laptop's Ethernet port to the appropriate settings. Because this device defaults to an IP address of 192.168.1.245, configure the laptop's IP settings to 192.168.1.200 with a subnet mask of 255.255.255.0. To see an example of the WAP54G that you're configuring, refer to Figure 4.4 in Chapter 4.

When you first access this access point by connecting to 192.168.1.245, enter the password **admin** in the logon dialog with no user name. On the very first screen, change the IP address to **192.168.12.2** and the default gateway to **192.168.12.1**. Click Save Settings and wait for the access point to restart.

After logging on again, you configure the wireless settings. The SSID and channel are both configured on the same screen shown in Figure 12.18. Leave the device in mixed mode, as this allows both 802.11b and 802.11g devices to connect to the network. This device is located in *cell 2,* so place it on channel 6.

The next settings you'll configure are the wireless security settings, as shown in Figure 12.19. Select WPA-Personal. (This setting is the same as the WPA-PSK settings in the Buffalo Air Station router.) Use the same settings for Passphrase and Key Renewal as used for the Air Station.

The final setting to configure is the logon password for the management interface. It defaults to admin, and because this is well-known, you must change it to something more secure.

Now repeat these steps with the second Linksys WAP54G access point. Configure the channel to **11** and the IP address to **192.168.12.3**. Other than these settings, everything else is the same.

The final step is to run the cable and connect the access points to the network using two 150-foot Ethernet cables to connect the access points to the central switch in the closet. These cables run under the floor to the locations of the access points in *cells 2* and *3*, shown previously in Figure 12.9. With the cables installed and the access points plugged into the Ethernet and outlet power, the infrastructure installation is now complete.

FIGURE 12.18   Configuring the basic wireless settings

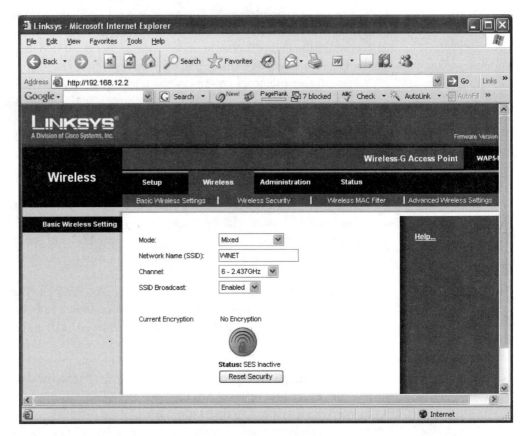

Test the Implementation

Test the implementation to verify proper configuration. You can test at each stage along the way or after the entire infrastructure has been installed. Connect a client device to the network using the appropriate security settings. If the device connects and has ample throughput and data rates, the infrastructure is working as planned. If you notice problems, you may need to perform some of the troubleshooting tips listed later in this chapter.

Installing the Clients

Now that the wireless infrastructure devices are in place, it's time to install the client devices. Some of the systems in this organization will use PCI

FIGURE 12.19   Wireless security configuration

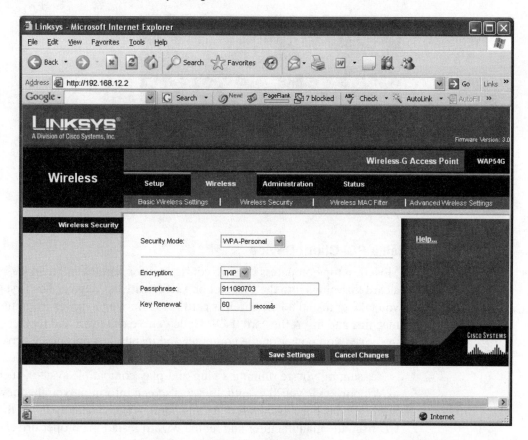

devices in desktop computers and others will use either built-in wireless
or PC card wireless devices in laptops. To understand the steps needed
for all client connection types, I'll show you how to perform the following
configuration tasks:

- Install a PCI client device.
- Install a PC card client device.
- Configure a built-in wireless device.
- Configure a client to connect with VPN.

FIGURE 12.20   D-Link wireless PCI card

Install a PCI Client Device

Most desktop computers that are configured for wireless networks use a card that plugs into the PCI slot or a USB wireless device. The first step you take to install a PCI wireless card is to remove the cover from the machine and insert the card itself. Once you've done this and replaced the cover, you power on the computer and install the appropriate drivers. Figure 12.20 shows an example of a wireless PCI card being installed.

Assuming you're running a plug-and-play compatible system, such as Windows XP, you'll eventually see a screen informing you that new hardware has been discovered. At this point, you can usually insert the CD from the manufacturer and let the wizard install the proper drivers.

 Some devices require that you install the drivers before you install the card in order for the installation to complete successfully. In addition, the specialized client software that comes with the device is not usually installed if you just install the drivers in this way. Don't be alarmed if a warning about unsigned drivers pops up, as long as you know the drivers you are installing come from a credible source. These warnings are part of the Windows 2000 and XP operating systems and do not necessarily indicate that the drivers will be problematic.

Now that the drivers are installed, you can configure the card to access the installed wireless infrastructure. The method you use for this configuration varies depending on whether you are using the wireless client software written for the device or the Windows XP built-in wireless services. In this example, you'll configure the device with the built-in wireless services.

Assuming the drivers have been installed correctly and your system is configured to use the Windows Wireless Zero Configuration (WZC), you can connect to the wireless network easily by clicking the Start button and selecting Connect To and Wireless Network Connection. You'll see the dialog shown in Figure 12.21.

If you're connected to a wireless network, this dialog box gives you the connection information. This information includes the name of the network, the length of the connection, the speed and strength of the connection, and the data packets that have been sent and received. If you're connected to a wireless network, you can see the available networks by clicking the View Wireless Networks button. A screen similar to the one in Figure 12.22 appears.

The network you've configured uses WPA for securing the wireless links. If you select the network and click Connect, you'll be asked for the passphrase. Type in the phrase used earlier (**911080703**) and then connect to the network. Once completed, the PCI card is configured and operational.

FIGURE 12.21   Wireless Network Connection dialog

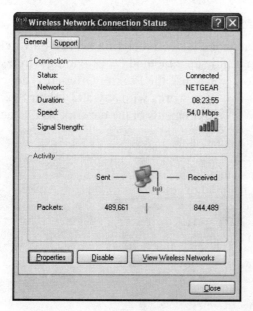

FIGURE 12.22 Available wireless networks screen

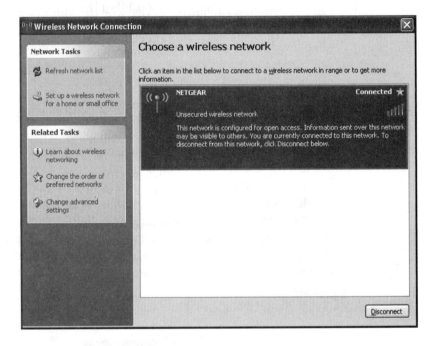

Install a PC Card Client Device

If your installation includes laptops without built-in wireless connectivity, you'll have to decide on a method for providing wireless support. For this installation, you'll use the Proxim Orinoco 11b/g card shown in Figure 12.23. This card works with any 802.11b or 802.11g network and supports the WPA requirements of the network you've built.

FIGURE 12.23 Orinoco 11b/g Gold card

Another advantage of the Orinoco 11b/g Gold card is its support for an external antenna. Other PC Cards provide this support as well, but most cards include a built-in antenna with no expandability. The use of an external antenna with this card is valuable for site surveys and security penetration-testing scenarios.

Similar to the PCI device, the first step to installing this card is to install it physically in the computer. Because the card is a PC Card, you can install it while the laptop is on, or you can install it while the laptop is off and then power the laptop on. I suggest installing the software from Proxim first and then inserting the PC Card. When you insert the accompanying CD-ROM and launch the SETUP.EXE program, you'll see a screen like the one shown in Figure 12.24.

When you click the Next button, installation begins. You'll be asked to accept the license agreement and then you must decide if you want to install the driver only or the driver and the Orinoco Wireless Utility.

FIGURE 12.24   Orinoco installation program

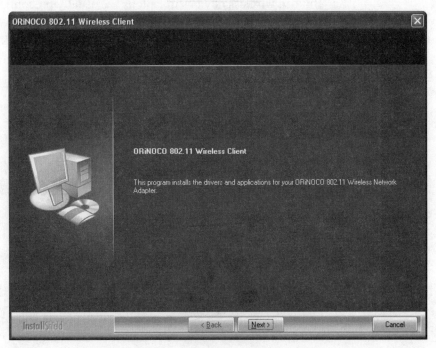

For this example, you'll install both. After selecting the file location and the Program Group name, the file copying process begins. Once it's complete, a quick click of the Finish button finalizes the operation.

When you insert the wireless card into an available PC Card slot, it's detected automatically. You can then launch the wireless client utility from Orinoco. If WZC is turned on, the utility gives you the option to turn it off. Elect to do so and you are presented with the screen shown in Figure 12.25.

To configure the device for the WINET wireless network, select the Profile Management tab and click the Modify button. Here you can enter the SSID. Then, click the Security tab where you can configure the WPA settings. Figure 12.26 shows the resulting dialog screens.

With these configuration parameters set, the client is ready to use the wireless network. If a wireless client is receiving weak signals or dropped connections with this configuration, provide them with an external antenna (using an MC connector type) to provide better signal reception and transmission. Remember, the MC connecter type is susceptible to damage, so use them with caution.

Configure a Built-In Wireless Device

Built-in wireless devices in laptops are usually preconfigured from the manufacturer; however, newer device drivers may be available and may

FIGURE 12.25 Orinoco client utility

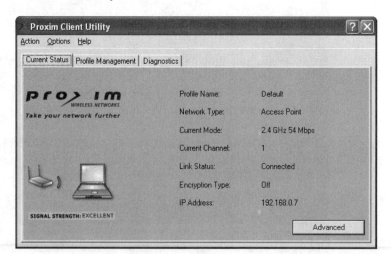

FIGURE 12.26   Security configuration screens

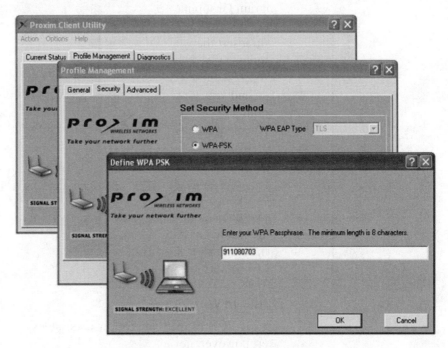

improve performance, so you should evaluate this. Once the drivers are installed, you can usually configure the device through the Device Manager in Windows-based systems. The screen in Figure 12.27 shows the configuration interface provided by the Device Manager.

Configure a Client to Connect with VPN

As you may remember, the original specifications for this installation stated that a user should be able to connect to the network from home using an Internet connection and a VPN client. You configured the VPN service in the Buffalo Air Station router, so all that's left to do is configure the clients to connect to the VPN server. You can do yourself, or users can do it based on your instructions. Either way, assuming they are using Windows XP, you can create a VPN connection to a PPTP-based VPN server easily.

FIGURE 12.27 Configuring a built-in wireless device

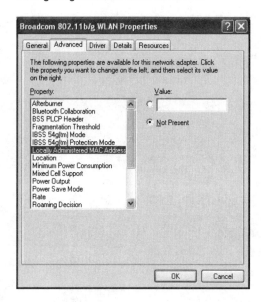

To create the VPN connection, follow these steps:

1. Click the Start button and select Connect To and Show All Connections.

2. Click the Create a New Connection option on the left-side menu (Figure 12.28).

3. Click the Next button.

4. Select Connect to the Network at My Workplace and click the Next button.

5. Select Virtual Private Network Connection and click the Next button (Figure 12.29).

6. Enter a company name or a name for the connection and click the Next button.

7. Enter the domain name **pptp.vpn4-winet.net,** which is the name used through dynamic DNS to connect to the Buffalo Air Station router (refer back to Figure 12.17 earlier in this chapter).

8. Click the Next button and then click the Finish button.

You've created the connection, and because of the default settings, you can actually connect immediately. After configuring the connection, you'll

FIGURE 12.28   Create a new connection.

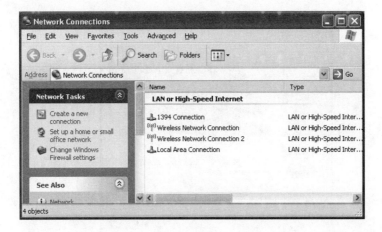

see the dialog in Figure 12.30. Here, you enter a user name and password created in the internal database on the Buffalo Air Station PPTP server.

If you want to verify the settings for the VPN connection, click the Properties button in the connection authentication dialog. After the Properties dialog is displayed, click the Networking tab. Here, you can select either PPTP or L2TP for the VPN type. You can also choose Automatic and let the software determine what the server supports. The client uses whatever the server supports that is the most secure. Figure 12.31 shows this screen.

FIGURE 12.29   Selecting Virtual Private Network

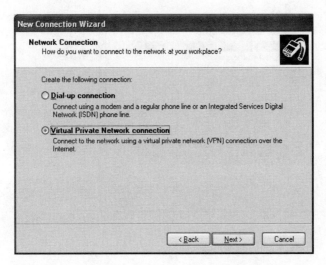

FIGURE 12.30 Connection authentication dialog

FIGURE 12.31 Selecting the VPN tunnel type

Maintaining the Network

Installing a wireless network is only the beginning of your responsibility if you're the network administrator for the organization. Once you've installed the network, you must transition to maintenance mode. In this mode, you install updated drivers and apply updated firmware from the manufacturers to keep your environment secure and provide users with the latest features and capabilities of the Wi-Fi world. There are three major tasks you must perform to keep your environment stable and secure:

- Applying firmware
- Updating client drivers
- Updating clients and servers

Applying Firmware

Depending on the manufacturer, you can receive updated firmware automatically, or you can download it manually. Some manufacturers release new firmware revisions on a near quarterly basis while others release a fix rollup shortly after the product is released with few revisions or updates after that. It is usually your responsibility to go to the website and download the firmware. Figure 12.32 shows the firmware download page for the Linksys WAP54G used earlier in this chapter.

Updating Client Drivers

Because a wireless client device may have been stored in a warehouse for months, or even years, check for newer drivers after the install. The Orinoco Gold card used earlier in this chapter shipped with drivers at version 3.0.1.6; however, version 3.1.2.19 is available for download from the Proxim website at the time of this writing. You can view the version of the installed driver in the Device Manager if you are using a Windows-based computer. Figure 12.33 shows the Version tab for an installed Proxim card before and after the driver upgrade.

Updating Clients and Servers

Much of the literature related to wireless security and installation assumes the wireless network exists in some sort of black hole all by itself. The reality is that the wireless network is just the point of access to the much larger organizational resource pool. To keep your wireless network secure,

FIGURE 12.32   WAP54G Firmware Download Page

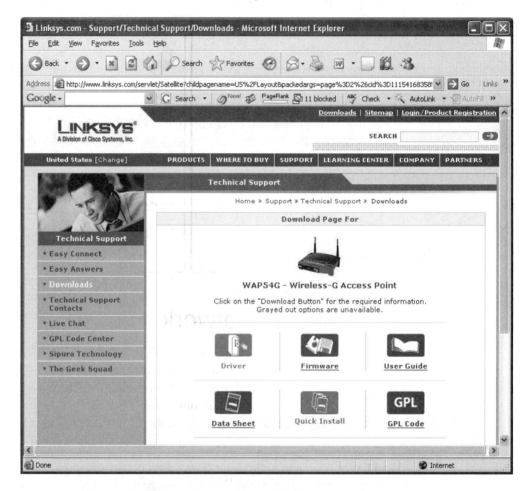

you must keep the devices on the network—clients and server—secure as well by patching the machines when security vulnerabilities are discovered and applying appropriate service packs and updates.

You might consider using automated update services such as Microsoft's Software Update Services (SUS). These services download patches from the manufacturer and allow you to distribute them automatically to your network computers. You can also configure the service to download the updates and wait for approval before distributing the update to the computers on the network. Either way, these services can save you many hours of labor.

FIGURE 12.33   Proxim drivers, old and new versions

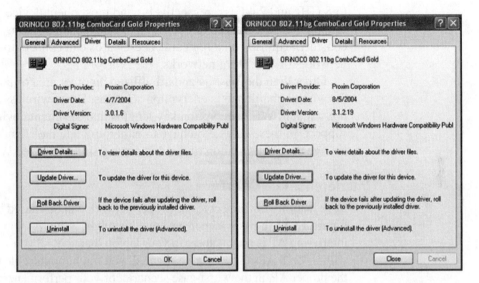

Troubleshooting the Network

There are many problems that can creep into your wireless network installations. These problems can be caused by improper installation and changes made to the environment after the installation. Many problems are the result of faulty drivers, and still others are caused by the users themselves. Among the problems you will encounter, the following are common:

- No connectivity
- Intermittent connectivity
- Decreased throughput
- Weak signal strength

No Connectivity

If you can't connect to the wireless network, it's usually because of one of three problems: incompatible hardware, interference, or configuration errors.

Incompatible Hardware

If you don't see the wireless network at all, you may have an incompatible hardware problem. You can't use an 802.11a client device to connect to an

802.11g-only network. These two technologies use different frequencies (5.8 GHz and 2.4 GHz, respectively) and most client devices support one or the other. If you need to connect to both types of systems, you should consider acquiring an a/b/g card. These cards can connect to either 802.11a networks or 802.11b/g networks.

Other than the Wi-Fi standard utilized, another area of incompatibility for wireless hardware is encryption schemes. Some wireless APs may use nonstandard WEP encryption key lengths that the client device may not support. In these cases, you have to either upgrade the client device or change the configuration of the AP to use a standard-sized WEP key.

Interference

Your inability to connect to the proper network can be caused by interference. Figure 12.34 shows a scenario where this might occur. As you can see, the interfering AP is much closer to your laptop than the AP you want to connect with. If both APs use the same channel, you might not be able to connect to the proper AP, in the worst-case scenario, or your performance will be poor, in a best-case scenario.

FIGURE 12.34   Interference from neighboring networks

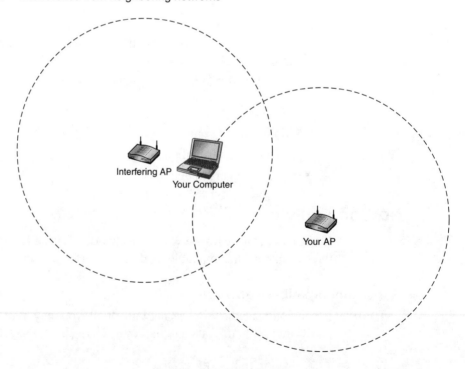

To resolve these problems, consider changing the channel of the proper access point so it does not compete with the neighboring devices. You could also use 802.11a, if the neighboring network uses 802.11g. Your final option is to relocate the laptop farther from the neighboring network.

Configuration Errors

The final common reason connectivity cannot be achieved is improper configuration. Always verify that WEP keys or WPA passphrases are entered properly. Be sure you have provided the correct SSID. Double-check the IP configuration if you can connect to the wireless network but can't actually access resources. It's not uncommon for users to think they aren't connected to the wireless network because they can't communicate on the network. The reality is that their wireless connection can be strong, but if their configuration is problematic, they can't communicate.

Intermittent Connectivity

As with no connectivity, intermittent connectivity can be the result of interference; however, it can also be caused by two common wireless problems: the hidden node and near/far.

Hidden Node

The concept of the *hidden node* problem in wireless networks is rather simple. A wireless client sees the access point, but it can't be seen by the other wireless client or clients. Because of how wireless networks deal with collisions (they try to avoid them by communicating only if no other device is communicating), problems occur when a hidden node situation is in play. Assume that the hidden node is called client01 and another node is called client02. Client02 is communicating on the network, but client01 won't realize it because it can't hear the other client. For this reason, client01 communicates on the network when it shouldn't and corrupts packets, which requires a retransmission from client02 to the access point.

Hidden nodes are normal in wireless networks, but when they decrease performance, they can be a problem. There are a number of possible solutions to the hidden node problem should it become an issue for you. These include

- Enable RTS/CTS so each client requests transmission before it transmits.
- Increase power to the nodes.

- Remove any obstacles between the nodes that cannot see each other.
- Move the hidden node to an area where the other clients can see it.

 For more information about the hidden node problem and how to deal with it, see the *CWNA Certified Wireless Network Administrator Official Study Guide (Exam PW0-100), Third Edition* by Planet3 Wireless (McGraw-Hill/ Osborne 2005).

Near/Far

The *near/far* problem is one of location. This problem occurs when one or more clients are close to the AP and using high power, and another client is far from the AP and using lower power. The client that is far from the AP may not be strong enough to overpower the closer clients. The "far" node is effectively "drowned out" of the communications.

To solve the near/far problem, increase the power of the remote node to give it the ability to communicate "over" the closer clients. You could also decrease the power of the clients closer to the AP. You could move the remote node or the AP so they're closer to one another, or you could add another AP closer to the remote node. Any of these options should solve the near/far problem.

Decreased Throughput

Decreased throughput is caused by the same issues that affect intermittent connectivity. Over time, however, another common cause of decreased throughput is the continual addition of more nodes on the wireless network. Over-utilizing the network can cause throughput levels to drop to unacceptable levels. Table 12.3 provides a breakdown of expected throughput levels per client based on the number of clients communicating on the wireless LAN at any given time. As you can see, the average throughput can become unacceptable with more than 20–25 clients communicating at the same time. Depending on the QoS needs of your implementation, even 20–25 clients may be too many.

Using 802.11g, you can install three access points in the same area and get a total available throughput of approximately 80–85 Mbps (remember, 50 percent of the bandwidth is consumed by management overhead). With 802.11a, you can install many more access points in the same area and achieve well over 200 Mbps total throughput. However, 802.11a networks have smaller coverage areas. You usually lose the 54 Mbps signal between 30 and 50 feet.

TABLE 12.3   Expected Throughput for 802.11g Based on Number of Clients

Number of Clients	Average Throughput per Client
1	26–29 Mbps
5	5–6 Mbps
10	2–4 Mbps
20	1–2 Mbps
50	.1–.5 Mbps

Weak Signal Strength

If your client can connect to the access points, but the signal strength is weak, there are four major things to verify:

- The distance between the client and the AP
- The number of walls and wall types between the client and the AP
- The output power settings on the AP
- The antenna gain at the AP and at the client

Fixing any of these problems can help, though sometimes you'll be required to change a combination of things. For example, you may have to move to an area without as many walls between you and the AP. If this is not an option, you may have to install a more powerful antenna on the client side. With the default built-in antenna, the Proxim Gold b/g PC card gives me a signal strength of 38 when I'm 20 feet from the AP with a floor between me and the AP. By connecting an external range extender antenna to the MC connecter of the card, I increase the signal strength to as much as 57 without changing any settings on either the AP or the client computer. The antenna can make that much of a difference by itself.

You can also increase the signal strength with a signal booster. Linksys has manufactured a signal booster that works with their 802.11b access point. The difficulty with signal boosters is FCC certification. According to the FCC rules, the device needs to be certified as a system, and this means connecting the Linksys signal booster to an 802.11g network; while this may work, it could be a breach of FCC regulations and you could be fined. Hawking Technologies also sells a signal booster that is certified to work with their access points. In the end, you need to be careful to use signal boosters only with devices with which they are clearly certified to operate.

Summary

Installing a wireless LAN is about understanding both the wireless hardware and the needs of the organization. To master the latter, performing a site survey is essential. The site survey reveals the needs of the organization and any potential problems that might occur during installation. It also allows you to determine the best location for the different hardware components in your wireless LAN.

Troubleshooting a wireless LAN is about understanding the behavior of wireless technology and proper configuration options and settings. By solving common problems such as no connectivity, intermittent connectivity, and weak signal strength, you can resolve most situations that arise in wireless networks.

Key Terms

- ☐ **business process analysis**
- ☐ **feasibility study**
- ☐ **hidden node**
- ☐ **interference**
- ☐ **near/far**
- ☐ **site survey**
- ☐ **technical requirements**

Review Questions

1. What is the purpose of a site survey?

   A. To discover if wireless technology really works

   B. To ensure the installation plan provides for the users' needs

   C. To make sure you have the best equipment on the market

   D. To be certain that the network supports streaming video and audio applications

2. Select the three objects from this list that you should include in a site survey toolkit.

   A. Wireless AP

   B. Wireless client device

   C. Battery pack

   D. Wireless switch

3. A user says they need to achieve fast transfer speeds on a consistent basis. Which of the following should you consider during the planning stage of the wireless implementation? Select one.

   A. The manufacturer that produced the APs you will be using

   B. The speed of the RRAS server's processor

   C. The number of users in that coverage cell

   D. The number of cells in that coverage area

4. What benefit does observation provide that polls and surveys do not usually provide?

   A. Observation reveals steps in the users' work that they often forget when they tell you what they do.

   B. Observation allows you to critique the users' processes so they can do their job better.

   C. When you observe the users, you can find out where they're having problems.

   D. There is no benefit to observation over polls and surveys.

5. What is a benefit of detached antennas during site surveys?

   A. They provide greater RTS/CTS tolerance.

   B. They can be moved around more easily than the AP itself.

   C. The antenna supports either 2.4 GHz or 5.8 GHz frequencies.

   D. You can convert your AP into a switch with the right antenna.

6. What happens to the average bandwidth available to each user as new active users are added to a coverage area serviced by a single access point?

   A. The total available data rate increases.

   B. The total available data rate decreases.

   C. The average available bandwidth decreases.

   D. The average available bandwidth increases.

7. Which of these listed items are common causes of decreased data throughput? Select two.

   A. Interference

   B. Number of users

   C. Use of wireless switches

   D. Use of generic client devices

8. Which one of these options is a possible solution to the near/far problem in wireless networks?

   A. Increase the power of the near nodes

   B. Increase the power of the far nodes

    C. Decrease the power of the far nodes

    D. Buy a newer access point

9. You notice reduced throughput in your wireless network and an increase in retransmissions according to the Proxim client utility's statistics dialog. What common wireless problem might this indicate?

    A. Outdated firmware

    B. Improper configuration

    C. Hidden node

    D. Shadow coverage

Review Answers

1. **B.** A site survey determines the best way to provide wireless coverage in the needed areas regardless of size and in accordance with the users' needs.

2. **A, B, C.** You probably won't need a wireless switch during the site survey. Although these devices are useful in wireless implementations, they are not that helpful during the site survey.

3. **C.** The factor with the most impact is the number of users in that coverage cell. If the only user in the area is the one who needs sustained fast transfers, you won't have a problem. For every user added to that area, however, the transfer speed decreases for the high-speed user.

4. **A.** When you become familiar with a process, you often forget some of the steps taken along the way. Observing the users' work processes allows you to catch these oversights and consider them for your wireless implementation plan.

5. **B.** You can reposition a detached antenna more easily than the AP itself, which allows you to test results when positioning the antenna in different locations. Antennas are either 2.4 GHz or 5.8 GHz, but not both because of the difference in the wavelength sizes between the two frequencies. For best use, the antenna needs to be a factor of the size of the wavelength.

6. **C.** The more users you have in a coverage area the less bandwidth each user has on average because all the users are sharing the same medium. Think of it as cars on a highway. When one automobile is traveling on a highway, the car can go as fast as it wants; however, when hundreds of automobiles are on that same highway, they limit the speed of each other.

7. **A, B.** Interference and the number of users in a coverage area are common causes of decreased performance. Generic hardware may perform better or worse and that can only be discovered through testing. Because wireless switches do not communicate directly on the wireless air waves, they aren't limited to the standard 54 or 11 Mbps data rates. They often provide 100 Mbps rates or even 1 GB and are therefore not the common cause of reduced throughput.

8. **B.** By increasing the power of the far node, decreasing the power of the near nodes, moving the far node closer, moving the AP closer to the far node, or installing another AP closer to the far node, you can resolve the near/far problem.

9. **C.** A hidden node is often revealed through the corruption of wireless frames and, therefore, more retransmissions occur than normal. You can resolve this by relocating the objects on the network so the hidden node is no longer hidden or by removing any obstacles creating the problem.

Standards and
Specifications Tables

802.11 Standards and Specifications

Standard	Purpose
802.11	Defines general wireless networking for PHY and MAC.
802.11b	Defines wireless networking up to 11 Mbps in 2.4 GHz spectrum.
802.11g	Defines wireless networking up to 54 Mbps in 2.4 GHz spectrum.
802.11a	Defines wireless networking up to 54 Mbps in 5 GHz spectrum.
802.11i	Defines security for wireless networks.
802.11e	Defines quality of service for wireless networks.
802.11n	Defines high bandwidth for wireless networks.

802.11a Channels

Channel	Frequency	Lower (L)/Middle (M)
36	5.18 GHz	L
40	5.20 GHz	L
44	5.22 GHz	L
48	5.24 GHz	L
52	5.26 GHz	U
56	5.28 GHz	U
60	5.30 GHz	U
64	5.32 GHz	U

802.11b/g Channels

Channel Identifier	Frequency in GHz	Regulatory Domains				
		Americas	EMEA	Israel	China	Japan
1	2.412	X	X	—	X	X
2	2.417	X	X	—	X	X
3	2.422	X	X	X	X	X
4	2.427	X	X	X	X	X
5	2.432	X	X	X	X	X
6	2.437	X	X	X	X	X
7	2.442	X	X	X	X	X
8	2.447	X	X	X	X	X
9	2.452	X	X	X	X	X
10	2.457	X	X	—	X	X
11	2.462	X	X	—	X	X
12	2.467	—	X	—	—	X
13	2.472	—	X	—	—	X
14	2.484	—	—	—	—	X

Standards and Data Rates

	802.11	802.11a	802.11b	802.11g
Frequency	2.4 GHz	5 GHz	2.4 GHz	2.4 GHz
Data Rate(s)	1, 2 Mbps	5, 9, 12, 18, 24, 36, 48, 54 Mbps	1, 2, 5.5, 11 Mbps	6, 9, 12, 15, 24, 36, 48, 54 Mbps
Modulation	FHSS, DSSS	OFDM	DSSS	OFDM
Advertised Range	300 feet	225 feet	300 feet	300 feet

RF Math Factors

dB	Factor
+3 dB	multiply times 2
+10 dB	multiply times 10
−3 dB	divide by 2
−10 dB	divide by 10

DRS Rate Adjustment Estimates

Rate	Distance (feet)	Frequency	Power
54 Mbps	60	5 GHz	40 mW
48 Mbps	80	5 GHz	40 mW
36 Mbps	100	5 GHz	40 mW
24 Mbps	120	5 GHz	40 mW
18 Mbps	130	5 GHz	40 mW
12 Mbps	140	5 GHz	40 mW
9 Mbps	150	5 GHz	40 mW
6 Mbps	170	5 GHz	40 mW
11 Mbps	140	2.4 GHz	100 mW
5.5 Mbps	180	2.4 GHz	100 mW
2 Mbps	250	2.4 GHz	100 mW
1 Mbps	350	2.4 GHz	100 mW

WiMAX Specifications

WiMAX Standards: Data Rates and Throughput

WiMAX Standard	Expected Throughput	Advertised Data Rates
Fixed LOS (802.16-2004)	40 Mbps	70–75 Mbps
Mobile NLOS (802.16e)	15 Mbps	30 Mbps

802.16-2004 Frequencies, Duplexing Schemes, and Channel Widths

Frequency (GHz)	Duplexing	Channel Width (MHz)
3.5	TDD	3.5
3.5	FDD	3.5
3.5	TDD	7
3.5	FDD	7
5.8	TDD	10

Types of WiMAX Access

Type of Access	Devices Used	Locations/Speeds	Handoffs	802.16-2004	802.16e
Fixed	Outdoor/Indoor CPEs	Single/Stationary	No	Yes	Yes
Nomadic	Indoor CPEs,PCMCIA cards	Multiple/Stationary	No	Yes	Yes
Portability	Laptop PCMCIA or mini cards	Multiple/Walking speed	Hard	No	Yes
Simple Mobility	Laptop PCMCIA or mini cards, PDAs, or smartphones	Multiple/Low vehicle speeds	Hard	No	Yes
Full Mobility	Laptop PCMCIA or mini cards, PDAs, or smartphones	Multiple/High vehicle speeds	Soft	No	Yes

Bluetooth Specifications: Power Classes and Ranges

Power Class	Range
1	100 meters (300 feet)
2	10 meters (30 feet)
3	1–3 meter (3 feet)

IrDA Specifications

Remote Controls and IrDA Comparison

Feature	Remote Controls	IrDA Devices
Communications	Unidirectional	Bidirectional
Data transfer	Small amount	Larger amounts
Distance	Many feet	1 meter
Wavelength	880 nm to 950 nm	850 nm to 900 nm
Protocols	No error checking; human monitoring required	Error checking protocols; automatic retransmission

IrDa Standards

Serial Infrared (SIR)	September 1993
Link Access Protocol (IrLAP)	June 1994
Link Management Protocol (IrLMP)	June 1994
Fast Infrared (FIR)	October 1995
Infrared Mobile Communications (IrMC)	January 1997
Infrared Object Exchange (IrOBEX)	January 1997
Infrared Wristwatch (IrWW)	October 1998
Infrared Financial Messaging (IrFM)	October 1999

IrDA Link Types and Data Rates

Link Type	Data Rate
SIR	2.4 Kbps–115.2 Kbps
MIR	0.576–1.152 Mbps
FIR	4 Mbps
VFIR	16 Mbps

ZigBee Specifications

ZigBee Frequencies

Frequency	U.S.	Europe	Worldwide
868 MHz	No	Yes	No
915 MHz	Yes	No	No
2.4 GHz	Yes	Yes	Yes

FFD vs. RFD ZigBee Devices

	Coordinator	Router	End Device
Purpose	Network establishment and control	Data routing, can talk to other routers and the coordinator as well as end devices	Only talks to routers and/or the coordinator
FFD (full function device)	Yes	Yes	Yes
RFD (reduced function device)	No	No	Yes

ZigBee Frequencies and Data Rates Provided

Frequency	Usage Areas	Channels	Channel Numbers	Data Rates
868 MHz	Europe	1	0	20 Kbps
915 MHz	U.S.	10	1–10	40 Kbps
2.4 GHz	Worldwide	16	11–26	250 Kbps

RFID Tag Types

RFID Frequencies

	UHF	HF	LF
North America	902–928 MHz	13.56 MHz	125–134 kHz
Australia	918–926 MHz		
Europe	865.6–867.6 MHz	13.56 MHz	125–134 kHz
Japan	950–956 MHz	13.56 MHz	125–134 kHz

RFID Tag Type Comparisons

Tag Type	Power Source	Memory	Communication Range
Active	Battery	Most	Greatest
Semi-Passive	Battery and reader	Moderate	Moderate
Passive	Reader	Least	Least

RFID Interface Protocols

Protocol	Frequency	Capabilities	Pros	Cons
Generation 1 Class 0	UHF	Preprogrammed tag; end user cannot write new id to tag	Lower cost	Cannot be customized
Generation 1 Class 1	UHF and HF	Write once, read many (WORM)	Open standard	Can be written to only once
ISO Standard 18000	LF, HF, and UHF	Write once, read many	Manages standard	Can be written to only once
Generation 2.0 Class 1	HF and UHF	Write once, read many	Globally accepted protocol	Write once, read once

WEP and WPA Security Combinations

Lowest Security	Highest Security	Resultant Security
None	WEP	None
WEP	WEP	Weak
WEP	WPA-Personal	Weak
WPA-Personal	WPA-Personal	Moderate
WPA-Personal	WPA-Enterprise	Moderate
WPA-Enterprise	WPA-Enterprise	Strong

EAP Types and Supported Clients and Certificate Demands

EAP Type	Common Supported Clients	Certificate Requirements
EAP-TLS	Linux, MAC OS-X, Windows 9x and NT-based systems (NT, 2000, XP, 2003)	Required for both server and client
EAP-TTLS	Same as above	Required for server: optional on client
PEAP	Windows XP	Required for server: optional on client
EAP-MD5	Most clients	No certificates; password-based; considered insecure compared to others

Throughput Tables (802.11g)

Number of Clients	Average Throughput per Client
1	26–29 Mbps
5	5–6 Mbps
10	2–4 Mbps
20	1–2 Mbps
50	.1–.5 Mbps

Glossary

3DES   An encryption standard based on the Data Encryption Standard (DES) but that uses stronger keys and key processing and is supported by many systems still today.

802.1x   An IEEE standard for port-based network access control. Utilizing various implementations of extensible authentication protocol (EAP), 802.1x provides the authentication framework to determine if a client should be allowed access through the wired or wireless port.

802.11   802.11 is the base standard specified by the IEEE on which all 802.11 technologies, including 802.11b, 802.11g, and 802.11a operate. The original 802.11 specification provided for lower bandwidth capabilities of 1 and 2 Mbps and specified the medium access control and physical layers.

802.11a   The 802.11a standard is a revision to the original IEEE 802.11 standard and specifies use of the unlicensed 5 GHz band. This standard supports data rates of up to 54 Mbps and uses OFDM technology.

802.11b   A revision of the IEEE 802.11 standard defining the use of direct sequence spread spectrum (DSSS) and supporting data rates up to 11 Mbps.

802.11e   Defines a set of Quality of Service (QoS) standards for 802.11-based wireless networks. These standards are intended to provide optimized and prioritized bandwidth for network intensive applications such as streaming media and Voice over IP.

802.11F   An Inter-Access Point Protocol (IAPP) intended to provide a set of specifications for use in roaming scenarios to allow more efficient hand off between access points in a wireless network. The goal is to achieve interoperability between multiple access point vendors.

802.11g   Similar to 802.11b, 802.11g works in the 2.4 GHz band and provides up to 54 Mbps data rates. This IEEE revision to the 802.11 standard uses a form of OFDM modulation for wireless communications. 802.11g and 802.11b are compatible in that both client types can connect to an 802.11g access point when it is configured in mixed mode. Neither 802.11b or 802.11g are compatible with 802.11a.

802.11i   Referred to as WPA2 by the Wi-Fi Alliance, 802.11i provides recommendations for stronger security in an 802.11-based network. 802.11i requires the use of AES encryption and helps to prevent attacks that are easily formed against the older WEP specification. 802.11i utilizes 802.1x authentication, which uses some form of extensible authentication protocol (EAP), and an authentication server such as a RADIUS device.

802.11n   Multipath has traditionally been viewed as a problem in wireless networks, but 802.11n devices will take advantage of this to increase bandwidth through spatial multiplexing. The popular term for this solution is *multiple input/multiple output (MIMO))* as multiple antennas are used for communications. This term should not be confused with *antenna diversity* in which only one antenna is used at a time.

802.15   The IEEE working group is responsible for wireless personal area network (PAN) standards and specifications. Four task groups are included: 802.15.1 (Bluetooth), 802.15.2 (Coexistence), 802.15.3 (High Rate), and 802.15.4 (Low Rate).

802.16   The IEEE broadband wireless access working group. Their aim is to provide standards for deployment of wireless metropolitan area networks (WMANs).

802.16-2004   Fixed line-of-site standard for WiMAX or broadband wireless access.

802.16e   Mobile non-line-of-site standard for WiMAX or broadband wireless access.

802.1x   An IEEE standard for port-based access control. The standard provides access through the port if authentication succeeds and denies access should authentication fail. This standard is used in wireless networks with various types of EAP authentication.

absorption   The process in which radiated RF energy is retained by material rather than reflected off or passed through. RF energy can be absorbed into moisture in the air or visible physical objects.

access point (AP) A device that provides access to a wired network or the Internet. This device may also act as the center of a wireless-only network when no wired networks are present. Many APs can also act as bridges and repeaters by changing a configuration setting.

active mode One of two power management modes in which a wireless client may operate. In active mode, the wireless client is always powered on and listening for wireless communications intended for the device.

active RFID tags When a RFID tag has its own power source, such as a battery, it's known as an *active tag*. These tags usually provide more memory and processing capabilities than the passive tags that do not have their own power source.

adaptive frequency hopping An added feature to modern Bluetooth standards that allows devices to shift automatically to frequencies that are not being utilized by other Bluetooth devices or wireless networks. This feature helps to prevent interference between Bluetooth and other wireless technologies.

ad hoc mode A mode of operation for Wi-Fi networks in which devices communicate directly with each other without the use of an access point.

Advanced Encryption Standard (AES) Also known as *Rijndael,* AES is a block cipher adopted by the U.S. government for encryption purposes and is used by WPA2 or 802.11i standard devices. AES and Rijndael differ in that AES uses keys of 128, 192, and 256 bits in length and Rijndael can use keys in any multiple of 32 bits with a low of 128 and high of 256 bits. However, AES is based on the Rijndael cipher.

antenna diversity The use of multiple antennas to overcome multipath problems. Only one antenna is used at a time and this should not be confused with MIMO or 802.11n.

antennas A device that radiates and/or receives radio signals. In a wireless network, antennas propagate the radio frequency waves into the area and receive them from other antennas.

association The relationship that is created between a wireless client and the access point.

attack surface   A term used to reference the totality of the attack points in your network or system. *Attack surface reduction* is the reduction of this surface size by removing unneeded systems and/or interfaces among other things.

authentication   The process of identity verification. In a wireless network, it is the process a station uses to provide its identity to another station (such as a client to an access point). The IEEE 802.11 standard defines two forms of authentication for wireless LANS: *open system* and *shared key.*

base station   In a WiMAX network, the base station is the hub or central location to which subscribers connect. A single base station can serve multiple subscribers.

Basic Service Set (BSS)   A group of Wi-Fi (802.11) stations and a single access point that function as a wireless network.

Basic Service Set Identifier (BSSID)   Not to be confused with the SSID, the BSSID is a unique identifier that is used to identify a unique network of Wi-Fi devices. In an infrastructure network (having an access point), the MAC address of the access point is used. In an ad hoc network, the first station in the IBSS (Independent Basic Service Set) generates a random 48-bit value for the BSSID.

Bluetooth   A standard for wireless personal area networks (WPANs) that is used in close range communications. Bluetooth uses frequency hopping spread spectrum technology and communicates in the 2.4 GHz spectrum.

CardBus   An interface available on most newer laptop computers. Similar to PCMCIA in form factor, it offers a 32-bit bus and is based on PCI. PCMCIA devices usually function in a CardBus slot.

channel   A defined frequency range used for communications in wireless networks and with wireless devices. Some wireless technologies use the entire channel as a single carrier and others divide each channel into subcarriers or subchannels.

colocation   The act of placing multiple wireless infrastructure devices in the same coverage area while avoiding conflicts.

Compact Flash (CF)   A form of storage medium or device interfaces for small devices and portable situations. Used in cameras, PDAs, and for device interfaces such as Bluetooth or Wi-Fi.

coordinator   In a ZigBee network, the device or devices responsible for forming and managing the network.

cracker   A person using hacking skills to perform illegal or unethical activities. In the technology community, *cracker* is not synonymous with *hacker,* though the lay community often sees a hacker as one who performs technical actions with ill intent; in fact, the lay community is mostly unfamiliar with the term *cracker* as it relates to computer crimes.

data encryption standard (DES)   Data encryption standard (DES) is an encryption standard adopted by the U.S. federal government in 1976. It is a symmetric encryption algorithm, meaning it uses the same algorithm to encrypt as it uses to decrypt. This encryption standard has been replaced by the Advanced Encryption Standard (AES).

data rates   The raw speed of communication in a networked system. This total speed is reduced for data throughput because of management overhead.

dBm   A measurement of power relevant to 1 mW – decibel milliwatt. Used to measure power gain and loss. It is said that 0 dBm equals 1 milliwatt (mW) and other power levels are defined from this starting point.

dBi   A relative measurement of the gain of an antenna. If an antenna has a gain of 3 dBi, it doubles the output power of the RF energy in the direction of the antenna. For example, if an antenna with 3 dBi of gain receives 50 mW of power to transmit, the power is transmitted at 100 mW based on the directionality of the antenna.

decibel (dB)   A unit of measure used to indicate the relative strength between two signals. In wireless systems, it is used to measure the gain and loss of RF energy (signals).

Denial of Service (DoS)   An attack designed to overwhelm or shut down a system so service is denied to valid users.

diffraction   Diffraction is the action of RF waves turning or bending around obstacles.

direct sequence spread spectrum (DSSS)   One of the two types of spread spectrum technologies used in wireless LANs. DSSS uses single channels for communications and provides greater bandwidth than frequency hopping spread spectrum (FHSS) systems.

electromagnetic   The combination of electronic and magnetic wave forms to create a new wave used to carry information in wireless systems.

encryption   An algorithmic-based procedure used to convert plaintext (or plain information) into cipher text (or encoded information) that can then be decrypted to retrieve the original information often after transfer or after a period of time in storage. There are many different algorithms, but AES, DES, 3DES, and RC4 are among the most common.

European Telecommunications Standards Institute (ETSI)   A nonprofit organization that establishes telecommunications standards for Europe.

Extended Service Set (ESS)   Multiple Basic Service Sets connected together through a distribution system and having a shared name (SSID).

Extended Service Set Identifier (ESSID)   The term used to refer to the SSID when it is used in a network with multiple access points configured to use the same SSID for roaming purposes. This term should not be confused with the BSSID, which is a 48-bit number used to identify a single network: either ad hoc or infrastructure.

extensible authentication protocol (EAP)   A widely used authentication mechanism. EAP authentication is often used in wireless networks based on the 802.11 standards. The 802.11i standard specifies the use of EAP for authentication purposes.

fast infrared (FIR)   The second revision of the IrDA Physical layer specification. FIR defines speeds of 0.576 Mbps and 1.152 Mbps.

Federal Communications Commission (FCC)   The governing body, in the U.S., for telecommunications law.

fixed WiMAX   An implementation of WiMAX used to provide last-mile delivery of Internet or other network access. An antenna is usually connected to the outside of the building, and the signal is transferred to a receiving device in the building that is connected to the local network or devices.

frequency hopping spread spectrum (FHSS)   One of two types of spread spectrum technologies used in wireless LANs. FHSS uses many different frequencies and hops between them at specified intervals. FHSS does not provide the faster data rates of DSSS.

Fresnel Zone   An ovular zone around the main signal of an RF transmission. This zone should remain 60–80 percent unblocked to provide effective communication links.

full function device (FFD)   In a ZigBee system, a device that can function as a coordinator, router, or end device.

gain   (1) The focusing of the lobes of an antenna in a specific direction. (2) The increasing of an RF signal's strength through some means.

hacker   An individual with in-depth knowledge of computer systems. These individuals may perform penetration testing or software security testing for organizations. To the lay person, they are criminals, and to the technology community, they are computer experts whereas crackers are the criminals.

hash   A one-way algorithm that generates a code often used for integrity analysis. Data is passed through the algorithm to generate a hash (sometimes called a *message digest*). The data can be evaluated later, and if the same hash results, the data has not changed (it has integrity).

hidden node   A situation in which a wireless client can be seen by the access point but not by the other wireless clients on the network. This can result in collisions and reduced network throughput.

highly directional antennas   Antennas that focus most of their energy in a particular direction. These include parabolic dish and grid antennas.

hijacking   An attack where a user's layer 2 and/or layer 3 connections are removed from an authorized network and placed on a rogue network. The attacker may perform this attack for many reasons, including the capture of user data such as logons and passwords.

HiperMAN   High Performance Radio Metropolitan Area Network (HiperMAN) is a standard put forth by the ETSI (European Telecommunications Standards Institute) for developing wireless MAN networks.

IEEE (Institute of Electrical and Electronics Engineers)   An organization responsible for creating standards in the electronics and computer markets. They have specified the 802.11 standards and others related to wireless networking.

Independent Basic Service Set (IBSS)   The technical phrase for an ad hoc wireless network. An IBSS does not use an access point.

infrared   A portion of the electromagnetic spectrum that lies between the visible light and the microwave. It is said to be a red light that the human eye cannot perceive.

infrastructure mode   The nontechnical phrase for a wireless network that is operating as a BSS (Basic Service Set) or ESS (Extended Service Set). When in infrastructure mode, an access point is utilized.

initialization vector (IV)   Used in encryption systems to make a message unique based on random or pseudo-random numbers.

interface protocols   The protocols used for communications between RFID tags and readers.

interference   A term used to define the conflict created when two or more sources of RF energy on the same frequency propagate in the same coverage area. Interference can be caused by other wireless devices or microwave ovens and even incidental devices such as motors.

IrCOMM   An IrDA specification used to allow communication over infrared by serial and parallel devices.

IrDA   The Infrared Data Association (IrDA) is a group that specifies standards and protocols for data communications over infrared links.

IrFM   The infrared protocol used for Financial Messaging—Infrared Financial Messaging (IrFM).

IrLAP   Infrared Link Access Protocol (IrLAP). Manages the negotiation establishment and the maintenance of the data link and is part of the core IrDA stack.

IrLMP   Infrared Link Management Protocol (IrLMP). Enables multiple service connections over one IrDA link created by IrLAP. Also works with the Information Access Service to provide a directory of available services on the infrared device.

IrOBEX   IrDA Object Exchange (IrOBEX). The IrDA protocol for object exchange across an infrared link, including the exchange electronic business cards or any other object.

IrPHY   A term used to reference the Physical layer of the IrDA stack. The IrPHY determines link types such as FIR, SIR, and VFIR.

IrSimple, IrSMP   An IrDA specification that allows for faster data rates. According to the IrDA, 16 Mbps data rates have been reached.

last mile   A phrase used to refer to the provision of network access in areas that are unreached by wired technology (or any existing connection). WiMAX is said to provide a last mile solution for remote areas, and other wireless technologies have also served this need in the past. Last mile can also refer to any connection to an end point (in other words, the end point connects to no other network and it is therefore the "last" mile).

line-of-sight (LOS)   Visual LOS is the ability to see along a virtual line between two points. RF LOS must also consider the Fresnel Zone to ensure effective communications.

loss   The lowering of a signal's strength. Often measured in decibels in wireless networks.

MAC filtering   Each networking device has a Media Access Control (MAC) address that is unique to the device. Wireless networks can allow or disallow device connectivity based on the MAC address of the device and this is known as *MAC filtering*.

mesh network   A mesh network is a network having two or more paths to any node. Examples of possible mesh networks include ZigBee, TCP/IP, and other routed protocols.

message integrity code (MIC)   The IEEE term used for a message authentication code; it is a hash used for verification of data integrity. MIC uses a keyed hash, which means that both the encryption key and the message (data) are passed through the hashing algorithm to generate the hash.

milliwatt   1/1000 or a watt. Used to measure RF signal strength because of the low levels of strength needed to communicate on wireless networks.

mini-PCI   A form factor used for devices mostly in laptop computers. Many wireless devices, installed in laptops, are actually mini-PCI adapters.

mobile WiMAX   In WiMAX implementations, a link that can be maintained while moving. Mobile WiMAX is also known as 802.16e. Because it is mobile, it does not require line-of-sight (LOS) and is said to be non-line-of-sight (NLOS).

modulation   The process used to transmit information on a carrier signal by varying one or more of the properties of the signal.

multipath   RF signals arrive at a receiver from a single transmitter but along different paths. These different paths are the direct path and reflected paths. This can result in signal loss because of the signals arriving out of phase or at differing times. However, MIMO takes advantage of multipath to improve bandwidth.

Multiple Input/Multiple Output (MIMO)   A technology, upon which 802.11n is based, that takes advantage of the normally detrimental problem of multipath to create more data bandwidth in wireless networks by reducing bit error rates and improving throughput.

near/far   A term used to describe the problem that arises when wireless nodes are far from the access point transmitting with low power and other wireless nodes are closer to the access point or transmitting with higher power. This results in the far node not being "seen" by the access point and, therefore, having difficulty communicating.

nomadic WiMAX   Nomadix WiMAX access is another term used to describe *portable WiMAX*. It should not be confused with mobile WiMAX. Nomadic or portable WiMAX is intended to be used while stationary or moving at pedestrian (walking) speeds. It differs from fixed WiMAX in that you can move to different locations and still access the network once you are stationary as long as a signal exists.

omni-directional antennas   Antennas that radio energy in a donut fashion around the antenna. These include dipole and rubber-ducky antenna types.

open system authentication   The default authentication for the IEEE 802.11 specification. The authenticating station sends a frame to the other station (an access point in infrastructure mode) requesting authentication and containing the authenticating station's identification. The receiving station (again, the access point in an infrastructure network) sends back a frame that either authenticates access or denies access to the authenticating station.

passive RFID tags   RFID tags that get their energy from the RF signal being transmitted from the reader. They usually contain low memory and little or no logical processing capabilities. The memory data is transmitted to the reader, which makes analytical determinations.

PCI   Peripheral Component Interconnect (PCI) is a high-speed connection port for devices attached to computers. Some wireless network interface cards (NICs) use PCI slots for their interface connections.

PCMCIA   Personal Computer Memory Card International Association (PCMCIA) is an interface used to connect devices to laptop computers. Some wireless network interface cards (NICs) use PCMCIA interfaces. PCMCIA cards often function in the newer CardBus slots on modern laptop computers. Today, PCMCIA devices are often called *PC Card devices*.

piconet   A group of devices connected using Bluetooth standards and protocols. A piconet can contain up to eight devices with seven acting as slaves and the eighth acting as the master. The master controls which Bluetooth device gets access at which time and negotiates between the devices.

polarization   The plane of the electrical field in an RF signal. Antennas are usually said to be vertically or horizontally polarized. This polarization determines, to a great extent, the direction of the RF signal.

point-to-multipoint   A wireless link that includes multiple points connecting to a single central point. This is much like a star network topology in that all the sites communicate back to the central location.

point-to-point   A wireless link where one system connects directly with only one other system.

portable WiMAX   An implementation of WiMAX that allows for connections to be created to one or more base stations from multiple locations but does not allow roaming while connected.

Power over Ethernet (PoE)   A technology that allows for the transmission of power over standard Ethernet cables. PoE can be used to power access points and other wireless devices in locations where local power outlets are not available.

power save mode   One of two power management modes in which a wireless client may operate. In power save mode, the client wakes at predetermined intervals to check for packets intended for the client.

push-button security   A newer security technology used in many wireless devices. While vendors use different names for it, the concept is the same: the access point negotiates the best security that is compatible with the access point and the connecting client.

radio frequency (RF)   A generic phrase used to refer to radio-based technology.

radio frequency identification (RFID) A technology used for identification without the need for UPC (Universal Product Code) labels. RFID is also used for many tracking purposes and automatic payment processing and inventory management.

RADIUS (Remote Authentication Dial-In User Service) An authentication, authorization, and accounting (AAA) service for applications such as wireless network access. RADIUS can also be used in relation to virtual private networks (VPN) and remote access dial-up connections.

range A term used to describe the distance a communications link supports. At different ranges, wireless link properties must change. For example, the greater the distance the lower the data rate.

reflection A behavior of RF signals where the majority of the signal is bounced off an obstacle and focused in a different direction.

refraction A behavior of RF signals where some of the signal is reflected but much of the signal passes through the obstacle and is redirected out the other side so the direction of the signal changes.

reduced function device (RFD) In a ZigBee network, a device that cannot act as a coordinator or a router.

RFID readers A device that can read the unique code and information stored in RFID tags.

RFID tags A small device that can contain information and function as either an active or passive device and is read by RFID readers.

RF shadow The space behind an obstacle that diffracts the RF signal. When the RF signal is diffracted around an obstacle, there is often a space behind the obstacle (the side opposite the transmitter) that has no RF coverage. This lack of coverage is called RF shadow.

roaming The act of disconnecting and then connecting to another access point, in a wireless network, without losing the link state. Seamless roaming allows you to transfer from one access point to another while continuing to transfer data.

rogue access point   An access point that is installed, either intentionally or unintentionally, without the authorization of the network support staff. These can be used to gain access to your wired network or to gather information from users who connect to the rogue access point.

scattering   A behavior of RF signals where the signal is split and reflected in different directions. This can cause an extreme reduction in signal strength and is often caused by obstacles that have smaller edges or sizes than the RF wavelength.

scatternet   A group of piconets connected together through some form of sharing devices.

SDIO   Secure Digital Input/Output (SDIO) is an interface for connecting devices to hosts such as PDAs or computers. There are wireless network interface cards (NICs) that connect through SDIO interfaces.

semi-directional antennas   Antennas that focus a larger portion of their transmitted energy in a specified general direction. These antennas include patch, panel, and Yagi.

Serial Infrared (SIR)   Serial Infrared is an IrDA Physical layer specification for infrared communications. Communication speeds include 2.4 k, 9.6 k, 19.2 k, 38.4 k, 57.6 k, and 115.2 k. This was the first Physical layer specification.

shared-key authentication   A form of authentication for wireless networks where each station is aware of a secret key. Using shared-key authentication requires the use of WEP (Wired Equivalent Privacy) encryption.

signal to noise ratio (SNR)   Ratio of the wireless signal to the RF energy noise floor in an environment.

site survey   A set of procedures performed to ensure accurate coverage of RF energy in a given area and the fulfillment of user needs within the area. To be performed, the engineer must understand intermediate to advanced RF behavior and have the needed tools to test the behavior in the specific environment.

SOHO (Small Office/Home Office)   A term used to describe small businesses that have just a few users and home offices where individuals work out of their own homes.

subscriber station   In a WiMAX network, the client side of the wireless connection. The subscribe station connects to a base station to establish a communications link.

technical requirements   In a technology project, the requirements that are technical in nature, such as the system must be 802.11g compatible. Technical requirements are determined to ensure proper technology is selected and implemented.

Temporal Key Integrity Protocol (TKIP)   A protocol created to repair the weaknesses found in WEP (Wired Equivalent Privacy). Improvements include 128-bit encryption keys, 48-bit initialization vectors (IVs), and a message integrity code (MIC).

throughput   The actual bandwidth available for transfer of business or organizational traffic other than network management overhead. In wireless networks, this is usually one-half the data rate of the system.

Tiny TP   The Tiny Transport Protocol (Tiny TP) provides flow control and segmentation with reassembly on IrDA connections.

Universal Serial Bus (USB)   An interface for connecting devices to personal computers and other electronic hosts. Common USB devices include wireless interfaces, memory sticks, external drives, and mice and keyboards.

very fast infrared (VFIR)   The May 2001 IrDA Physical layer specification. This standard allows for speeds of 16.0 Mbps.

virtual private networking (VPN)   A term used to explain the process of creating an encrypted network link across an untrusted network for data transfer. There are many VPN protocols including PPTP, SSH, LT2P/IPSec, and naked IPSec.

Voice over IP (VoIP)   A technology that allows for voice communications over Internet protocol (IP) networks. Wireless VoIP simply uses wireless technology to implement the IP network and then wireless VoIP client devices to communicate on this network.

war driving   The act of discovering wireless networks, usually while driving slowly through a community or business district. Tools used include PDAs, laptop computers, and wireless scanning software such as NetStumbler.

WiBro   The Korean standard for WiMAX network implementations.

Wired Equivalent Privacy (WEP)   The security protocol defined by the base 802.11 IEEE standard. This protocol is known to be very weak with simple tools available for easy attacking. If at all possible, use the newer WPA and, preferably, WPA2 technologies should be used.

Wi-Fi Alliance   An organization that creates certification programs to verify interoperability among hardware based on IEEE standards and recommendations. This organization created the Wi-Fi, WPA, and WPA2 certifications among others.

WiMAX   A term used to refer to the WiMAX Forum's specifications for 802.16 wireless MAN implementations. This is not the same as Wi-Fi, and the two should not be confused.

wireless bridge   A device that creates a wireless connection between two separate networks and performs no routing—only forwarding.

wireless hotspot gateway   A device that can share network access and provide authentication, authorization, and accounting internally. These devices usually allow for separation of public and private networks internally.

wireless media gateway   A device that can access media (video, auidio, images) on a media server and display the media on a video screen.

wireless presentation gateway   A device that connects directly to a monitor or projection unit and receives video signals over wireless (usually 802.11g) connections with one or more computers. They are used mostly for delivering slideshow presentations as the throughput is seldom useful enough for streaming video.

wireless print server   A device that can share printers on a wireless network.

wireless repeaters   Wireless devices that can extend the range of a wireless network by "repeating" the signal. They generally act as a wireless client to the wireless network and act as a wireless access point to the remote wireless clients.

wireless routers   A device that routes between a wireless network and a wired network or, possibly, between two wireless networks.

wireless switch   Usually a switch to which wireless access points connect and by which they are managed.

WPA (Wi-Fi Protected Access)   The Wi-Fi Alliance created the WPA certification to provide a standard against which pre-802.11i hardware could be developed that included interoperability between multiple vendors. WPA uses Temporal Key Integrity Protocol (TKIP) but is not as secure as WPA2.

WPA2   The Wi-Fi Alliance's certification for 802.11i-compatible equipment. This certification requires the use of Temporal Key Integrity Protocol (TKIP) and AES.

ZigBee   A specification for small, low power RF-based radios based on the IEEE 802.15.4 standard for wireless PANs. ZigBee devices may be used to implement wireless mesh networks for monitoring and controlling of environments.

ZigBee router   A ZigBee device that can communicate with other ZigBee networks as opposed to only communicating within a defined network.

Index